T0370998

JEREMY LEE

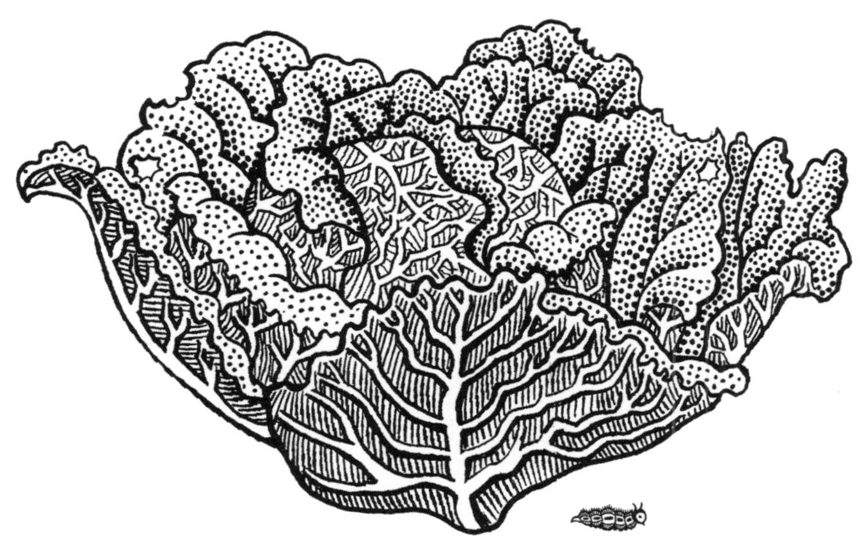

COOKING

About the Author

Jeremy Lee joined Sam & Eddie Hart at Quo Vadis in Soho in early 2012, becoming Chef Proprietor of this venerable restaurant. Jeremy had previously manned the stoves of the Blueprint Café on the first floor of the Design Museum, which Sir Terence Conran created on the south bank of the River Thames near Tower Bridge.

This singular cook has worked with such distinguished restaurateurs as Simon Hopkinson and Alastair Little, who all played a considerable part in the great resurgence in British cooking.

Jeremy, originally from Dundee, Scotland, came from a family where home cooking of a high order was daily fare. His parents and grandmother taught him the mysteries of finding good produce through good shopping. Having been brought up thus, Jeremy applies this to the menus at Quo Vadis, where the cooking is bright, fresh, light and quintessentially British in a manner most modern.

His menus change monthly, reflecting the seasons, and are full of his favourite things, using produce expertly sourced from his enviable list of suppliers. Jay Rayner described him as 'one of those rare phenomena in the London food world; a chap everyone agrees is a good thing'.

In 2012 Jeremy and Quo Vadis won the Catey for Best Restaurant Menu of the Year and in 2013 they won the Tatler Award for Best Kitchen. He writes for numerous newspapers and periodicals and has appeared on television in *The Great British Menu* and *Could You Eat an Elephant?* for Channel 4.

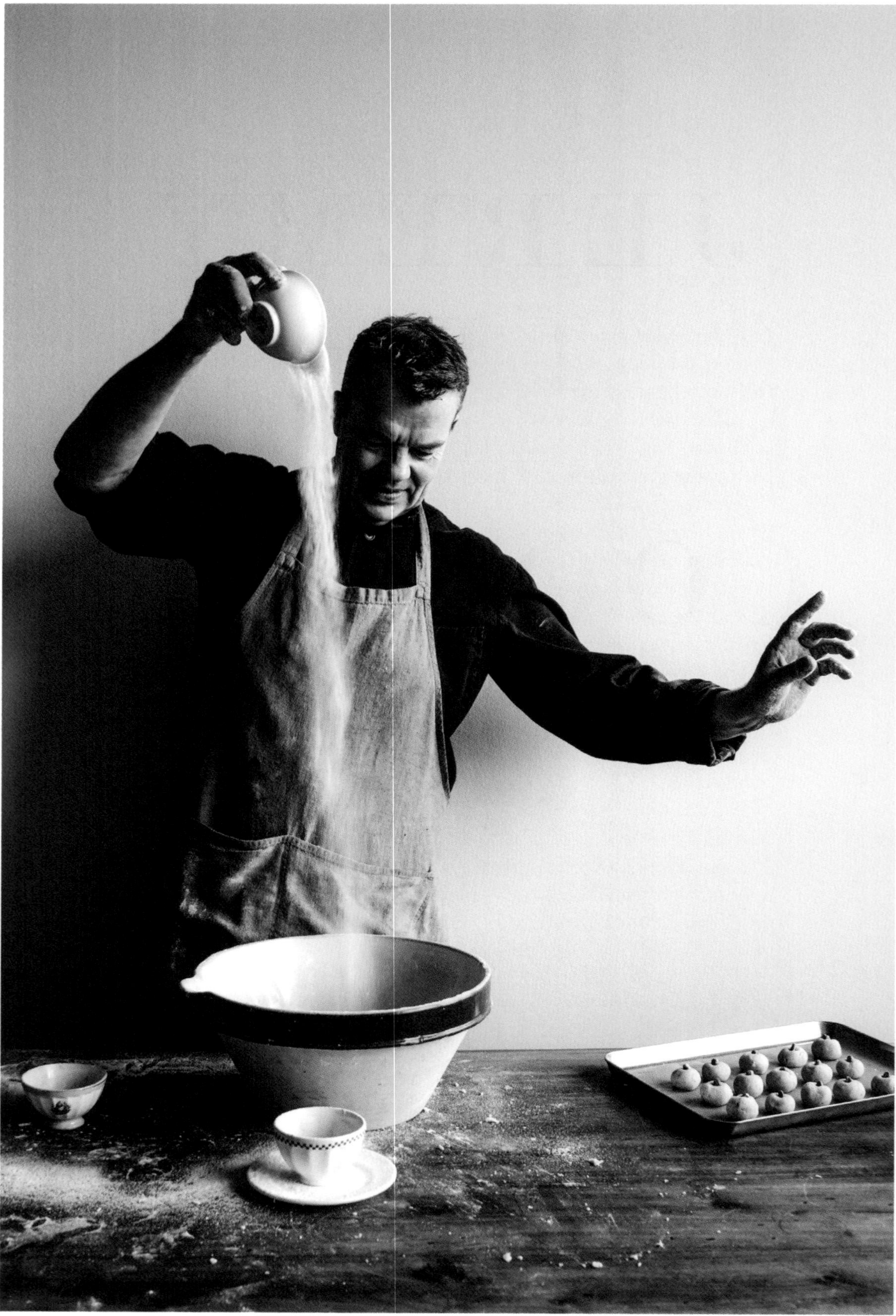

JEREMY LEE

COOKING

Simply and well, for one or many

PHOTOGRAPHS BY ELENA HEATHERWICK
DECORATIONS BY JOHN BROADLEY

4TH ESTATE • *LONDON*

4th Estate
An imprint of HarperCollins*Publishers*
1 London Bridge Street
London SE1 9GF
www.4thEstate.co.uk

HarperCollins*Publishers*
1st Floor, Watermarque Building, Ringsend Road
Dublin 4, Ireland

First published in Great Britain in 2022 by 4th Estate
2

Edited by Carolyn Hart
Designed by Julian Roberts

'This is Just to Say' from the collection *Collected Poems Volume II 1939–1962* edited by Christopher MacGowan, and written by William Carlos Williams, is reprinted by kind permission of Carcanet Press, Manchester, UK

Extract from 'Little Gidding' from the collection *Four Quartets* by T. S. Eliot is reprinted by kind permission of Faber and Faber Ltd.

Photograph on page 405 used by kind permission of Christopher Hirsheimer.

A catalogue record for this book is available from the British Library

ISBN 978-0-00-815620-6

Always follow the manufacturer's instructions when using kitchen appliances.

Typeset by GS Typesetting

Printed and bound by GPS Group

MIX
Paper from
responsible sources
FSC™ C007454

This book is produced from independently certified FSC™ paper to ensure responsible forest management.

For more information visit: www.harpercollins.co.uk/green

To
Mum and Dad,
who put so much into
the day-to-day pleasure of cooking,
curiosity, shopping and eating

Acknowledgements

AS WITH ALL STORIES, it is best to start at the beginning, which was a commission from the distinguished publisher Louise Haines for a cookbook for 4th Estate. Of course the book took somewhat longer than promised, but Louise awaited the manuscript with only words of encouragement and the most intuitive kindness, care and consideration towards a chef juggling restaurant life and all the daily distractions therein. There was too the splendid and able Mia Colleran, assisting and gently choreographing the incredible detail required to deliver the final manuscript. Thanks must go to Alex Gingell, and to all at 4th Estate for the great effort taken to publish a book. There came a timely offer of the greatest of gifts, an editor. Enter Carolyn Hart, the lady with the keyboard, with so many thanks for coming to my aid, editing with patience, persistence and support and the simple edict 'just keep writing' forever in my ears while tapping away at a manuscript. Thanks in abundance to my agent Lizzy Kremer – and all at David Higham Associates – who, from the first day we met, has always encouraged me and kept nudging me forward.

Needless to say, the idea for the book was simplicity itself, an arbitrary collection of favourite dishes and ingredients in a form inspired by so many favourite writers. I quickly learned the many differences between writing a book and writing a menu. But, as with all good things, what you learn is priceless, quite beyond measure. And so, a journey began at the top left-hand corner of a page, starting with my family and our many years cooking and eating together and in particular Mum and my grandmother. There are a fair few friends too who have shared many of my adventures in kitchens and at tables near and far, who have remained true despite my absence more often than I dare admit when juggling restaurant and manuscript. The title came through the simple act of cooking, the very spine of the book.

I must thank all the chefs I have worked with past, present and future, starting with those in Scotland who gave a young lad an apprenticeship that resulted in an incredible grounding in restaurant kitchens and which paved the way towards working in kitchens with some of the greatest names in British restaurants, such as Simon Hopkinson, Alastair Little, Terence Conran and the Hart Brothers, feeding a hearty appetite and inquisitiveness. To all the restaurants and the folk who make them so special, who have delighted and inspired through the years, I thank them collectively they are so many.

With these must go grateful thanks also to all the suppliers and producers who have vitteled this book and kitchens I love to cook in at home and at work. Particular thanks must go to the crew at Natoora, at H G Walter, George Bennel & Co at Belazu, Andy & Kate at the Vinegar Shed, Leila's Shop, The Ealing Grocer, Ben & Silvy Weatherall, Lucy & Anthony Carroll, Ben's Fish, Jane Scotter at Fern Verrow; Jason Hinds and the crew at Neal's Yard Dairy; Patricia Michelson at La Fromagerie; James at Cabrito Goat Meat Ltd; and to Monica and Rudi at Brindisa, who inspired many a pot of beans. Their vision, generosity with knowledge, produce and kindness cannot go unmentioned.

I salute and thank the food writers who penned a vast body of work, many of which have become constant companions, sources of inspiration for recipes and writing alike. I have revelled in the works of Elizabeth David, Julia Child, Jane Grigson, Arabella Boxer, Marcella Hazan, Colman Andrews, Christopher Hirsheimer, Melissa Hamilton, Rachel Roddy, Olia Hercules, Michael Smith, Michel Guérard and Roger Vergé to name but a few.

And this leads me to thanking Elena Heatherwick, ably assisted by Lesley Lau and Billy Barraclough, not only for beautiful photography and a peerless eye but also for effortless, joyous company who, with one click, makes magic out of pots and pans, bowls, dishes and everything else we could find tucked away at home.

I thank Julian Roberts for his friendship, great company and his incredible mind brimming with ideas that brought to the book all the vision, wit and style that he has brought to the menus at Quo Vadis. Thanks must also go to John Broadley, whose illustrations grace the walls and menus of Quo Vadis with a humour and penmanship like no other, a truly unique illustrator. Thanks, too, to Priscilla Carluccio and Kate Friend.

My thanks to Annabelle and Stephen Harty, Mary Lou Sturridge and Lloyd Stanton for those times I needed to lock myself away.

I must thank Matthew Fort for encouraging me to write, giving a chef the remarkable opportunity of writing a column for the *Guardian* for many years when it was still a broadsheet. An adventure in itself, it begat many others.

Thanks go to Sam, Eddie and James Hart and all at Quo Vadis and Hart Brothers for the endless support through the production of this book.

I must thank Annie Bell, my sister Annabel and Lindsey Bareham and those who took the time to read the manuscript as it took shape. And Annie Lee – it cannot go unmentioned that an editor has the same name as my sister – and Louise Tucker, both vital to this book.

And thanks to Susannah Hunt and Jake Farley for making the journey through the recipes such a joy, always so chirpy going about the weighing, washing, peeling, whisking and myriad preparations required.

Jeremy Lee
Hackney 2022

Author's note

COOKS SHOULD SEASON LIGHTLY AS THEY GO, having a care not to add so much salt, more of which can be added when checking that the seasoning is just right prior to taking to table.

The recipes in this book were cooked in a conventional oven. Fan-assisted oven temperatures should be lowered by 10°C or even 20°C depending on your oven.

A note on soup spoons: thank you in advance for indulging a cook measuring much in soup spoons. It is an old habit inherited from Mum, who had a great array of spoons, often old, some silver, some stainless steel, and often using soup spoons for tablespoons in the kitchen when measuring ingredients. For the recipes in this book, 1 soup spoon and 1 tablespoon can be used interchangeably.

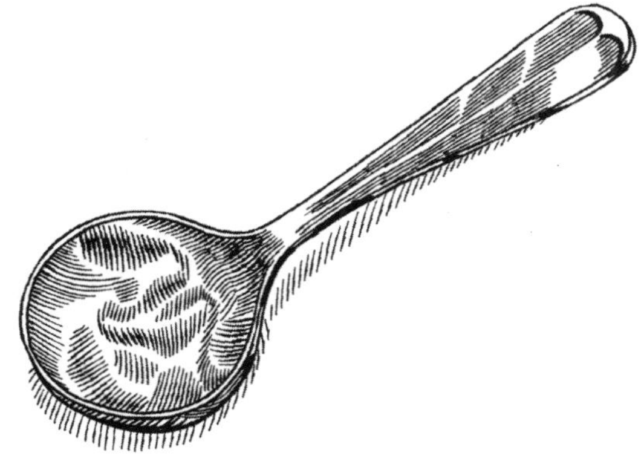

Contents

Jeremy Lee as a young apprentice, by his father, Norman S. Lee

THE SIMPLE TRUTH I'VE LEARNED FROM A LIFETIME of cooking is that good food is honed from fine ingredients. Regardless of whether it is a particularly good bundle of asparagus, its paper collar announcing where the stems were grown, a great box of artichokes or a fish-shop window full of nets of mussels and tubs of oysters, it is invariably the ingredients that spark the thought of what the next meal will be.

This being the case, I find I am unable to pass market stalls or food shops without a swift and thorough investigation of all that is offered. I love markets. There is nothing quite like approaching a market and catching the first scents of produce carried on the breeze, rich with freshly picked wild garlic announcing itself with a heady, sweet scent, followed by early raspberries, peaches and melons. It's an aromatic blend of warm fruit and fresh leaves that piques both curiosity and appetite, and in doing so, fuels the desire to cook and, of course, to scoff on that punnet of perfect strawberries.

A childhood memory that never diminishes is the smell of raspberries laid out in front of our greengrocer in Dundee, raspberries from the Carse of Gowrie, so famous they warranted a train waiting at Cupar to take the day's pickings south to London and beyond. They were so fresh they had never seen the inside of a fridge and my mother bought them by the tray. Nowadays, there are rumours of trying to make raspberries seedless. So silly. Spend the money feeding school kids and keep the esteemed berries as they are.

Through the summer months when I was growing up, as well as raspberries there were gooseberries, and currants, strawberries too, turned into jam or, a great favourite, piled on top of freshly churned ice cream, my appetite for which has never diminished, to the chagrin of the pastry chef at Quo Vadis, who finds the contents of the vanilla ice cream pot all too often much reduced. The trays of fruit and all the other bags and boxes of shopping came into the house to be unloaded by us kids and tumbled in bowls and baskets in and around the kitchen. This was a job I always liked, for the promise they held of good things to come.

As an adult, I find it nigh on impossible to return home without having stopped off at least once at a greengrocer or market stall, even for just a bag of oranges. As a result, my kitchen table is usually spilling over with so much produce that there's only one question: right then, just what are we going to do with all this?

I hope this book will answer that question. In the following pages are recipes for dishes that have become constants in my life, as well as for those cooked when an ingredient is in season or, quite simply, when the appetite arises, all inspired by the produce from markets, growers and independent shops. Many of these shops and growers appear throughout the book, some very often.

Much as they love to shop, cooks also love to cook, and are thus drawn to the kitchen by the simplest of impulses (often, as in the case of this cook, greed). This certainly explains why, when away from the bustle of a busy restaurant, I often find myself back in the kitchen at home, whiling away time halving apricots or peeling pears, making pastry, lightly rubbing cuts of meat in olive oil and herbs, reaching for lemon, bay leaves, garlic and thyme, or curing fish and chopping vegetables, sorting through heads of lettuce and other leaves, and simmering beans put to soak the night before.

It's in the kitchen that I immerse myself in the enjoyable process of weaving together old and new recipes, adding in some good sense and much generosity of spirit as well as good cooking, quite often with what's at hand while looking forward to the return of asparagus and gooseberries, wondering why the peas are so late, the pear tree a little shy and why plums seem to increase in amount and variety every year.

I like the contrast in pace between the boisterous, ebullient daily life of a restaurant chef, and the peace of a kitchen at home, often cooking for one. When staying with friends, at home or abroad, after moseying around the shops, or a market, or a foreign supermarket – always so much more glamorous than those at home, mysterious aisles of oils, sea salts wet, coarse and fine, and tins of sardines and anchovies – it is to the kitchen I find myself straying. I love those rare mornings at home, or abroad, when, breakfast done, with a last cup of coffee from the pot, there is nothing to do except decide what to cook that day and, for that matter, later in the week.

Being born into a boisterous family where a great part of growing up was centred round the kitchen, these thoughts seem to come naturally. Mum was an intuitive and elegant cook, a natural with an instinct for cooking good food, be it a pan of lentil soup, a daube of beef or a plate of asparagus with poached eggs and a nut of butter, dishes fashioned from produce bought locally and always in season. When I was growing up, I was often perched on a stool at the counter with half an eye on the kitchen as I fretted over homework or doodled on a sketch pad as Mum went about the business of cooking for her family, rolling pastry, stirring a pot, dipping fillets of haddock in breadcrumbs, grating a lemon or nutmeg.

Home was on the east coast of Scotland in the county of Angus, just outside Dundee, which sits on the north bank of the Tay River, famous for salmon. The hinterland of Dundee contributes much to the superlative larder of Scotland and my parents took just as much pleasure in exploring and acquiring the produce to be found there as they did cooking and eating it. No journey was too long, no detour too convoluted, when we were in search of Angus beef or lamb from George Irving our garrulous butcher, lobsters and crabs from the East Neuk of Fife, sea kale and asparagus from Eassie farm just down the road from our village, porridge oats from Cupar, a favourite honey made from bees feasting on heather, often found in Mr Braithwaite's tea and coffee shop. Even the neeps were the best I have ever eaten, turning as bright as pumpkins when cooked and mashed. There were smokies from the village of Arbroath, otherworldly good when lifted fresh from the smoker and eaten on buttered baps, or the flesh flaked, warmed and served with sea vegetables, or simply leeks and potatoes. Smokies are very good with scrambled eggs too.

These adventures are indelibly printed in my memory – an education for a chef in the making, even if unknowingly. My path to the kitchen began as a detour from a plan to attend art college. I got a holiday job as a waiter in a small country house hotel, was moved to the kitchen and found I liked it there. I was lucky to work with chefs with more bark than bite and was given enough encouragement to persevere with the hours and duties demanded of a trainee chef. In return for pushing on through, I was catapulted by my mentors into their alma mater at Boodle's Club in London.

Looking back, I realise even at that early stage I was drawn to kitchens where ingredients and cooks were as important as the menu and the customers. From Boodle's I went to a catering company called Duff & Trotter, named for the caterer in the books by P. G. Wodehouse, prior to rekindling my love of restaurants at Bibendum and Alastair Little, and began to be aware that I was cooking food in restaurants with an ethos similar to how I would, when I could, cook at home: preparing dishes from scratch with impeccable ingredients.

When I started heading up my own kitchens, first at a tiny restaurant in Islington, then at the Blueprint Café in the Design Museum, overlooking the Pool of London at Tower Bridge, the menus were always led by ingredients that were in season, and, of course, a hearty appetite. Good cooks always want to eat what they cook; no dish will appear on a menu if the chef doesn't want to eat it. Some days, a morning's work involves as much chat and planning with the suppliers as with the crew. What fish was landed that morning? Can you age some bellies of pork? When are gooseberries due?

The position of the Blueprint, overlooking the Tower of London and the river, was spectacular – an urban miracle of huge eastern skies reflected in the tidal waters of the Thames. Just as beguiling are the streets behind the restaurant. A hop, skip and a jump away from the river were to be found many of our suppliers. Some were at the then fledgling farmers' market at Borough Market, dating back to the twelfth century, the last of its kind in the capital's centre.

The market abuts London Bridge station, the terminal for trains that run over the largest viaduct in the capital. Underneath them, in the viaduct's arches, are the market's traders, counted among the best in the country, selling to businesses and public alike. The arches in Borough Market and at Maltby Street and Spa Terminus have become an ingenious reimagining of the defunct High Street – here you will find the finest meat, fish, fruit and vegetables, ferments and coffee, bread, cheese, wine and a fair few eateries too.

It was a magic time when I could cycle from Hackney, where I lived, to the restaurant, choosing a different bridge to cross most mornings. I liked Southwark best, for it is the prettiest and quietest bridge, and I would detour for coffee just round the corner at Borough Market. On the fringes of the market was a favourite greengrocer, Mr Booth, who fed my curiosity as much as he fed our menu at the Blueprint Café.

Originally a trader in Leadenhall Market, Tony Booth was a gentle, kindly man with a jovial smile and a mane of white hair swept back. He was always there, standing before tables piled with fruits, vegetables, salad leaves and herbs, chatting to customers about the produce he had in from around the British Isles and abroad. Queuing for my turn, I would already have spied wild garlic, tomatoes and artichokes, apricots and cherries, melons, figs, quinces, bitter leaves, herbs, onions and garlic, before even being shown what was backstage waiting to make an appearance. It was a splendid start to the day. After much rummaging and chatter, a stack of boxes filled with produce would be loaded onto a van which would then head off to the restaurant, with me on my bicycle following in its wake.

Tony was famous for mushrooms and always had the best of what was in season: the biggest and darkest of Portobello mushrooms, the best parasols, so huge in diameter two or three would fill a box, their gills richly coloured with dark browns of many hues and the earthy smell of soil still clinging to the stems bright from recent cutting. This was the kind of produce designed for an urban chef who craved the wild foods of the countryside. At the restaurant, we baked them whole in the oven, dotted with butter punchy with garlic, rested them slightly before slicing and served them with onglet or roast sirloin of beef.

From time to time there would be huge puffballs of such quality you felt you were cutting into a cloud. Any plans made were put to one side to prepare and feast upon this bounty. Similarly with boxes of ceps and luminous gold Scottish girolles, stuff of rumour when I was growing up.

The fruit was just as good, always seasonal, new arrivals mixed with the usual suspects. Oranges of every kind and lemons along with pink rhubarb kept us happy through the early months of the year, before the first gooseberries and elderflowers appeared. Then the first apricots arrived, heralding peaches of all sorts, some as green and velvety as fresh almonds with flesh veined the deepest red, and nectarines even more veined, and stained crimson.

After that, strawberries (always try to get those that have not been watered or rained on the day before; the flavour is more concentrated and makes the best jam, too), raspberries, gooseberries and currants too. Tony could even get the odd punnet of huckleberries and wild blaeberries. When I despaired of the sweet, tasteless, shiny black fruits masquerading as blackberries you find in supermarkets, Tony always seemed to have a few brambles too.

He loved to know what our intentions were towards his produce and I would tell him how the pastry chefs always joked about the 365 fruit compotes, curds, jams and preserves filling the fridge, to be served with cakes, tarts, trifles and meringue tumbles. As I left, he would often hand over a small bunch of perfumed leaves, suggesting, 'Here, why don't you try these scented geraniums for your fruit, simmer them in syrup or custard.'

Bouquet in hand, thoughts would turn swiftly to apricots and custard with an almond tart, a pudding I have enjoyed since childhood and never tire of baking. It's been a fixture on the pudding menu in almost every restaurant where I have cooked, baked freshly every day at the Blueprint Café and Quo Vadis. It's made with whole, blanched Marcona almonds ground to a coarse crumb, stirred into a mix of butter, sugar and eggs and poured into a case lined with pastry. The tart has to be placed on a rack over a tray to catch the butter that escapes regardless of every attempt to stem this eccentricity caused by the oil in the almonds. I must confess to a stubborn refusal to add flour to the recipe as it makes the tart too 'cakey' (see page 150 for the recipe).

Just shy of a first decade, eight years or so into my time at Quo Vadis, Covid happened. It arrived with a shocking suddenness, turning our lives upside down and catapulting us into lockdown hibernation. Quo Vadis was shuttered for the duration. When the dust had settled a little, removed from the daily business of a restaurant, I set to in the kitchen at home to cook the days away. I turned my flat into a field kitchen and found myself, like my mother had always done, sitting at a table, ever a coffee pot on the stove, poring over cookbooks and notebooks, considering what to cook next.

As with all stories, a good beginning is required, and as the beginning of the day demands breakfast, I started each morning with a pan of oats I had steeped the night before to make porridge. I make it the way my mum taught me, stirring gently with a spurtle until a soft, yielding porridge forms (no spoon should ever stand to attention in a pan of porridge), crumbling a little dark muscovado sugar atop, covering with a plate for a minute to allow the sugar to dissolve into syrup. When sitting down to a bowl of porridge, I take an auld Scots leaf out of Dad's book and pour on a spoonful of cream, then dip a spoonful of porridge in a small bowl of chilled milk to cool it. This is a breakfast that challenged me as a child but as an adult, it's one I have grown to love for its calming effect while cooking and its soothing warmth when eating.

Through the morning there was always some amusement to be had wondering what might arrive through the post. Mostly it was vegetables, fruit and herbs I had ordered, often too much, and mornings were whiled away picking, peeling and chopping to make a braise, a salad, an omelette or a soup, or a pot with chard or a whole riot of different vegetables forever ticking over on the stove or in the oven. Forget your five-a-day rule; most days it was more like twelve as I chopped celery, onion and garlic, occasionally a carrot or two and perhaps a bulb of fennel. To the pot would be added peas and broad beans, asparagus or celeriac, spinach and chard or both, parsley by the handful, the day's choice of potato from the arrival that morning of a delivery of four different varieties, lemon, olive oil, and perhaps pinches of summer savory, borage and thyme.

For the cook locked up at home, Robinson Crusoe with a kitchen, the ability to order from restaurant suppliers as well as shop locally rather than in a supermarket was pretty remarkable. There was a certain charm seeing someone who normally delivered to the restaurant standing at my own front door with a box of chicories and oranges, another with a delivery of mackerel, smoked cod's roe and a kipper, cheese of course, a can of olive oil, a bag of almonds, beans, chickpeas and rice, and on occasion tears were shed for a duck lost in transit. I would set to making a big pan of soup, or a braise always with a host of vegetables, sometimes with a ham hock, a bone or a lamb shank, or fish, and often with beans or chickpeas.

Although I began this book thinking it would be a collection of recipes learned during my time spent in restaurant kitchens, I've come to realise that it was those warm, comforting, nourishing dishes that I made during lockdown that form the heart of it. Home cooking rediscovered after a lifetime spent in professional kitchens.

As the world keeps spinning, evolving and moving forever onwards, the seasons ever changing, perhaps one thing lockdown has done for us is underline that time spent in the kitchen is something to cherish and celebrate, a vital part of daily life, making us healthier and happier. As T. S. Eliot wrote in 'Little Gidding', in *Four Quartets*, 'We shall not cease from exploration/And the end of all our exploring/ Will be to arrive where we started/And know the place for the first time' – the kitchen at home.

SHRUBS
JAPANESE FOOD
A CALEDONIAN FEAST
THE LEOPARD
GIUSEPPE TOMASI DI LAMPEDUSA
HERRING
Lisboeta
Nuno Mendes
YQUEM
THE GASTRODROME
GERALDENE HOLT · FRENCH COUNTRY KITCHEN
The Best of JANE GRIGSON
EAST
MEERA SODHA
CITRUS FRUIT
THE ART OF COOKERY
the omelette book
REINVENTING THE WHEEL
BUTTER
FRENCH CHEESE
The Royal Cookery Book
the natural baker
JANE GRIGSON
The Pastry Chef's Guide
In Praise of the Potato
LINDSEY BAREHAM
THE SECOND CLASSIC ITALIAN COOKBOOK
THE CLASSIC ITALIAN COOKBOOK
Kettle Broth to Gooseberry Fool
CANAL HOUSE
COOK SOMETHING
The Savory Way
Deborah Madison
EVERY DAY COOKERY
THE ENGLISH Bread Book
THE COMPLETE NOSE TO TAIL
ON WINE
GERALD ASHER
THE GEOMETRY OF PASTA
ONE GOOD DISH
DAVID TANIS
MARKET COOKING
THE CARVED ANGEL COOKERY BOOK
JOYCE MOLYNEUX
ENGLISH FOOD
JANE GRIGSON
SICILIAN FOOD
MARCELLA HAZAN
A TASTE OF SCOTLAND
YORKSHIRE
IRELAND
LAKE DISTRICT
WALES
THE LAST COURSE
ENGLISH BREAD AND YEAST COOKERY
CAKE DOUGHNUT PUDDING
CHOCOLATE DESSERTS
Geraldine Holt's CAKES
DAN LEPARD
BAKING SCHOOL
RONALD SEARLE
Ah Yes, I Remember it Well · PARIS 1961-1975
BRITISH
VEFA'S KITCHEN
WINE GRAPES

Michael Smith's AFTERNOON TEA
Good Housekeeping's Cakes and Pastries
PICTURE COOK BOOK
IL MUSEO IMMAGINARIO DELLA PASTA
JASPER CONRAN COUNTRY
The Ballymaloe Bread Book
Much Depends On Dinner
CLASSIC CHINESE COOKBOOK
THE FIFTH QUARTER AN OFFAL COOKBOOK ANISSA HELOU
GOURMET GUIDE
Favourite Food from AMBROSE HEATH
GOOD FARE
gather
Jane Grigson
FIRST SLICE YOUR COOKBOOK
A SECOND SLICE
the modern preserver kylee newton
FROM JULIA CHILD'S KITCHEN
LA BONNE CUISINE
Harvest of the Cold Months ELIZABETH DAVID
ALASTAIR LITTLE
CITRUS FRUIT
South Wind Through the Kitchen THE BEST OF ELIZABETH DAVID
HOW TO EAT NIGELLA LAWSON
The DOWNRIGHT EPICURE
Citrus
Colman Andrews My Usual Table
Cook and Housewife's Manual Dods
Broths to Bannocks CATHERINE BROWN
FERN VERROW
The Taste of ITALY
Heritage Fruits & Vegetables
ENGLISH COOKING
BRITISH COOKERY JANE GRIGSON
ARABELLA BOXER'S GARDEN COOKBOOK
Arabella Boxer's Book of English Food
ENGLISH
FOOD
The Taste of Britain
MARK HIX BRITISH SEASONAL FOOD
THE SPORTSMAN
THE SCOTS CELLAR
A TASTE OF INDIA MADHUR JAFFREY
BALTIC

ARTICHOKES

Kitchen thistles

Artichokes cooked in olive oil

Artichoke vinaigrette

Artichoke, squid and green beans

THEY CAME FROM ROME: Rachel Roddy, an estimable writer as well as cook, and Sarah Levi, sous-chef at the American Academy in Rome. They arrived to cook a dinner at Quo Vadis which was to be memorable for one of Rome's most famous vegetables – the artichoke. There are many images that have lingered from that evening, but the most beguiling by far is of those two cooks standing whittling their way through boxes of artichokes piled high, prior to cooking and layering them between incalculable lengths of pasta for a superb lasagne. It was an unforgettable dinner.

Artichokes stir that most vital of qualities in a cook: curiosity. With their long stalks of varying thickness, and large-leafed, they are as unlike other vegetables as they are versatile. They are equally splendid raw in salads or can be simply boiled, cooked in wine, herbs and olive oil, eaten whole, or sliced and fried until crisp and golden to strew over griddled fish, meat or other vegetables.

There are numerous varieties of artichoke and as ever it pays to ask suppliers and shopkeepers where they are from and when they were picked. Smitten after driving through fields of artichokes in Brittany on a first holiday to France, a fondness for those noble Breton artichokes has never diminished. They rival the bundles of small artichokes that appear throughout Italy, a land blessed with superb produce.

Because of their variety and versatility, artichokes have a special place in the restaurant (there is often an illustration of an artichoke or a thistle to be found somewhere on the menu at Quo Vadis) and should be equally welcome in the kitchen at home. The young, smaller artichokes arrive at different times throughout the year, making an appearance in the autumn months, and in January brightening the winter months. Being so tender, they can be sliced raw, as thin as possible with a sharp knife, and dipped in water with a squeeze of lemon to arrest any swift discoloration. Once all are done (the stalks too, if still attached and firm, can be peeled boldly of their fibrous casing, sliced and added to a simmering pot or pan), they are splendid tossed with leaves, perhaps some beguiling chicories, dressed with anchovies, capers, lemon and a good olive oil. Add to this some peeled crevettes or potatoes and celery, or poached salt cod, maybe some swiftly fried squid, and you open up an intriguing choice of dishes.

As winter secedes to spring, most artichokes, depending on their freshness, need cooking as they grow and become firm. Slice and fry the prepared artichokes gently in oil, adding a glass of water to simmer the slices until they are tender and just begin to colour in the residual oil, but dress them simply as before. Or simmer them gently with cooked chickpeas, cuttlefish and herbs to make a memorable dish. The Roman vegetable dish that exalts the artichoke, *la vignarola,* or in Sicily *la fritteda*, is a pot of all the tender green summer vegetables simmered slowly, added one at a time so they cook correctly.

As summer advances, the supply of smaller artichokes dwindles, the heads grow larger and the more familiar globe artichokes begin to appear. The sheer simplicity and elegance of a globe artichoke with an accompanying bowl of vinaigrette spiked with extra mustard and, on occasion, enriched with chopped fresh herbs and a hard-boiled egg makes for a dish as peerless as it is timeless.

Britain is often too shy of sunshine to grow artichokes in abundance and there often seems to be a corresponding reluctance to engage with the kitchen thistle, perhaps because of the armour of leaves, each tipped with a tiny spike that keeps the choke within such a prize. A bowl of cold water with slices of lemon, a bowl for the leaves and a small sharp knife are all that is required, along with a modicum of patience. The large globes are so beautiful, I cannot recall the last time I trimmed one, but the smaller artichokes are swiftly despatched. The fresher and firmer they are, the less trimming required.

PS: The cardoon, another variety of thistle, wild, with leaves coloured a ghostly silver, is prized for its stalks, which can be peeled, plunged into boiling water and cooked until tender, to be eaten with anchovies melted gently in olive oil. I also like to cook cardoons with vegetables to then be baked in pastry.

The tins and jars of prepared artichokes, often in oil, tend to be cooked until softened to such a degree that further cooking is impossible. Small jarred artichokes halved and cooked in a little oil until crisp pass muster for an impromptu lunch along with cheese, sliced meats and bread. Artichoke bottoms, tinned or frozen, sliced thin and fried with some finely chopped shallot or sliced spring onion, a little lemon zest, chopped garlic and parsley, are good tossed with griddled squid or cuttlefish. They are good too in a salade Niçoise.

Artichokes cooked in olive oil

AT THE RESTAURANT AND AT HOME, a container of small artichokes cooked in olive oil over a gentle heat is estimable, so I'd encourage cooking a few more than are required, keeping the remainder stored under the cooking oil for other occasions. Lifted from the oil, drained and sliced, they can be fried crisp in a frying pan and sat on toast spread with goat's curd or ricotta – a great favourite with a glass of something cold and delicious.

The remaining olive oil (as with oil used to cook fennel or whole heads of garlic) can be used for cooking vegetables for salads or soups, brightened with fresh herbs, lemon and chilli flakes or a pinch of ground fennel seeds.

Commercial varieties of tinned or jarred artichokes abound but rarely deliver the promise of those cooked at home.

Feeds 6

1 lemon
12 small artichokes
2 bay leaves
a tiny sprig each of rosemary and thyme
3 cloves of garlic, peeled
6 black peppercorns
300ml olive oil

Slice the lemon and add to a bowl of water big enough to hold all the artichokes. Trim the tip of the small artichokes and dip into the lemon water. One at a time, pull away and discard the leaves until the pale-coloured heart is revealed, then trim with a small sharp knife, dipping the hearts in lemon water to deter any discoloration, which is almost instant. Trim the stalks so often discarded to reveal the heart within. Place in the bowl of water and sliced lemon and continue until all are done.

Put the bay leaves, herbs, garlic, peppercorns and olive oil into a heavy-bottomed pot and place on the gentlest heat. Drain the artichokes, the stalks too, if using, and add to the pot.

The artichokes require between 45 minutes and 1 hour or so until a small sharp knife or skewer inserted feels no resistance. Remove

the pot from the heat and leave to one side until cool. Lift the artichokes into a scrupulously clean container and store somewhere cool. They keep remarkably well for several weeks and can of course be refrigerated.

When using, lift from the container with a slotted spoon, letting the residual oil drip back into the container for further use. Slice or quarter the artichokes and fry gently until crisped and golden, to strew on salads, dishes or slices of bread, baked crisp and spread with goat's curd or ricotta.

Artichoke vinaigrette

THE QUINTESSENTIAL DISH, cooked as they are, artichokes rejoice in their singularity. I have cooked artichokes with their leaves closed, giving a familiar pleasing roundness, and open, with an almost fearsome appearance as if cut from a lance. A favourite table is one laid with a whole globe artichoke with its own bowl of mustard vinaigrette at each setting. The preparations require only the patience to let the artichokes simmer in a pot with a few spoonfuls of olive oil, a few bay leaves, peppercorns and a small bundle of thyme before being set on a tray to cool. (They prefer not to sit in a fridge.)

And vinaigrette. We make such large quantities at the restaurant, most often in a food processor; the olive oil combines with the Dijon mustard, emulsifying and becoming almost creamy. As already mentioned, the adding of chopped soft herbs and hard-boiled eggs to the vinaigrette is a happy consideration.

Feeds 6

75ml olive oil
4 bay leaves
a small pinkie-sized bundle of thyme
12 black peppercorns
6 whole globe artichokes

For the vinaigrette

2 soup spoons organic cider vinegar
1 soup spoon lemon juice
2 heaped soup spoons Dijon mustard
300ml extra virgin olive oil

Fill a large pot with water and bring to the boil, adding the olive oil, bay leaves, bundle of thyme, peppercorns and a big pinch of sea salt. Carefully place the artichokes in the water, and cover. Depending on their girth, artichokes will take roughly 45 minutes to an hour to cook fully. They are done when the leaves attached to the stalk can be pulled free with no resistance. Once cooked, lift carefully from the pot with slotted spoons or that most useful of implements, a spider, so called because of its woven concentric circles of metal or mesh, attached to a long handle ideal for lifting from a simmering pot. Let cool.

To make the vinaigrette, stir a pinch of sea salt with the vinegar and lemon juice until dissolved, then add the Dijon mustard and mix well. Whisking all the while, add the olive oil in drops a little at a time, then add freshly ground pepper.

If so wished, add a handful of chopped tarragon, chervil, parsley and chives along with 2 or 3 hard-boiled eggs, chopped coarsely, seasoning accordingly.

Artichoke, squid and green beans

ARTICHOKES TRIMMED AS ON PAGE 20, sliced and cooked gently in a pan, are particularly good with griddled squid or cuttlefish. Tumbled with a few varieties of green beans such as runner, bobby and French, spiked with green olives and capers, a salad of great charm is made.

PS: Flakes of poached salt cod, boiled new potatoes and slices of grilled courgettes can be added to this salad.

Feeds 6

6 small artichokes
a glass of white wine (optional)
4 soup spoons best olive oil
100g green beans
100g runner beans
50g samphire
50g monksbeard
a bunch of spring onions or Tropea onions
a bunch of flat-leaf parsley, leaves picked, washed and dried
50g green olives (stones removed)
1 clove of garlic
75g spinach
a bunch of watercress
1 lemon
300g cleaned and trimmed squid or cuttlefish (see page 125)
30g salted capers, soaked for 30 minutes in cold water

Trim the artichokes as on page 20, then slice thinly. Lay the slices evenly in a wide shallow pan, or two, depending on size. Cover with water and a glass of white wine, if at hand, along with a soup spoon of olive oil. Add a little sea salt and black pepper and place over a moderate heat to simmer until the artichokes are tender, the water evaporated and the slices beginning to colour slightly round the edges, roughly 15 minutes or so. Cover and leave to one side.

Top and tail the beans and cook in salted boiling water until tender, then drain, cool and chop coarsely. Trim the samphire and monksbeard and rinse, plunge into boiling water for 15 seconds, then drain and leave to cool.

Trim and thinly slice the spring onions. Chop the parsley. Coarsely chop the olives. Peel and finely slice the garlic. Carefully pick through, wash and dry the spinach and watercress. Finely grate the zest of the lemon, then halve and juice.

Place a griddle over a moderate heat. Slice the squid into thin strips, roughly 2–3mm wide. Dress the squid with the juice of half the lemon, 1 soup spoon of olive oil and season with salt and pepper. Lay the strips evenly on the griddle, turning after 2–3 minutes and cooking for a further 3 minutes. Remove from the heat.

Place the squid slices in a large bowl with the rest of the olive oil, lemon zest and juice, green olives, garlic and drained capers. Add the beans, spring onions, samphire and monksbeard, the chopped parsley and the leaves. Add the cooked, sliced artichokes, season with salt and black pepper, and mix deftly and swiftly before serving.

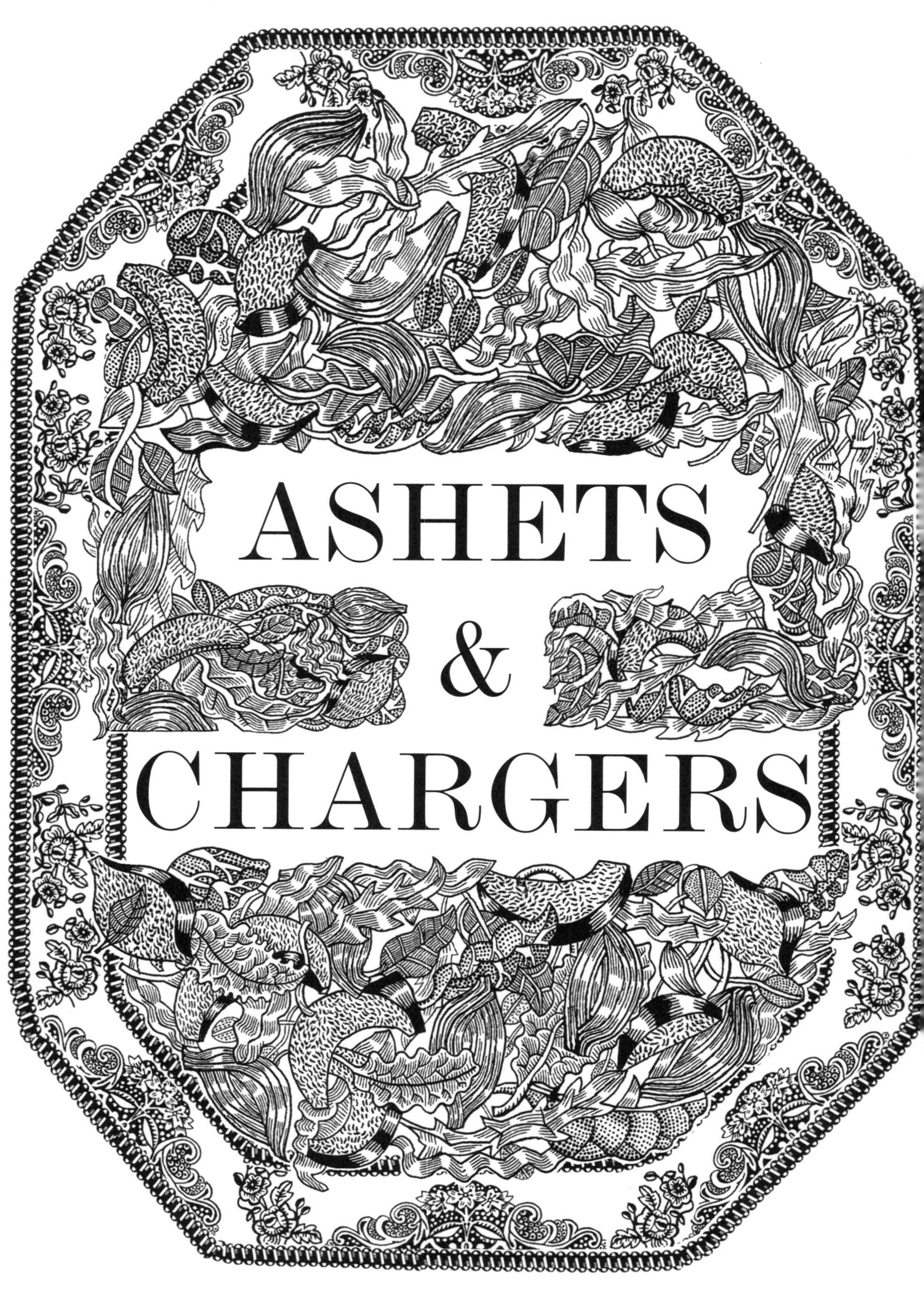
ASHETS
&
CHARGERS

A FEW BIG DISHES SIMPLY DONE

Salmagundy

A dish of lamb

A pot of spring vegetables

Venison with caramelised pears & pickled prunes

Roast leg of pork with bitter leaves

Marinated chicken with roast pumpkin salad

Salt duck with pickled damsons & gooseberries

Barley & beetroot salad

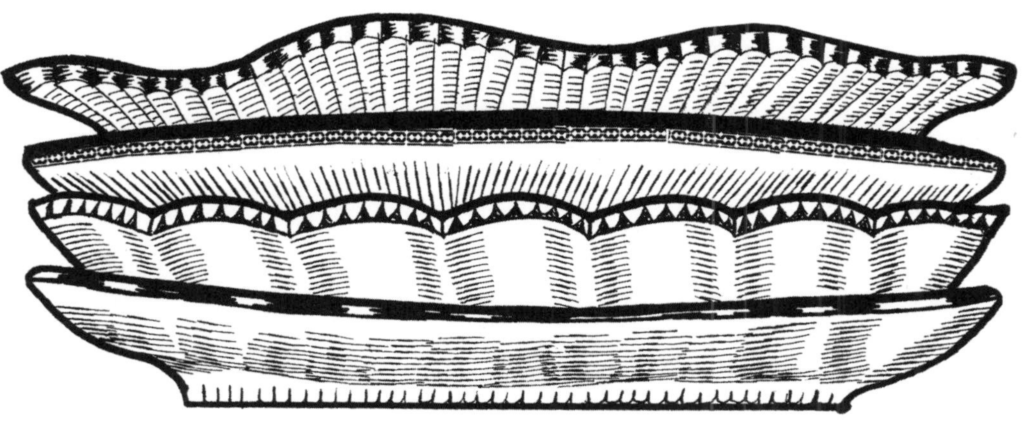

ASHET IS AN OLD SCOTS NAME FOR A SERVING DISH, possibly deriving from the French *assiette*, meaning a dish or a plate; a charger derives from the thirteenth-century word *chargeour*, for a large plate or platter. There seems to be no particular rule as to what the plate should be made of – tin, porcelain, pewter, Scottish pottery, plain or engraved or extravagantly decorated, large, small, round or oval. They are dishes good for piling high with abundantly generous salads for large gatherings. All heaped together, these dishes make a splendid show on the table and are a pleasing alternative to a fleet of bowls, dishes and boards.

One of the dishes I recall Mum making was a salmagundy. Salmagundy (aka sallet magundi, solomongundy or salmagundi) has as many variations in its spelling as it has ingredients and thus makes good use of an ashet. It's an abundant salad made with leaves, fruits, vegetables, herbs, meats and fish. The particular dish prepared by Mum came from the book *Fine English Cookery* by Michael Smith, who used a recipe that dates back to the Tudors.

The salmagundy Mum made was a summery delight, light and elegant, and made a lasting impression on me probably for the simple reason that it was far removed from the food I was trained to prepare as a commis chef in restaurants. Salads, though, are not just for summer, but for journeying through the seasons, making judicious use of all that is in abundance and plentiful.

When I was a young commis chef, *Le Répertoire de la Cuisine* by Louis Saulnier was the chefs' handbook, listing all the ingredients for a great many dishes, all French. Among them was an astonishing list of salads, mostly named after nationalities, nobles, battles or generals. The composed salads, or, to use the curious term, compound salads, were mostly prepared by juniors and, as with pastry, were something more senior chefs seemed not to take seriously.

An apprentice chef therefore becomes well versed in salads and cold foods and I found I enjoyed them immensely, becoming a rather well-practised 'chef garde manger', better known as a larder chef. Apprentices were to be seen and all that was to be heard was a busy knife upon a chopping board – in theory anyway.

Salmagundy requires some thought and preparation beforehand, the reward being a reasonably swift assembly before taking to the table. The cook can take much solace from the fact that the preparations are for small amounts of each ingredient, excepting perhaps the star turn, which might be a poached or roast bird such as duck, a guinea fowl or pheasant, or a chicken.

When composing these huge plates of meats and salad, I enjoy echoing the colours of the season. For instance, an early summer menu shot through with the delicate feather-like leaves of young mustard and rocket, both possessed of a coltish exuberance that so excites a dish, or the simple joy of newly picked peas, or one of the huge heads of the blousiest lettuces, their soft folds layered in every colour from the palest greens to the darkest reds.

The ravishing abundance of summer yields to the beauty of autumn: the first game, along with late-harvest raspberries, rare and wild plums, medlars and quinces, not to mention apples and pears. From there to a quixotic mix of bitter, peppery winter leaves: the chicories that are served both cooked and raw alongside leaves such as land cress and wild cress, cress tops and chickweed, to mention but a few. Should fortune smile, perhaps there might even be the delicate pretty stems of pink and wood sorrel which add a winning zip and zing to a salad, be it of vegetables or meats, game or fish.

All the seasons have their own unique qualities, and as each approaches I look to the shelves for the old familiar books, often charmingly illustrated with calendars and lists of what's best in which month, to help inspire new dishes. There is much pleasure to be had sorting through all this bounty and thinking what to pair with what, or, even better, what dish might best suit using the lot. Inevitably it is a dish inspired by a salmagundy, an exuberant delight in many good things.

Other thoughts for piling on big dishes or ashets might be roast and marinated joints of less familiar ingredients that aren't used on a daily basis, such as kid, boar, venison, goose, game feathered and furred, even offal. Perhaps thin slices of a roast Middle White pig or wild duck or pheasant strewn over a great dish of caramelised apples, prunes steeped in red wine, roast onions, and fried sage and parsley leaves.

Grilled or roast guinea fowl or rabbit, when laid upon a salad of clean, bright chicories such as puntarelle and cicoria, dandelion and watercress, with the thinnest slices of fennel, slivers of blooded and non-blooded oranges spiked with capers, and judiciously dressed in a fine vinegar and oil, makes for a dish as handsome as it is good to eat.

Similar dishes can be made with lightly cured fish such as poached cod or trout, strewn over a salad of potatoes, cabbages, celery and leeks, carrots and beetroots, and lemon, with a vinaigrette of finely chopped onions and capers, herbs and olive oil, akin to the classic sauce ravigote.

A vegetarian alternative might be a great heap of celeriac and fennel braised with onion and celery, lemon juice and olive oil, a little garlic, and a mustardy green sauce, a derivative of the great salsa verde. Add a few bitter greens for a welcome bite. This dish can also be used to accompany roast birds and meats or fishes like cod and hake.

Make use of cheeses and curds such as ricotta and feta and their numerous counterparts from other countries. They can be scattered across salads or over grilled breads spread with olive oil, along with olives and herbs, capers and anchovies. There are infinite variations to such dishes, depending on the season.

Salmagundy: warm roast chicken salad with summer slaw

THIS ANCIENT DISH makes marvellous use of abundant seasonal produce. The ingredients listed will make an epic, splendid salad, so very much worth a great effort. Fear not adding, subtracting, swapping and tailoring the salad with other salads and leaves, herbs and vegetables along the way. Prior to assembly, have ready all the prepared ingredients, each in their own bowl.

Feeds 6–8

1 whole very, very good chicken, roughly 1.5kg in weight
3 soup spoons olive oil
1–2 different blousy lettuces such as Bibb or Webbs
a small bunch of mint, leaves picked and torn
a bunch of bright, fresh watercress
150g new potatoes, scrubbed and boiled
3 soft-boiled organic eggs, peeled and cut in half
150g green beans, topped, tailed, boiled and cooled
4 ripe tomatoes, cut into quarters or sixths
a pinch of fresh marjoram, and summer savory too, if possible, leaves carefully picked
2 oranges, peeled and segments removed from between each membrane
6–8 anchovy fillets
1 soup spoon salted capers, soaked for 30 minutes in cold water, then drained
24 black olives, Niçoise or Kalamata (stones removed)
1 heaped soup spoon chopped flat-leaf parsley

For the slaw with which to dress the dish

1 small Savoy cabbage
the leafy heart of a head of celery
6 spring onions
juice and grated zest of 1 unwaxed orange
juice and grated zest of 1 unwaxed lemon
3 soup spoons extra virgin olive oil
1 soup spoon organic cider vinegar

Preheat the oven to 200°C. Rub the bird with the 3 soup spoons of olive oil, and season with salt and black pepper. Place in a roasting tin and roast, basting from time to time, for 1 hour, or until the juice runs clear after piercing the thigh. Let sit until cool. Carve the meat and keep covered. The resulting juices in the pan can be kept for stock or boiled and mixed with the dressing when ready to serve.

To make the slaw, chop the cabbage and celery small. Slice the spring onions thinly. Place in a bowl with the orange and lemon zests and the juice, then add the olive oil and cider vinegar. Season with salt and black pepper and mix very well. Cover and refrigerate.

Place each prepared ingredient in its own bowl.

Clear the decks in readiness to assemble in a pleasing choreography.

The salad is layered on a bed of lettuce leaves laid holus-bolus over the whole of the dish. Strew with the torn mint. Arrange the watercress around the borders of the leaves. Lay the slices of chicken over the leaves. Spoon half the cabbage and celery slaw over the chicken. Tumble on the potatoes, then settle the halves of the soft-boiled eggs in among the potatoes, swiftly following suit with the beans and the tomatoes. Scatter the marjoram on the tomatoes. Reserving the juice, lay the segments of orange over the tomatoes and lay the fillets of anchovy on top. Strew with the capers and then the olives. Add the last of the slaw.

When all is done, strew the salmagundy with the chopped parsley and take to the table.

A dish of lamb, braised root vegetables, lemon and dill

THIS INSPIRING RECIPE USING MANY WINTER VEGETABLES is an adaptation of a recipe by Claudia Roden. The vegetables are cut into pieces, piled into a pot and gently cooked in olive oil, then spiked with lemon and much chopped dill. They are wonderful eaten as is. In summer the dish should be made with lamb; in winter it's worth seeking out mutton or hogget (a year-old lamb).

PS: All legs in the following recipes, including the leg of lamb here, can be butterflied. This has the benefit of ensuring the skin is crisp all over, reducing the cooking time by half and making it easier to carve.

Feeds 6–8

1 whole leg of lamb, hogget or mutton, weighing somewhere in the region of 2kg
a light vegetable oil such as sunflower or rapeseed
1 teaspoon each black and white peppercorns, celery seeds, dill seeds and fennel seeds
2 lemons
3 small cloves of garlic
a generous bunch of flat-leaf parsley, leaves picked, washed and dried
2 soup spoons very good red wine vinegar
olive oil
2 small onions, peeled
1 bulb of fennel, trimmed and thinly sliced, fronds, stalks and all
1 head of celery, leaves reserved
1 clove of garlic
2 large, earthy carrots, peeled
2 parsnips, peeled
1 small swede, peeled
6 small fresh white turnips, firm to the touch, unpeeled
a small head of celeriac, about 400g, peeled
2 small bunches of dill

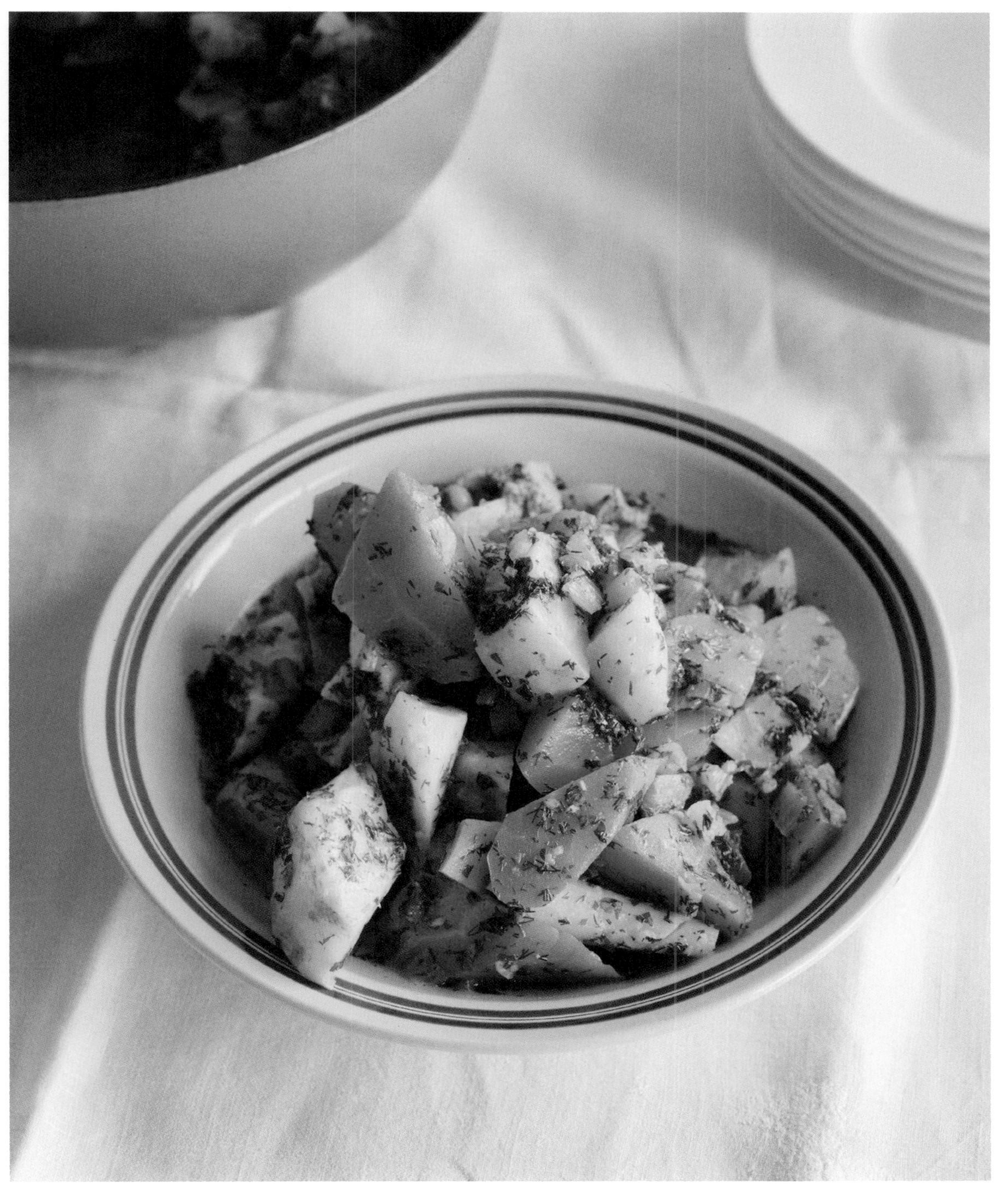

Heat the oven to 220°C. Rub the meat all over with a light film of oil and season with sea salt and black pepper. Place in a large heavy-bottomed roasting tin and roast fiercely for 20 minutes, then reduce the heat to 180°C for an hour (or half an hour for a butterflied leg) for a blush of pink in the lamb, or slightly longer, say 30 minutes, if you like your meat well done, bearing in mind that you will rest the lamb for at least 30 minutes after cooking so the meat settles prior to a 5-minute flash in the oven before carving.

Finely grind the peppercorns, celery seeds, dill seeds and fennel seeds.

Grate the lemon zest, peel and finely chop the garlic, and chop the picked parsley. Then chop these all together.

When the lamb is done, remove from the oven. Should there be an enthusiastic presence of fat, carefully spoon some of it away until there are about 4 or 5 spoonfuls left. Dust the ground spices over the joint, then strew with the chopped parsley, garlic and lemon zest. Spoon over the juice of a lemon, the red wine vinegar and 2 soup spoons of olive oil. Scoop up the residue in the tin and pour it over the meat. Let rest for at least 30 minutes, covered with foil.

Coarsely chop the onions, fennel and head of celery, reserving the celery leaves for later, and finely chop the garlic. Cook gently in 4 soup spoons of olive oil in a wide heavy-bottomed pot. Coarsely chop the carrots, parsnips, swede, turnips and celeriac, and add to the pot. Add a pinch of salt, a few grinds of pepper and two soup spoons of water, stir well and cover with a lid. Bring to the boil, then lower the heat to a simmer and cook gently for 30–40 minutes, until the vegetables are tender. Add a soup spoon of water now and again if the vegetables boil dry, but the cook will be surprised at the amount of water expelled by the vegetables through cooking.

Remove the lid, boil away any excess liquid and remove from the heat. Chop the celery leaves and dill. Add the juice of a lemon, the chopped celery leaves and dill to the vegetables and leave to sit, covered, until curtain up.

Carve the lamb in thin slices and heap upon a warmed dish. Spoon over all the resulting goodness gathered in the tray after the lamb has rested. Tumble the braised vegetables onto a second dish and take to table.

To adapt this dish for spring, replace the root vegetables with braised spring vegetables: broad beans, spring onions, peas, courgettes, asparagus, wild garlic and new potatoes (see opposite).

A pot of spring vegetables to accompany a leg of lamb

It is worth considering that the weights given are more for guidance, the cook encouraged to use the eye, as this is a celebratory and abundant dish and will enjoy a harmonious mix of vegetables, any leftovers happily reheated the following day or even made into soup.

Feeds 6–8

1 small onion, peeled
1 heart of celery (outer stalks are good for soup or stock)
12 new potatoes
2 soup spoons olive oil
6 small courgettes
250g peas (unpodded)
250g broad beans (podded weight, or use frozen)
2 bunches of spring onions, trimmed and sliced thinly
15 spears of asparagus, stalks sliced thinly, spears left intact

Chop the onion, pick the leaves from the celery heart, chop and put to one side, then chop the stalks coarsely. Scrub the potatoes well and halve any larger ones. Warm a wide, heavy-bottomed pot. Add the olive oil, 2 soup spoons of water, the chopped onion, celery heart, potatoes and a pinch each of salt and black pepper. Cover with a lid. Cook gently for 20 minutes or so over a moderate heat, stirring from time to time, until softened but uncoloured.

Coarsely chop the courgettes, then add them to the pan of vegetables, with 2 more soup spoons of water if required, then cover and cook for 15 minutes.

Pod the peas and broad beans. Tip them into the pot of potatoes and courgettes, add 4 soup spoons of water, a pinch more salt and pepper and stir gently. Cover and cook for 10 minutes. Add in the spring onions and the spears and sliced asparagus stalks. Simmer for a further 5 or 10 minutes, until all is tender, tasting to see if the seasoning requires adjusting, before adding the chopped herbs and giving a final gentle stir prior to serving. Add a small handful of wild garlic if available, and serve with the roasted leg of lamb.

Venison with caramelised pears and pickled prunes

THE RICH ABUNDANCE OF AUTUMN FARE has the cook conjuring dishes of game and fruit to warm and nourish. Pairing roast venison, marinated in wild pepper and herbs, with prunes simmered in wine spiked with black pepper and a superb vinegar, with pears cooked golden, makes a splendid dish. It is an excellent excuse too for going shopping, or for rummaging in the shelves through tins already at hand of different peppers, such as a wild pepper, cubeb and those Madagascan voatsiperifery peppercorns, rare and so worth the effort of seeking out. These peppers, ground with pinches of wild marjoram and sage to bestrew the cooked venison, result in a pooling of beguiling juices in the roasting tin to be spooned over the dish when serving.

PS: The bitter leaves accompanying the pork in the following recipe are equally good with this venison dish.

Feeds 6–8

For the pickled prunes

2 big soup spoons redcurrant jelly
350ml red wine
350g Agen prunes, stones removed
6 bay leaves
3 soup spoons red wine vinegar, e.g. Banyuls
½ teaspoon freshly ground black pepper

For the caramelised pears

2 lemons
6 pears
3 soup spoons caster sugar

1.2kg haunch of venison, hung well and not vacuum-packed if possible, bone removed and butterflied
5 soup spoons extra virgin olive oil, plus extra for greasing
2 cloves of garlic
6 sage leaves
a large pinch each of dried wild marjoram, sage and thyme (if at hand)

1 teaspoon thyme or summer savory, tiny leaves picked
1 level teaspoon each of freshly ground black and white peppercorns, wild if possible
2 soup spoons good-quality red wine vinegar, e.g. Banyuls (see page 198)

To serve
leaves such as watercress, rocket, mustard and escarole

Start with the prunes. Dissolve the redcurrant jelly in the red wine in a wide-bottomed pot over a moderate heat. Bring to the boil. Add the prunes and bay leaves. Return to the boil and add the vinegar and pepper, stir well and remove from the heat immediately. Do not be afraid of the bite of this pickle. As it cools it will temper dramatically. When cool, it'll store in the refrigerator for several weeks. This can be done well in advance.

To caramelise the pears, juice the lemons into a large bowl. Peel and core the pears and, depending on size, cut each pear into three wedges then roll the pieces in the lemon juice. In a wide, heavy-bottomed frying pan, gently dissolve the sugar over a moderate heat and cook until a beautiful golden caramel forms. When the caramel is bronzed and bubbling, tip in the pears and lemon juice and stand well back, as the sugar will splutter indignantly. When the fury is silenced, agitate the pears in the caramel and let cook, turning the pears frequently until evenly coloured and the caramel begins to bubble and thicken. Continue thus until the pears are tender. Remove from the heat. Tip the pears and juices out on to a flat dish.

To roast the venison, first heat the oven to 220°C, with a roasting tin inside. Lightly oil the haunch, and liberally season the skin side with salt to be lowered onto the roasting tin. Generously and evenly pepper the meat facing upwards, place in a heated roasting tin with a film of olive oil, then put into the heated oven.

Roast for 30 minutes or so, until the meat is just cooked. (Venison is best eaten when just cooked to a crimson blush.)

While the venison roasts, make the dressing. Peel and thinly slice the cloves of garlic. Grind together the dried and fresh picked sage leaves, summer savory or thyme, then mix with the pepper and marjoram. Mix all these with the extra virgin olive oil and red wine vinegar.

Remove the joint from the oven. Spoon the dressing over the haunch, lifting up any juices gathered in the tin around the meat. A pair of tongs is excellent for helping to move the venison in the tin for ease of dressing. Cover with foil and let rest for at least half an hour.

Lay an abundance of leaves on an ashet, then carve the meat into slices and put on top of the leaves. Arrange the caramelised pears and pickled prunes around the sliced meat, add 4 soup spoons of the pickled prune juices to the residue in the roasting tin, stir to mix, then spoon over the meat and leaves.

Roast leg of pork with bitter leaves, onions and sage

ALMOST ALL OF THIS LOVELY DISH can be cooked earlier in the day at a gentle pace. The gorgeous colours of the beguiling radicchio family such as Tardivo, Treviso and Grumola verde and rosso are worth asking for but are very rare. The leaves are beautiful and, when washed and dressed, eat well raw, but when cooked lightly in olive oil in a frying pan the subtle, elusive depth of flavour acquired more than makes up for the reduction in colour – doneness is observed as the leaves closest to the heat curl and turn a muted sepia.

Feeds 6–8

a whole piece of pork leg, off the bone, roughly 2kg
6 shallots, peeled and halved lengthways
2 pink Roscoff onions, peeled and each cut into 6 pieces through the root
8 cloves of garlic, unpeeled
a small sprig each of thyme and summer savory, leaves picked, stalks reserved
1 head of Treviso
1 head of Tardivo (or 2 large heads of radicchio)
2 soup spoons olive oil
1 soup spoon red wine vinegar
18 sage leaves
50ml light vegetable or sunflower oil

To roast the meat, heat the oven to 220°C (leg of pork should be cooked for 18 minutes per 500g). Liberally salt and pepper the joint. Spread the shallots, onions, garlic and herb stalks over the bottom of a roasting tin and put the leg on top. Roast in the heated oven for 10 minutes, then turn down the heat to 180°C and cook for 1 hour. Take out of the oven and carefully remove the onions and garlic with a spoon onto a dish, cover and put to one side. Remove and discard the herb stalks. Dust the joint with half of the finely chopped herb leaves and plenty of black pepper, then cover and let rest for at least half an hour. Turn the oven up to 200°C.

Preheat a cast-iron pan over a moderate heat. Trim away any blemished outer leaves from the Treviso and Tardivo, or the radicchio. Cut the heads in half through the root. Lay the halves cut side down on the pan and leave to cook. Foods do not like being meddled with while getting along with the business of cooking. The leaves closest to the heat will curl and colour like paper. 'Tis rather lovely. After 5–10 minutes, moderating the heat so it is not too high, turn the halves and continue cooking until each half yields to the insertion of a small, sharp knife. Remove the halves to a dish, laying side by side so they cool and do not steam. Mix together the 2 soup spoons of olive oil, 1 soup spoon of vinegar and the picked thyme and summer savory leaves, season with salt and pepper and spoon over the leaves.

Pick the sage leaves from the stalks. Heat the vegetable oil in a heavy-bottomed pan over a brisk heat (Mum always used the ends of her bottles of olive oil for such tasks – her collection filled a tray in the kitchen like an array of perfume bottles on a dressing table). Have too a slotted spoon in hand. Add a few leaves to the hot oil at a time. With care, flip the leaves and when they colour a dark green, which is swiftly done, lift them out and put them on a plate lined with kitchen paper to drain. Continue thus until all are done. Lightly season with sea salt. Lift from the paper on to a clean plate and set aside.

Now all is ready for assembly. Coarsely chop the cooled radicchio halves into two or three pieces. Dress these with the onions and the peeled garlic cloves and season with salt and pepper. Add any juices remaining in the onion dish to the pork juices. Lift the pork on to a tray, and carve. Fill the middle of the ashet with slices of the pork and arrange the radicchio and onion and garlic mix around the edges.

Heat the juices in the roasting tin for a minute, until bubbling, then spoon over the leaves and the pork. Scatter the sage leaves over the top and serve.

Marinated chicken with roast pumpkin salad

IDEAL FOR GRILLING OR ROASTING OVER EMBERS, this recipe, inspired by Hamersley's Bistro in Boston, USA, is one I have cooked often since my time at Alastair Little. The eager cook might consider spatchcocking a whole chicken, marinating and roasting it whole.

Feeds 6

6 breasts of chicken, wings still attached
1 soup spoon extra virgin olive oil

For the marinade

4 sprigs of thyme
8 cloves of garlic, peeled
4 branches of rosemary
1 small onion, peeled and chopped
½ teaspoon freshly ground black pepper
a large bunch of flat-leaf parsley, leaves picked
100ml extra virgin olive oil
juice of 1 lemon
100g Dijon mustard

Place the thyme, garlic, rosemary, onion and black pepper in a food processor and grind to a coarse purée. To this add a handful of parsley leaves at a time, adding a few spoonfuls of olive oil as you go, until you have made a thick green paste. Add the lemon juice and the rest of the olive oil. Stir in the mustard. Evenly spread the marinade over the chicken, cover well and leave to marinate at least overnight.

Preheat the oven to 200°C. Heat a large roasting tin in the oven and, when hot, remove, strew with sea salt and a spoonful of oil and lay the chicken skin side down on the salt. Place in the oven and cook undisturbed for 45 minutes. With care, lift the chicken from the oven, check for doneness, then cover with foil and rest for 20–25 minutes.

Return the chicken to the oven to ensure it is heated thoroughly before serving with the roast pumpkin salad (see below).

Roast pumpkin and almond salad

This is a salad that makes excellent use of the great many varieties of onion, pumpkin and squash around. Crown Prince, Violetta or some other dark green or grey-skinned pumpkin are often the best for cooking. The same applies to lettuces, leaves and cresses – seek out different varieties. The giddier the mix, the more joyful the salad. Here too is an opportunity to try other vinegars of single grape variety rather than the Banyuls mentioned, or an organic cider or fruit vinegar such as pear, plum, quince or prune.

1kg pumpkin
30ml extra virgin olive oil, plus extra for the onions and dressing
3 red or Roscoff onions, peeled and sliced into rounds 5mm in thickness
2 soup spoons Banyuls (see page 198) or other red wine vinegar, plus extra for the onions and dressing
a small bundle of thyme
a small bunch of sage
3 cloves of garlic, finely chopped
grated zest of 1 unwaxed lemon
a big pinch of dried chilli flakes
salad leaves, a handful of each, e.g. large-leaf rocket, young spinach, watercress, wild cress, land cress or escarole, Grumola, picked and washed
a bunch of mint, leaves picked and torn
a bunch of flat-leaf parsley, leaves picked and chopped
75g blanched almonds, roasted at 150°C for 8 minutes or so until golden, then coarsely sliced

Preheat the oven to 220°C. Split the pumpkin, remove the seeds and cut into handsome wedges redolent of a Viking longship. Heat a large roasting tin in the oven for a few minutes, add the extra virgin olive oil and the slices of pumpkin and return to the oven. Cook for 20 minutes undisturbed, checking from time to time that the slices are not colouring too fast and may need turning. Add a little more oil if necessary.

Meanwhile, place a wide griddle or frying pan on a moderate heat, and lay the red onions in the heated pan to colour well. Cook for 5–8 minutes, then turn and repeat for a further 3–4 minutes. Remove the onions to a dish, cover and set aside for 5 minutes. Remove the cover and discard any burnt pieces of onion. Lightly dress with 1 soup spoon of vinegar and 2 soup spoons of extra virgin olive oil.

Pick the thyme and sage leaves and chop small, then mix with the garlic, lemon zest and chilli flakes. Season with salt and black pepper. Remove the pumpkin from the oven and insert a knife into the slices, which should offer no resistance. If still firm, return to the oven for a further 5–10 minutes.

Strew the herb seasoning over the roast pumpkin. Pour over 1 soup spoon of vinegar. To assemble the dish, carve each breast in 3 and keep warm. Tumble all the leaves onto a big dish. Lay the pumpkin on the leaves, along with any juices still in the tin, and scatter the onion over the pumpkin. Tumble on the slices of chicken. Strew the mint leaves, parsley and sliced almonds over the salad, finishing with one last flurry of Banyuls vinegar and olive oil.

Salt duck with pickled damsons and gooseberries

EQUALLY GOOD AS A STARTER FOR MANY or as a main course. The original recipe for salt duck is Welsh, from Lady Llanover's cookbook *Good Cookery from Wales*, and was then suggested by Elizabeth David to Anne and Franco Taruschio, founders of the Walnut Tree Inn, Abergavenny, who in turn made the dish a classic at their restaurant. The suggested companions for salt duck are an array of pickles and preserves such as pickled damsons, pickled gooseberries, crab apple, medlar or rowan jelly.

Feeds 6

For the duck

a crown of excellent duck, dry-plucked preferably
for every 2.8kg of duck, 225g coarse sea salt

To serve

pickled gooseberries (see below)
pickled damsons (see opposite)

Rub the duck all over with the salt, place in a dish, cover well and refrigerate. After a day and a half, turn the duck and leave for a further day and a half. Rinse the duck of any lingering salt.

Preheat the oven to 160°C. Place the duck comfortably in a deep lidded dish or casserole, allowing room enough to cover with cold water. Lay a disc of greaseproof paper on top to keep the steam in. Cover, place in the oven and cook for 2 hours. Carefully lift the dish from the oven. Remove the duck and discard the water, then let the duck cool before wrapping it in baking parchment and storing in a sealed container in the fridge for up to two to three days.

When ready, slice the duck thinly and arrange on an ashet. Serve alongside little bowls of pickled gooseberries and pickled damsons (see opposite), medlar jelly and rowan and crab apple jelly.

Pickled gooseberries

Excellent with many things. Make sure the jars for both pickles are scrupulously cleaned and dried (best done in the oven at 120°C).

Makes a good 2kg

1 teaspoon whole allspice
12 cloves
½ teaspoon coriander seeds
a thumb of ginger, peeled and thinly sliced
1 teaspoon mustard seeds
600ml white wine vinegar
1kg gooseberries, topped and tailed
150g caster sugar

Put the spices and vinegar into a stainless-steel pot. Bring to the boil and simmer gently for 10 minutes. Leave to cool.

Strain the vinegar and return to the boil in a wide pan. Add the gooseberries and sugar and simmer until the berries are tender (roughly 5–10 minutes for ripe fruit; 10–15 if your gooseberries are firm and sharp). Lift these out and place carefully in clean jars. Reduce the pickling liquid until it becomes syrupy, say 5–10 minutes. Pour this over the gooseberries in the jars and seal. Store in a cool place.

Pickled damsons

.2kg damsons

Prepare the pickling liquid as for the gooseberries above, using a stick of cinnamon and a heaped soup spoon of black peppercorns instead of the above spices.

Remove any stalks and leaves from the damsons.

Simmer the pickling liquid, cool, strain and return to the boil in a wide pan. Carefully add the damsons. Bring to the boil and simmer the damsons until tender, maybe 5 minutes.

Lift the damsons out carefully and spoon into clean jars. Reduce the pickling liquid until syrupy, about 10 minutes or so, then pour this gently over the damsons in the jars. Seal well and store in a cool place.

Barley and beetroot salad to accompany smoked and cured fish

SMOKED AND CURED FISH ARE ONE OF THE GLORIES of the British Isles, a tradition that spans the ages. Opening boxes of smoked fish at the restaurant and lifting apart the sheets of white paper within reveals the lustre of bronzed and golden skin, a trove with an appearance of ancient wealth: herring, whole or kippered, trout, mackerel, haddock or sprats from a trusted smokehouse or fishmonger. They are always worthwhile having in the fridge at home, as they keep well wrapped in paper in a sealed container. Smoked fish have a surprising delicacy, and when eaten with beetroot, cooked gently and dressed with the lightest of pickles on a small mound of soft, yielding barley, make a salad of great charm. The richness of the salad is dispelled with feisty horseradish and mustard.

PS: The cook might consider using a diable to cook the beetroots, as on page 370.

Feeds 6

a dish of one or a choice of smoked trout, herring, mackerel or sprats, depending on what is on offer

For the salad

500g bunched beetroot, leaves attached (roughly 6–8 small beetroots)
2 soup spoons olive oil
1 teaspoon red wine vinegar
200g cooked barley
a bunch of spring onions, thinly sliced
a large bunch of flat-leaf parsley, leaves picked and chopped
100g freshly grated horseradish (easy to find online, or buy a very good-quality jar such as Tracklements)

For the vinaigrette

1 soup spoon red wine vinegar
1 teaspoon Dijon mustard
4 soup spoons extra virgin olive oil

Preheat the oven to 180°C. Trim and scrub the beetroot and place on a piece of foil big enough to wrap them all. Lightly dress with a soup spoon of olive oil and season with salt and black pepper. Fold the foil into a tightly sealed package and place on a roasting tray in the oven. Roast for 40–45 minutes. Remove from the oven, carefully unfold the foil and check for doneness by inserting a sharp knife. If they yield fully, they're ready. Leave to cool. Once cool, peel the beetroots by rubbing them with your hands – the skin should peel off with great ease. Cut in half and dress with the vinegar and another soup spoon of olive oil. Set aside.

To make the vinaigrette, put the vinegar into a bowl with a little salt and pepper and whisk well until the salt has dissolved. Add the mustard, then the olive oil. Mix very well and taste for seasoning.

To assemble: tip the cooked barley onto a handsome dish and flatten slightly. Onto this spoon the beetroot and juices. Spoon over the vinaigrette. Then strew with the thinly sliced spring onions, the chopped parsley and the freshly grated horseradish.

Serve alongside a dish of smoked fishes.

BISCUITS

Roll out the barrel

Maple walnut biscuits

Cinnamon & hazelnut biscuits

Pistachio biscuits

Orange & fennel biscuits

Shortcake

Lemon thins

A VISIT TO EDINBURGH WHEN I WAS A LITTLE BOY always began with a trip to the greatly missed Laigh Bakery and Coffee House on Hanover Street. While Mum and Dad were revived with a coffee we ogled the cakes and the considerable pile of shortbread sitting beside a bowl of whipped cream. A sit-down in one of the great institutions of the day was concluded with a visit to the bakery and Mum buying a large bag of shortbread to take back home.

Those slabs of buttery goodness were eked out over time until the last crumbs were consumed and Mum, poor us, had to make her own shortbread. Oh, it was good. The smell alone of finely crumbed flour and butter so slowly baked to the palest wheaten hue had us all agog.

The favourite treat, though, was a delicate shortcake Mum only made as pudding when friends came for dinner, or, one on a heroic scale, sandwiched with strawberries or raspberries for Dad's birthday.

The memory of biscuits is curiously clear. I wonder if it's because a biscuit, buttery and crumblesome, eaten fresh with a scoop of just-churned ice cream, possibly with raspberries, remains a great favourite? Whether they're nutted or spiced, fruited or plain, the only rule for a biscuit is that it must be crisp and fresh. This is happily achieved by having a roll of biscuit dough in the fridge or freezer from which slices can be cut, laid upon a tray and baked in a hot oven until just coloured round the edges.

A few simple thoughts and rules when making biscuits:

- It is worth noting that these biscuits, baked fresh, make excellent quick puddings when served with ices and sorbets, custards, creams and syllabubs and seasonal fruits.
- The biscuit dough recipes in this chapter are a reasonably straightforward crew that behave well when made in advance.
- The dough, wrapped tightly in baking parchment, stores well in the fridge in sealed containers for 3–4 days and freezes excellently for at least 3 months, raw rather than cooked.
- As homemade biscuits are best eaten fresh, only slice and bake what is required with a few extra – known as the cook's perk.
- Once the biscuits are baked, remove from the oven and lift on to a rack to cool.

Pistachio
Maple &
Walnut

Maple walnut biscuits

ON A VISIT LONG AGO TO LOS ANGELES I ate at Campanile, founded by Nancy Silverton and Mark Peel. The food was wonderful and so too was their La Brea Bakery, as indeed are the books from this seminal restaurant, a testament to great shopping, cooking and eating. Nancy Silverton is famed for her baking, and these biscuits are inspired by her recipes.

Makes 48 biscuits; 24 for each cylinder

230g unsalted butter, at room temperature
100g caster sugar
½ a vanilla pod, split and seeds scraped
1 freshest organic egg yolk
2 soup spoons maple syrup
275g plain flour, sifted, plus extra for dusting
150g walnuts

Heat the oven to 180°C.

Cut the butter roughly into pieces and cream in a food mixer until pale. Add the sugar and vanilla seeds and continue to mix until pale again. Mix in the egg yolk and the maple syrup. Roast the walnuts for 5–10 minutes at 180°C, leave to cool and coarsely chop. Turn off the oven. Add the flour and chopped walnuts and mix until a dough forms. Knead this deftly and swiftly on a lightly floured surface. Once the dough is formed, shape into a cylinder roughly 30cm in length and 5–6cm in width. Cut in half and roll each half in a sheet of greaseproof paper, twisting the ends as if for a large bonbon. Refrigerate for at least 30 minutes; one of the halves can be frozen for another time.

Heat the oven to 180°C. Line a baking sheet with baking parchment. As these are best eaten fresh, slice and bake only what is needed, then rewrap, store and return to the fridge. Cut 3mm-thick slices and lay in serried ranks on the lined baking sheet.

Place in the oven and bake for 12–15 minutes. Cool on a rack.

Cinnamon and hazelnut biscuits

FIND THE BEST, FRESHEST CINNAMON there is for baking. Grinding cinnamon sticks from an excellent spice merchant makes an almighty difference. I buy mine from the Vinegar Shed. The same rule applies for nuts. I particularly love the hazelnuts from Piedmont in northern Italy, which tend to come peeled and roasted in tightly sealed packages and delight the cook no end.

Makes 48 biscuits; 24 for each cylinder

230g unsalted butter, at room temperature
50g caster sugar
90g dark muscovado sugar
1 organic egg, separated, the white reserved for coating
240g plain flour, sifted, plus extra for dusting
2 teaspoons freshly ground cinnamon
230g roast hazelnuts, ground, 90g reserved for the coating

For the coating

90g roast hazelnuts, ground (see above)
1 teaspoon freshly ground cinnamon
50g golden caster sugar
the reserved egg white

To make the biscuit dough, place the butter in a food mixer and beat until pale. Add both sugars and mix together thoroughly. Beat in the egg yolk. Sift the flour and cinnamon together and add to the mixture. Add 140g of ground hazelnuts and mix together thoroughly. Knead swiftly and deftly on a lightly floured surface until a dough forms, then shape into a cylinder roughly 30cm in length and 5–6cm in width. Cut in half and roll each half in a sheet of greaseproof paper, twisting the ends as if for a large bonbon. Refrigerate for at least 30 minutes; one of the halves can be frozen for another time. Set the rest of the ground hazelnuts aside for the coating.

To make the biscuit coating, mix the 90g of ground hazelnuts in a bowl with the cinnamon and sugar. Line a baking sheet with baking parchment. Evenly distribute the hazelnut mixture over the paper.

Tip the egg white into another bowl and beat well. Paint the dough with the beaten egg white and roll in the hazelnut mix until each cylinder is evenly covered. Wrap in baking parchment and refrigerate for at least an hour. Sadly, these do not keep so well once rolled in sugar, but the biscuits, once baked, keep well for 3–4 days in an airtight container.

Heat the oven to 180°C. Line a baking sheet with baking parchment.

Cut 3mm-thick slices from each roll and lay them neatly on the baking sheet. Bake in the oven for 12–15 minutes, until golden. Cool on a rack.

Pistachio biscuits

Makes 48 biscuits; 24 for each cylinder

220g unsalted butter, at room temperature
160g caster sugar
1 vanilla pod
a pinch of salt
40g ground almonds
60g ground pistachios (plus 1 whole pistachio to place atop each biscuit)
300g self-raising flour, sifted, plus extra for dusting

Cream the butter in a food mixer, then add the sugar and mix well. Split the vanilla bean lengthways, scrape out the seeds and add to the bowl, along with the ground nuts, and mix thoroughly. Add the flour and mix swiftly and deftly. Knead on a lightly floured surface until a dough forms.

Mould the dough into a cylinder and cut into 2 lengths, wrapping each in greaseproof paper, twisting the ends as if for a large bonbon. Refrigerate for at least an hour or overnight preferably.

Heat the oven to 180°C. Cut as required, but if baking all, cut the bonbon in half lengthways, then in half again, each quarter into thirds, then gently press each piece in the palm of your hand and lay them a few centimetres apart on a lined baking sheet. Pop a pistachio atop each.

Alternatively, slice each roll, cutting 3mm-thick biscuits to lay a few centimetres apart on a lined baking sheet. Place a pistachio atop each biscuit.

Place in the oven and bake for 10–15 minutes, until golden. Cool on a rack.

Orange and fennel biscuits

Makes 48 biscuits; 24 for each cylinder

230g unsalted butter, at room temperature
100g caster sugar
1 vanilla pod, split and seeds scraped
1 organic egg, plus 1 yolk
260g plain flour, sifted, plus extra for dusting
a pinch of salt
1 teaspoon ground fennel seeds
finely grated zest of 3 large oranges (or 4 to 5 smaller ones)
1 teaspoon whole fennel seeds

In a food mixer, beat the butter, sugar and vanilla seeds until creamed and pale.

Crack the whole egg and the egg yolk into a small bowl, whisk and add slowly to the butter and sugar, mixing all the while. Add the flour, salt, ground fennel seeds and orange zest. Mix all together and knead gently on a lightly floured surface into a dough, then shape into a cylinder roughly 30cm in length and 5–6cm in width. Cut in half and roll each half in a sheet of greaseproof paper, twisting the ends as if for a large bonbon. Refrigerate for at least 30 minutes; one of the halves can be frozen for another time.

Heat the oven to 180°C. Line a baking sheet with baking parchment.

Unwrap the dough, place on a board and cut into 3mm-thick slices, laying the slices in neat rows, not too close together, on the baking sheet. Rewrap any remaining dough and return it to a sealed container in the fridge. Place a few whole fennel seeds in the middle of each biscuit, pressing down lightly.

Bake in the oven for 10 minutes. Cool on a rack.

Shortcake

THIS IS MY MOTHER'S RECIPE, gleaned from her days as a student at Atholl Crescent in Edinburgh in the 1950s. Shortcake is the epitome of friable, a biscuit of such a delicate crumb it has a trembling fragility that requires careful handling when assembling. Best served with a bowl of raspberries or strawberries and cream. Bake as required, as fresh from the oven is best.

Makes about 48 shortcakes; 24 for each cylinder

190g unsalted butter, at room temperature
75g caster sugar
20g toasted breadcrumbs
145g plain flour, sifted, plus extra for dusting
75g whole blanched almonds, ground
grated zest of ½ an unwaxed orange

Cream the butter and sugar in a food mixer. Add the breadcrumbs, flour, ground almonds and orange zest. Beat gently until amassed into a ball of dough.

On a lightly floured surface, knead the dough gently into a ball, then work this into a cylinder roughly 30cm in length and 5–6cm in width. Cut in half and roll each half in a sheet of greaseproof paper, twisting the ends as if for a large bonbon. Refrigerate for at least 2 hours, preferably overnight; one of the halves can be frozen for another time.

Preheat the oven to 180°C. Line two baking sheets with baking parchment.

Unroll the shortcake mix and cut into slices about 3mm-thick. Lay these well apart on the baking parchment. Bake in the oven for 12–15 minutes. Cool on a rack.

Lemon thins

Makes 48 thins; 24 for each cylinder

250g unsalted butter, at room temperature
125g caster sugar
½ a vanilla pod, split and seeds scraped
1 organic egg
1 soup spoon double cream
grated zest of 2 large unwaxed lemons and 1 soup spoon of juice
300g plain flour, sifted, plus extra for dusting
1 level teaspoon baking powder
½ teaspoon salt

Place the butter in a food mixer and cream until peaked and pale. Add the sugar and vanilla seeds. Add the egg and the double cream. Mix in the lemon zest and juice, then add the flour, baking powder and salt. Mix deftly and swiftly into a dough on a lightly floured surface and shape into a cylinder roughly 30cm in length and 5–6cm in width. Cut in half and roll each half in a sheet of greaseproof paper, twisting the ends as if for a large bonbon. Refrigerate for at least 30 minutes; one of the halves can be frozen for another time.

Heat the oven to 180°C. Line two baking sheets with baking parchment.

Slice the dough into 2mm-thick discs and lay them well apart on the baking sheet. Lay on a similar-sized sheet of baking parchment and with a rolling pin, pressing gently, roll over the paper, joining the discs into one sheet. Place this in the fridge for 10 minutes. Then remove from the fridge, take away the top sheet and bake for 8–9 minutes. Remove from the oven. Cut into shapes that please, such as squares, rectangles and triangles.

BLOOD ORANGES

A SANGUINE AFFAIR

Campari & blood orange

Blood orange sorbet

THE VAST WINTER HARVEST of oranges and lemons imbued with summery oils and juices is vital for cooking, preserving, flavouring and, most assuredly, drinking. They seem miraculous when they begin to appear in the chilly UK January. And the most miraculous citrus of them all is the blood orange. Those from Sicily remain the best: dark-fleshed fruits, some of them almost black, resulting in a juice with a sanguine potency that makes a wonderful fruit sorbet, or when added to Campari a pretty good cocktail too.

Campari and blood orange

A UNIQUELY MARVELLOUS DRINK that sets the nerves a-tingle and dispels a winter's gloom like no other.

For each person
2 blood oranges, and a slice to serve
50ml Campari
25ml vodka
ice

Halve and squeeze the fruits. Pour the juice into a jug with the Campari and vodka. Stir well. Pour over ice in a glass and add a slice of blood orange.

PS: When on the hunt for blood oranges, should the cook find pomegranates with flesh as blood red as the sought-after oranges, scoop up a few to add to the mix. Roughly half a pomegranate added to the brew makes a most invigorating drink.

Blood orange sorbet

Makes 1.2 litres of sorbet, feeds 6

1 litre blood orange juice (roughly 12–15 oranges, depending on size)
1 lemon
350g icing sugar

Halve and squeeze the blood oranges and lemon. Blend 200ml of juice with the sugar until the sugar is dissolved. Mix well with the remaining juice. Pour into an ice cream machine and follow the maker's instructions.

As opposite, Campari and pomegranate juice make excellent companions to blood orange in this sorbet should such a thought please. Swap 300ml of blood orange juice for the darkest-stained pomegranate juice, freshly squeezed, and 50ml of Campari.

BREAD
CRUMBS

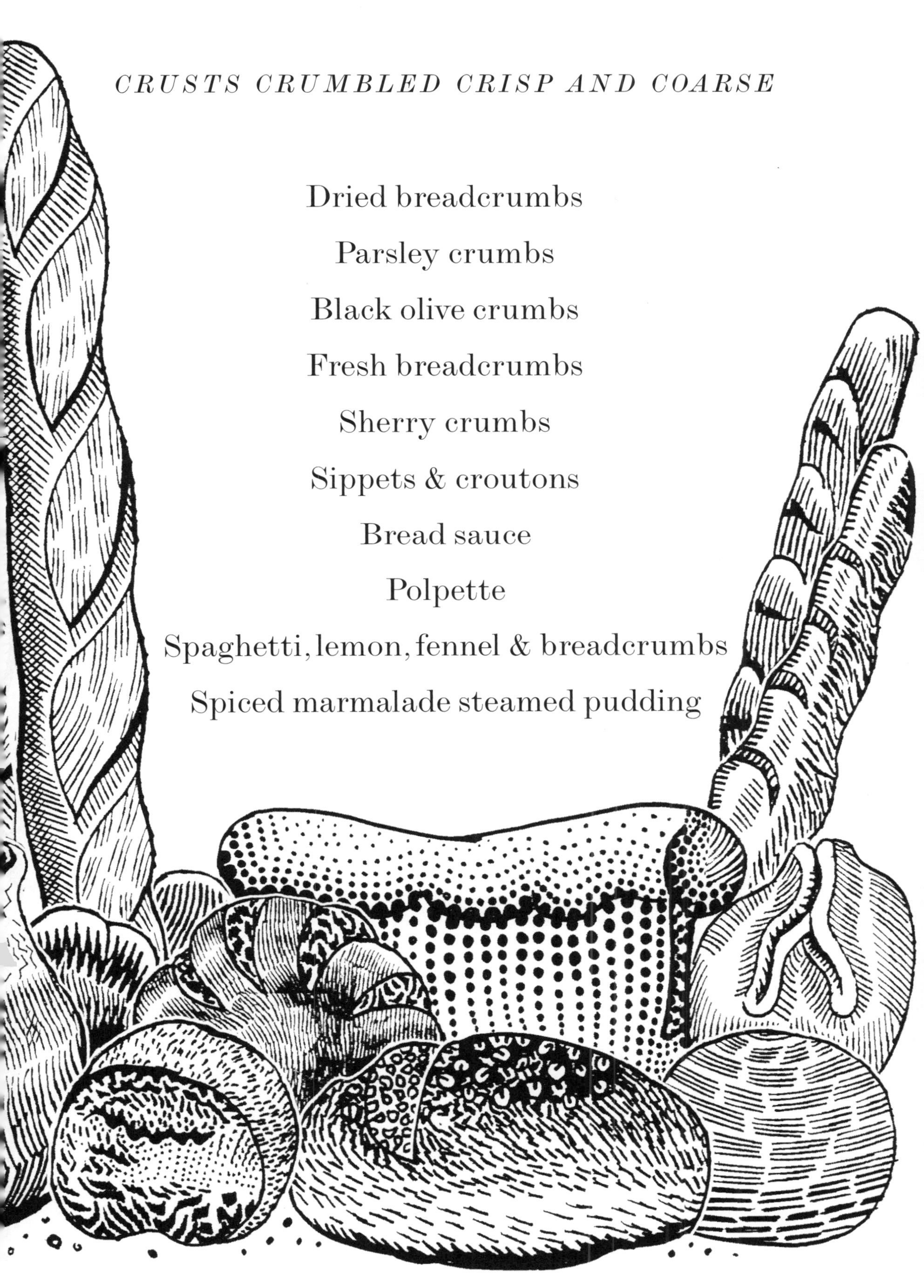

CRUSTS CRUMBLED CRISP AND COARSE

Dried breadcrumbs

Parsley crumbs

Black olive crumbs

Fresh breadcrumbs

Sherry crumbs

Sippets & croutons

Bread sauce

Polpette

Spaghetti, lemon, fennel & breadcrumbs

Spiced marmalade steamed pudding

THERE WAS ALWAYS A TRAY OF CRUSTS like ancient fallen ruins on, in or near the oven in my mother's kitchen. On occasion there would also be the most almighty racket, like someone felling a small tree, as Mum fed a food processor with these crusts, the fine-crumbed results being stored in big stoppered jars for use another day.

A favourite dish of fried fish (almost the national dish of Scotland) resulted every week when the fishman (sic) pulled up outside our house with an array of filleted fish laid out in the back of his van. Mum bought fresh haddock, which she lightly floured, dipped in beaten egg and then laid in a tray of those fine breadcrumbs. The breaded fillets were then cooked to a golden crust in a frying pan with an extra dot or two of butter.

Later, when I cooked at Alastair Little's restaurant in Frith Street in Soho, breadcrumbs, made from bread left over from the day before, took on a whole new meaning altogether. Thin slices of baguette or sourdough bread were laid out on trays and lightly brushed with olive oil, to be baked until golden. These were then ground in a food processor with parsley, olive oil, black pepper and a pinch of dried chilli flakes to a coarse crumb, then laid out on a tray and baked crisp once more. They are moreish in the extreme just as they are, but when strewn over a slow-roasted belly of pork or a shoulder of lamb spread with mustard and baked crisp, or over a salad of squid and octopus dressed with bitter leaves and celery, citrus, fennel and capers, they become very good indeed.

Spaghetti, when dressed with an infusion of olive oil and butter and much finely grated zest of lemon (the scent from the heat of the pasta on first contact with the lemon is otherworldly), can be mixed vigorously just before serving with handfuls of coarse crumbs. This is inspired by an old tradition from southern Italy, where breadcrumbs with a little olive oil were added to pasta. It's a vivid illustration of a good dish resulting from frugality and necessity.

Modern adaptations of old Italian recipes such as this simple dish include the addition of salted anchovies, lemon zest infused in butter and olive oil, or a little chopped chilli. And even on occasion that miraculous dust of powdered fennel pollen, fiore di finocchio, a spice most notably from Umbria and Le Marche, where fennel flowers are gathered in the early morning, dried and ground. They flavour the breadcrumbs beautifully.

Alastair Little's head chef Juliet Peston ground breadcrumbs with black olives, anchovies, garlic and capers to form a most delicious crust, heaped on a whole globe artichoke stuffed with goat's cheese beaten in a bowl with a spoon until smooth, seasoned with pepper and a pinch of thyme or summer savory, olive oil and baked.

My mother also stored fresh breadcrumbs. These were for the steamed treacle dumplings that were made by Granny, my dad, Mum and me.

It is a canny thought, having a store of little bags filled with fresh breadcrumbs, tied and then frozen. They are a boon to a cook needing to make bread sauce, so vital to giddy along a feast of roast birds, and also useful when fried in butter until crisp and golden, then made heady with a ration of sherry to accompany roast game birds. Or for making polpette – little patties of minced beef bound with bread soaked in milk then squeezed dry, brightened with finely grated lemon zest, chopped parsley and a whisper of garlic.

Along with breadcrumbs, other good uses of bread are sippets – slices of bread cut into little pieces – and croutons, larger and more coarsely cut, both cooked crisp in oil and visited upon soups and salads. There are those little croutons too that famously featured in a green salad at the original Chez Victor in Soho or indeed in Caesar Cardini's invention – an immortal pairing of croutons and hearts of Romaine to make his eponymous salad.

Bread, though, need not be fried. Torn into pieces, stale bread, as is, is invigorated with a steeping in olive oil and vinegar, then heaped with tomatoes or lightly cooked vegetables that thrill to a tumbling of cheeses and herbs.

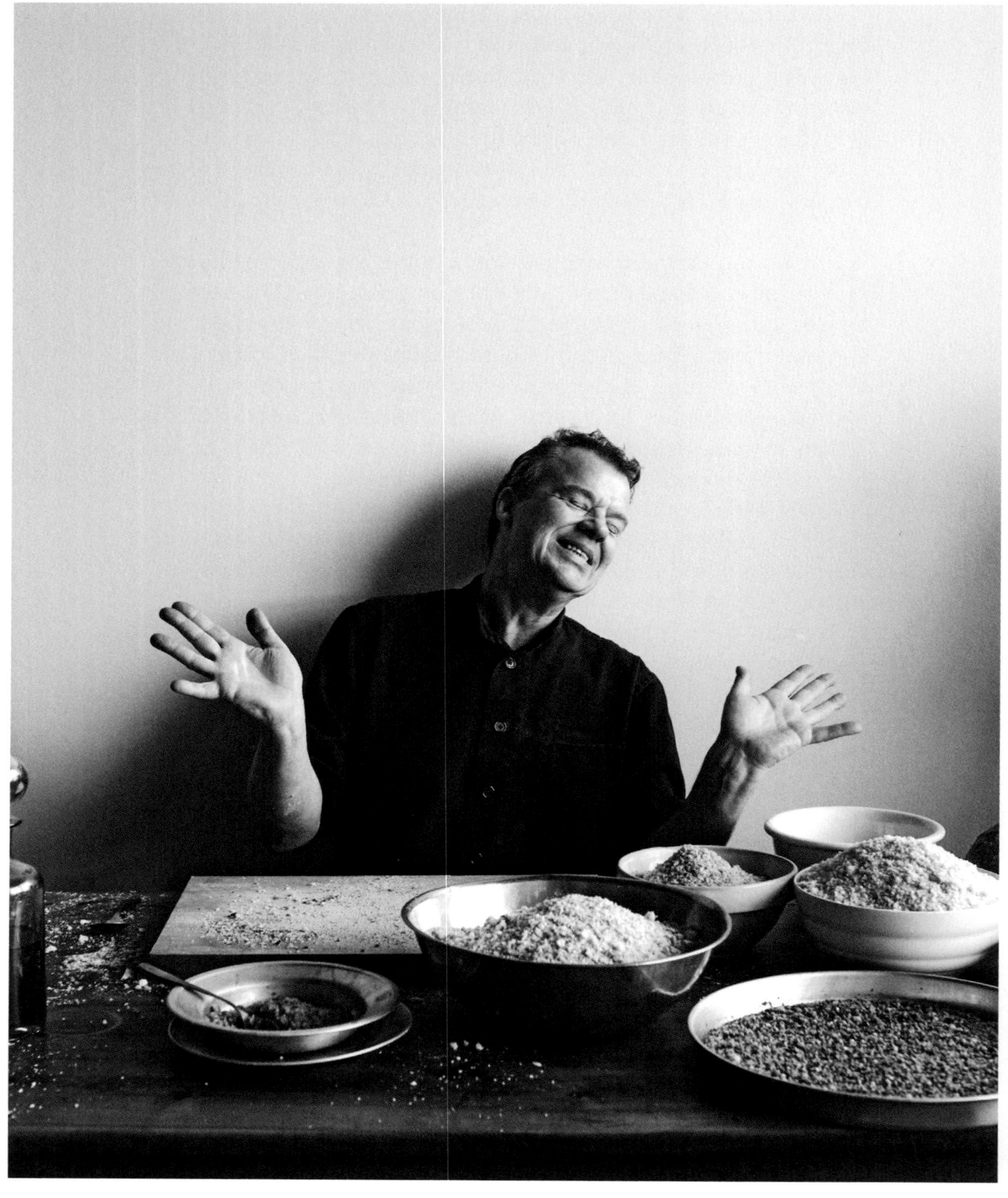

Dried breadcrumbs

DRIED BREADCRUMBS ARE MADE WITH THE LEAST EFFORT. Gather up husks, heels and buckshee slices of bread, then lay them out on trays to dry thoroughly. To avoid trays taking up valuable space, placing trays of bread in an unlit oven overnight is rather good, always remembering to check the oven for forgotten trays before turning it on. Once a goodly haul is amassed, heap a few pieces of the dried loaf at a time onto a large board and render them into a fine crumb with a rolling pin or give them a swift burst in a food processor. Keep the crumb coarse for a lighter, more interesting result. Make your crumbs a few hours before you start on the recipes, so that they have a chance to dry out.

Parsley crumbs

USE STALE BREAD FROM THE DAY BEFORE, or today's baguette, sliced thin, both requiring to be brushed with a little olive oil and baked golden and crisp, then mixed with parsley, garlic and chilli. These are best eaten swiftly within a few hours of making.

Enough for at least 10 decent scatterings

200g bread (baguette is best)
2–3 soup spoons olive oil, enough to dot each slice 2 or 3 times
30g flat-leaf parsley, leaves picked and coarsely chopped
3 cloves of garlic, coarsely chopped
a pinch of dried chilli flakes

Preheat the oven to 180°C. Thinly slice the baguette and dot each slice with 2–3 drops of olive oil. Place on a baking sheet and bake in the heated oven for 6–7 minutes. Remove from the oven and cool. Turn the oven down to 100°C.

Put the baked baguette into a food processor with the chopped parsley, garlic and chilli flakes, a pinch of salt and a few twists of a pepper mill. Whizz until a coarse crumb forms. Decant the crumbs onto a baking sheet and bake gently until crisp, turning occasionally, about 10–15 minutes. Excellent strewn on salads, with shellfish such as razor clams (see page 143) and with all sorts of pasta dishes (see page 79).

Black olive crumbs

Enough for 15 scatterings

150g sliced sourdough bread, crusts on
160g pitted black olives
1 heaped teaspoon salted capers, soaked for 30 minutes in cold water
1 large clove of garlic, coarsely chopped
6 anchovies, optional but to be encouraged
4–5 soup spoons olive oil

Preheat the oven to 120°C.

Put the bread, black olives, capers, garlic and anchovies into a food processor with the olive oil, then whizz until finely ground.

Spread the crumbs on a baking sheet and bake until crisp, turning occasionally. This can take 20 minutes to half an hour, maybe longer, so should be done well in advance to ensure they are crisp. Or prepare these the day before, then put them in a preheated oven (120°C) and leave overnight with the oven switched off. These keep remarkably well in a sealed pot or jar for up to 2 weeks. They are wonderful on many things really, in particular curds spread on grilled bread anointed with olive oil and baked crisp in the oven, and also on fish dishes, in particular roast cod with olive oil and rocket mash (see page 120).

Fresh breadcrumbs

THESE, OF COURSE, REQUIRE STALE BREAD, a day old at least. Remove the crusts, tear the bread into smallish pieces and then whizz in a food processor until a fine crumb forms. Have a care not to let the machine get carried away, resulting in clods of squidge, which, alas, are of little worth.

It is worth considering making several bags of these to freeze for cooking with when fresh breadcrumbs are required.

Sherry crumbs

THIS EXCELLENT RECIPE inspired by Simon Hopkinson comes into its own with the arrival of the game season, the first grouse in particular. But so delicious are these crumbs that you can also use them on dishes such as celeriac and potato gratin, Jerusalem artichokes and celeriac, as well as on warm salads of wild duck, venison, boar and hare. They are good, too, scattered over grilled and raw vegetable salads made from, say, chicories and fennel and perhaps with a few chopped, roast almonds on a tangle of green beans, made from several different varieties. A non-stick frying pan proves to be admirable in making these crumbs.

Enough for 6

60g unsalted butter
175g fresh white breadcrumbs
60ml medium-dry sherry

Over a gentle heat, melt the butter in a frying pan. Tip in the breadcrumbs. Let the pan sit for a minute before stirring the crumbs and continue thus until the crumbs have turned golden and crisp. Standing back from the splutter, add the sherry. Once the bubbling fury has abated, stir the crumbs well until all trace of sherry has been despatched, leaving only the allure of a rich aroma. Season with a pinch each of sea salt and freshly ground black pepper. Tip the crumbs on to a dish and put to one side to keep warm prior to serving.

Sippets and croutons

SIPPETS ARE SMALL PIECES of oiled, fried or baked bread, excellent in soups or salads. Croutons are a coarser variation on the theme. We make both from loaves of sourdough, rich in flavour and structure, resulting in croutons with bite and crunch.

Enough for 6 servings

3 slices of bread, from a good loaf of white bread or sourdough
60ml olive oil

Tear the bread into small pieces for sippets, and into larger pieces (say 1cm) for croutons. Heat the oil in a frying pan over a moderate heat. Once hot, tip in the bread and fry, stirring well, until golden brown and crisp. Drain and sit them on kitchen paper to despatch residual oil. Season with salt.

Bread sauce

BREAD SAUCE IS NOT JUST FOR CHRISTMAS; most birds enjoy the company of this singular sauce. Here, slices of bread are steeped in the infused milk and left to stand for a few minutes, longer being preferable should time permit, prior to warming and stirring, but not overheating, resulting in a textured but surprisingly light sauce, one so familiar but always so welcome at table.

Makes 500ml of sauce, enough for 6

1 medium onion
4 cloves
10 black peppercorns, cracked
4 bay leaves
500ml creamiest milk
250g fresh breadcrumbs
a fair few scrapes of nutmeg, to taste (I love lots)

Peel the onion and chop coarsely. Place in a heavy-bottomed pan along with the cloves, cracked peppercorns and bay leaves. Add the milk and bring to a simmer for about 1 minute, stirring well to ensure the milk does not catch on the bottom of the pan. Turn the heat off, cover with a lid and leave to one side to infuse for at least half an hour.

Place the slices of bread in a clean pan. Pour the infused milk through a strainer over the bread. Cover and let stand for 5 minutes. Place the pan over a gentle heat when ready to serve, warming through slowly. At the last minute, stir the sauce with a wooden spoon until softened and almost smooth, adding a splash more milk if the sauce is too thick. Season with a pinch of sea salt and grated nutmeg.

Polpette aka 'cecils'

SWIFTLY MADE AND AS SWIFTLY SCOFFED. Mrs David, presumably loath to conjure up the idea of a burger, likened these little beef patties to rissoles. In her book *Italian Food* she called them polpette and so they have remained – a favourite dish ever since. I also make them with lamb or pork, even kid, with equally pleasing results. Interestingly, this recipe for polpette is similar to one in *Mrs Rundell's Domestic Cookery* of 1863, where they are called 'cecils'. It is vital that only the freshest and leanest mince be used, preferably from a butcher, and, as Dad used to do, watch the beef going through the mincer.

Makes 25–30 small polpette, but makes fewer and larger if wished

a thick slice of white bread
3 soup spoons milk
500g lean beef, freshly minced
2 or 3 small cloves of garlic
a small handful of flat-leaf parsley, leaves picked and chopped
1 organic egg
¼ of a nutmeg, freshly grated
finely grated zest of 1 unwaxed lemon
2 teaspoons light oil, e.g. sunflower, to brush the grill pan

Remove the crusts from the bread and lay the slice on a plate, pouring on the milk. Put to one side.

Place the minced beef in a large bowl. Peel and finely chop the garlic. Squeeze the bread of any excess milk and add to the meat along with the garlic, chopped parsley, egg, nutmeg, lemon zest, and a little sea salt and freshly ground black pepper. Mix thoroughly and deftly with your hands. Tear the mixture into 25–30 pieces and shape into rounds with a diameter roughly of 2.5cm. Make a slight dent in each with your thumb, which (and this is true) makes them lighter.

Once all are done, cook them in small batches on a lightly oiled griddle or frying pan for 3 minutes each side until browned.

Mrs David suggests a green salad, or a potato or tomato salad with these, and as I enjoy all three, I have, on occasion, served all of them together.

Spaghetti, lemon, fennel flower and breadcrumbs

AN HOMAGE TO FRUGALITY AND NECESSITY but also to simplicity and delightful eating. I have enjoyed this just with the lemon, enjoyed it more with the breadcrumbs, with slices of artichokes, green beans, shredded runner beans, whenever these are in season, with squid fried swiftly in olive oil and a smattering of finely chopped chilli, and also with clams, mussels and sardines.

PS: It is worth mentioning that pasta is a most personal of dishes and quantities vary wildly according to taste and appetite, so here the cook is encouraged to gauge responses and adjust accordingly if required.

PPS: Fiore di finocchio is made from grinding dried fennel flowers, and was first encountered on a trip to Le Marche in Italy. I brought some home and have struggled to find any ever since. In times past I found it in La Fromagerie in London but not always. Though not as delicate or as aromatic as the dried flower, simply grind fennel seeds in a pestle and mortar for a fair alternative.

Feeds 6

finely grated zest and juice of 3 unwaxed lemons
a pinch of dried chilli flakes
50ml extra virgin olive oil
600g spaghetti, depending on appetite
1 teaspoon fiore di finocchio or fennel pollen, should this be at hand; if not, grind 1 teaspoon fennel seeds
350g parsley crumbs (see page 73)

Bring a big pan of water to the boil. Put the lemon zest and juice, chilli flakes and olive oil into a heavy-bottomed pot on the lowest heat and cook very gently for 15 minutes.

Plunge the spaghetti into the furiously boiling water with a soup spoon of salt, cover until the water boils once more, then remove the lid. Cook as per the packet instructions. Once cooked with a whisper of a bite left, drain, dress with the lemon-infused olive oil and mix well. Add a generous pinch of the fiore or ground fennel seed. Heap this into a dish and strew with the parsley crumbs. Serve swiftly.

Spiced marmalade steamed pudding

CLOSELY RELATED TO GRANNY'S ORIGINAL RECIPE, this pudding is made bold with whole ginger and spice, with a generous spooning of marmalade in the bottom.

PS: Steamed puddings keep very well, indeed improve mightily if kept for a day or two.

Feeds 6

unsalted butter for greasing
3 large soup spoons marmalade
150g preserved stem ginger and adhering syrup
125g self-raising flour
½ teaspoon cream of tartar
½ teaspoon bicarbonate of soda
2 teaspoons ground ginger
1 teaspoon ground allspice
½ teaspoon ground mace
1 teaspoon ground cinnamon
½ teaspoon baking powder
125g shredded suet
125g fresh white breadcrumbs
a pinch of salt
125g golden syrup
250g black treacle
1 organic egg
150ml milk

Lightly butter a 1.1-litre capacity pudding basin. Place a disc of greaseproof paper on the whole bottom of the basin. Spoon the marmalade on to the disc of paper.

Put the preserved stem ginger and syrup into a blender and whizz until smooth. Sift together the flour, cream of tartar, bicarbonate of soda, spices and baking powder and place in a large bowl. Add the suet and the rest of the dry ingredients, along with the blended ginger, golden syrup, treacle, egg and milk. Mix all this together very well.

Tip the batter into the pudding basin. Cover with a large piece each of baking parchment and foil, tied very tightly with string.

Smooth the foil over the paper and then fold and tuck neatly around the basin. Place the sealed pudding on a plate in a pan of simmering water, cover the pan and simmer for 2½ hours, checking every so often if the water needs topping up.

Once cooked, remove the string, foil and paper. Lightly loosen the pudding from the edges with a knife. Place a large, handsome plate atop. With the greatest care, flip the whole kaboodle. Lift away the bowl, carefully lift away the disc of paper and take to table. Serve with jugs of custard and a bowl of best cream.

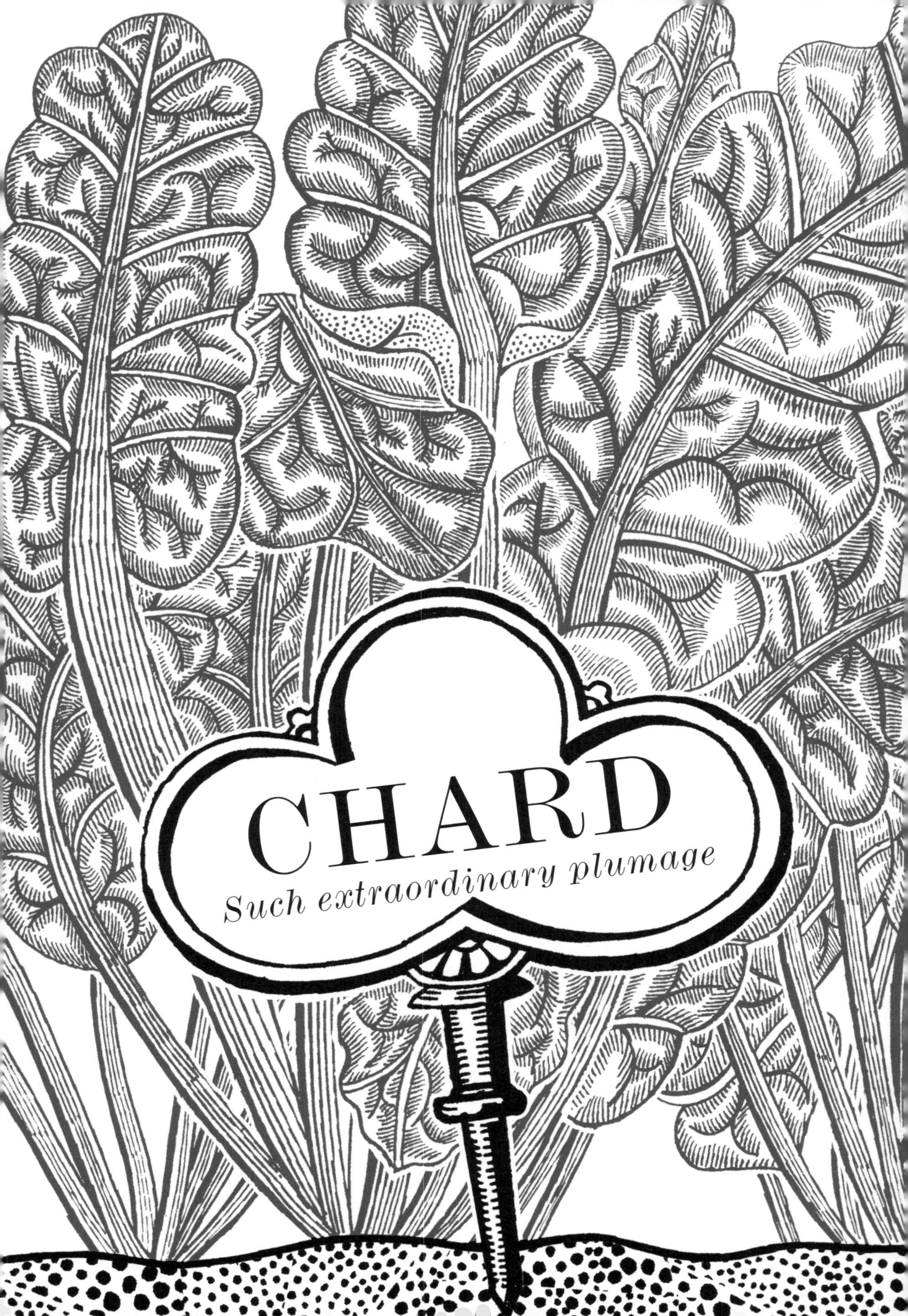
CHARD
Such extraordinary plumage

Chard, caper and lemon salad
Chard and cheddar omelette
Chard, potato and celeriac gratin

'CHARD IS BEST WHEN COOKED to look good and ancient. Done!!' said a very good friend as he watched me cooking these beautiful, plumed leaves. This is excellent advice.

Previously, I had always cooked chard as if it were spinach, plunging it into boiling water then draining it, barely cooked, the elusive flavour untapped, but allow chard to stew in a little olive oil in a lidded pot, and its true qualities come to the fore. The modest effort required to encourage chard is more than compensated for with a deep, rich flavour that is excellent in soups, salads, a gratin or indeed an omelette when chard is paired with a fine cheese such as Cheddar or Comté.

Chard is simple to cook: take one large bunch of billowing leaves. With a knife, separate the stalks from the leaves. Chop the stalks into 2–3cm lengths, tear the leaves into large pieces and wash the stalks and leaves separately.

Warm a wide pan with a close-fitting lid over a moderate heat, pour in 3 soup spoons of olive oil, add the stalks and fry swiftly for a minute, stirring often. Add the leaves, a pinch of salt and stir well until wilted. Place the lid securely on the pan, reduce the heat and let the chard cook gently. It is near miraculous how much water is released from the chard but perseverance pays a fine dividend.

Remarkably, the chard will cook happily like this for 20 minutes, depending on the stalks. It is done when no trace of water remains in the pan and the bottom of the pan begins to colour lightly. The colour will have become rather beautiful, a sort of olive green which matches the description given to me by the Italian friend who gave me this recipe, as 'good and ancient, not unlike, say, that of a hunting tartan or tweed'.

Once cooked, the cooled chard can be stored in a container in the fridge for several days. This manoeuvre is inspired by shopping in Italy and seeing bags of ready-cooked chard on the shelves of supermarkets, often beside bags of prepared artichokes for that matter.

Should chard prove to be elusive, spinach will do very well as a substitute in these recipes. A scrape of nutmeg is always good with spinach.

Chard, caper and lemon salad

Feeds 6

1 plump unwaxed lemon
500g cooked chard (roughly 1kg raw chard)
1 soup spoon salted capers, soaked for 30 minutes in cold water
4 soup spoons extra virgin olive oil
2 soup spoons organic cider vinegar

Put the lemon into a pan of water and boil gently for 15 minutes, until soft. Pour away the water and let the lemon cool.

Coarsely chop the chard and put into a large bowl. Cut the cooled lemon into quarters, cut away the flesh and discard, then chop the lemon peel into small pieces, about 2–3mm square. Add this to the chard in the bowl. Add the drained capers, olive oil, cider vinegar and a little sea salt and freshly ground black pepper. Thoroughly mix together and serve on a large dish.

Chard and Cheddar omelette

THIS IS A FLAT OMELETTE, as opposed to folded, not unlike a frittata, but still runny in the middle. An ovenproof non-stick frying pan is invaluable here.

Feeds 1–2

200g cooked chard (roughly 400g raw chard)
75–100g good farmhouse Cheddar
6 organic eggs
4 soup spoons double cream (optional)
15g unsalted butter

Heat the oven to 200°C. Chop the cooked chard coarsely and cut the Cheddar into small pieces, say 5mm square. Beat the eggs with the cream and add the chard and Cheddar, then season with black pepper and a pinch of salt.

Place an ovenproof, non-stick frying pan over a moderate heat. Melt the butter in the pan. Tip in the egg mixture and shake the pan slightly so that all settles happily. Place the pan in the oven and bake for 8–10 minutes, until a light wobble remains in the middle of the omelette and it has puffed up. Once done, remove from the oven, take the pan to table and sit it upon a trivet. A salad and chips are fine company for the omelette.

Chard, potato and celeriac gratin

THIS GRATIN IS WONDERFUL WHEN COOKED SHALLOW, just one layer of each vegetable spread over a large baking dish (roughly 30cm x 25cm), in lieu of the more familiar deep gratin.

Feeds 6

500g waxy potatoes
500g celeriac
500g cooked chard (roughly 1kg raw chard)
250ml double cream (you could substitute 250ml vegetable stock for the cream in this recipe)
½ a nutmeg, grated
30g unsalted butter

Heat the oven to 180°C. Peel the potatoes and the celeriac, rinse, then slice thinly, say 2–3mm thick, and put them into separate bowls. Wash both bowls of sliced vegetables until the water is clear. Drain the vegetables and roughly dry.

Cover the bottom of a large baking dish with the sliced celeriac, lightly overlapping the slices. Strew the cooked chard over the celeriac. Cover the chard with the sliced potato, again overlapping the slices slightly. Season the cream with salt, black pepper and nutmeg and pour this over the layers of sliced vegetables. Dot with butter. Cook in the oven for 45 minutes, until browned and bubbling at the edges. Let the gratin sit for 10 minutes or so before eating.

CHOCOLATE
BEHIND BARS

Les profiteroles au chocolat

St Emilion au chocolat

Chocolate & almond prunes

Chocolate & cinnamon tart
with Boodle's fool

THE ALLURE OF CHOCOLATE NEVER FADES. The memory of the chocolate cakes my mother made for us when we were growing up still exerts a hold over me. She made them for my sister's birthday, in her lovely battered old tins – holy relics which we still have at home. My preference was usually for a fruited spiced cake I was mad for as a kid. Cakes baked in these tins had a thin, delicate crust that when cooled resulted in great fissures and cracks – like looking at a lunar landscape.

Within the fissures, seams of rich chocolate released that familiar, much-loved scent. While the cakes were cooling, a huge bowl of cream was whisked into the softest of peaks and then heaped in clouds upon one layer of cake. Another layer was laid on top and then there was a final flurry of cream piped through the star nozzle of a gigantic piping bag. Little chocolate shapes – stars and moons, crescents and shards – were fashioned from a sheet of chocolate that had been melted and set upon paper and then scattered upon the cream in Mum's ineffable way.

Now cooks can take their pick from the extraordinary array of chocolate available in almost every food shop. I love shopping for the great blocks of chocolate under glass domes in Leila's Shop in east London. A most delicious chocolate called NearyNógs is made in Northern Ireland outside Belfast – as conched a chocolate as one could wish. I love bringing back a slab or two of Amadei's best from the airport shop at Pisa. Cru Virunga is delicious. And we also love Pump Street Chocolate from Suffolk. They are all costly but chocolate is costly, a great luxury and a wonderful ingredient with which to make wonderful recipes.

Les profiteroles au chocolat

MIRACULOUS CHOUX PASTRY PUFFS, baked golden with a delicate, crisp shell, stuffed with confectioner's custard, whipped cream and a scoop of vanilla ice cream. A jug of warm chocolate sauce is served alongside.

When making this admirable pudding, there are a few notes that might aid the cook. Make the choux pastry early on and keep it in a bowl in the fridge until required. The confectioner's custard can also be made earlier in the day, or even the day before. The ingredients for the chocolate sauce can be measured in advance but it should be made swiftly at the last minute, to prevent it cooling and setting.

So simple to prepare, these are peerless when fresh, retaining a delicate crust for several hours after baking.

Choux pastry

Makes 30 profiteroles, feeding 6 people

120ml whole milk
120ml water
110g unsalted butter
1 level teaspoon salt
140g plain flour, sifted
5 organic eggs

Put the milk, water, butter and salt into a pan and bring to the boil. Tip in the sifted flour and beat continuously over a high heat until the dough comes away from the sides. Still on the heat, continue to beat vigorously for a further minute.

Tip the dough into a bowl and smooth along the sides to cool. Crack the eggs into a jug and stir with a fork. Once the dough is cooled, add the eggs a little at a time, beating until the dough is smooth. The dough can now be placed in a bowl, covered and refrigerated, keeping remarkably well for 24 hours if made in advance.

When ready to bake, heat the oven to 180°C and line a baking tray with baking parchment. Use a teaspoon to make small walnut-sized rounds of choux dough on the tray, arranged in rows with room

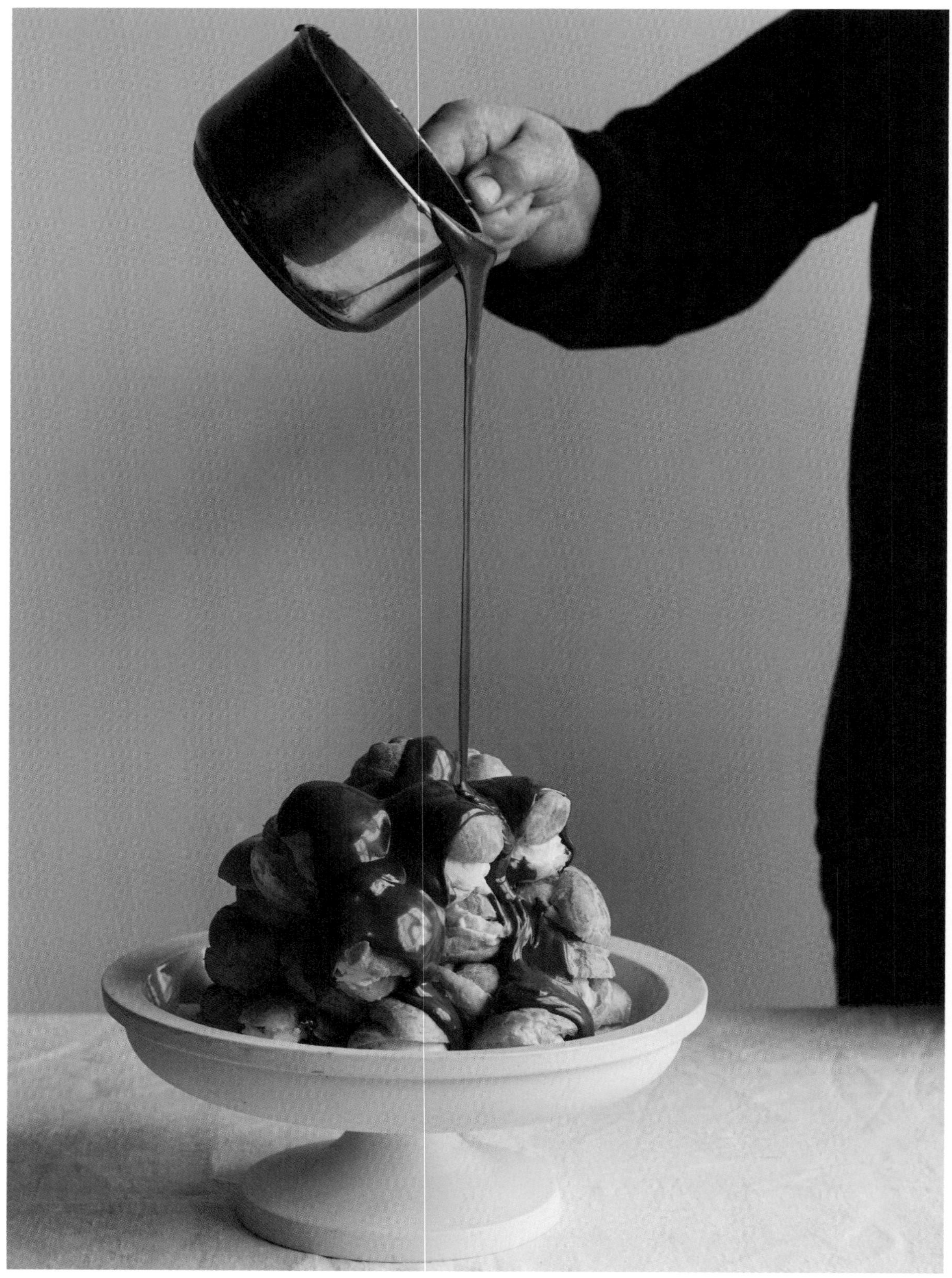

enough for each to expand and colour without invading any fellow profiterole's space.

Place in the hot oven and cook for 25 minutes. The profiteroles should be puffed and uniformly golden, so fear not cooking a few minutes longer if required. It is worth noting that it took us a while and a fair few attempts to achieve the profiteroles we now cherish. It may well be worth trying out a few to test the oven temperature.

Once baked, put aside to cool.

Confectioner's custard

This can happily be made the day before to settle overnight. And always rinse the vanilla pod once the custard is made, placing it somewhere to dry, then adding it to a jar of vanilla extract or caster sugar.

Feeds 6

6 organic egg yolks
25g caster sugar
20g plain flour, sifted
20g cornflour, sifted
500ml whole milk
½ a vanilla pod, split and seeds scraped
100ml double cream

In a bowl, beat the egg yolks and sugar until pale and increased in volume, about 4–5 minutes. Stir in the sifted flours.

Place the milk and scraped vanilla pod and seeds in a pan and bring to a simmer over a moderate heat. Lift out the vanilla pod. Pour the infused milk into the flour and egg mix, stirring well.

Scrape all back into the pan and return to the heat, stirring continuously. Bring to the boil and simmer, still stirring for a minute or two, until the custard is thickened and smooth enough to be poured through a sieve into a heatproof bowl. Continue whisking to dispel any lingering steam. Cool and refrigerate.

Put the cooled, set custard into a food processor, add the cream and whizz for 15 seconds. Pour into a bowl, then cover and refrigerate until needed.

Chocolate sauce

Makes 550ml, enough for 6
250g dark chocolate, at least 70% cocoa solids
300ml double cream

If the chocolate is in a bar, chop it into small pieces. Boil the cream in a pan, then remove from the heat and stir in the chocolate, continuing thus until melted and smooth. Keep warm.

Vanilla ice cream

My parents went into mourning when the last of the ice-cream makers in Dundee closed and you could no longer buy a tub of ice cream straight from the churn. Good ice cream is one of life's necessities and vanilla ice cream is one of the best. This recipe is based on the ice cream Frédy Girardet made at his restaurant in Crissier in Switzerland. You can use organic double cream in this recipe because you don't have to cook it and thus run the risk of it splitting (organic cream with a high fat content splits more easily when cooking).

PS: The discarded egg whites in this recipe can be used to make meringues. Heat the oven to 180°C, then weigh the egg whites and weigh out double the amount of sugar (e.g. if you have 50g of egg whites, weigh out 100g of sugar). Whisk the whites until stiff in a scrupulously clean bowl and beat in half the sugar with a large spoon. Continue beating until stiff peaks form, then fold in the second half of the sugar. Using a large tablespoon, scoop the meringue mix on to a baking sheet lined with baking parchment. Put into the oven, turn down to 120°C, and bake for 1 hour. The result is a delicately shelled meringue with a soft mallow interior.

Feeds 6

350ml organic whole milk
1 vanilla pod, split and seeds scraped
6 organic egg yolks
150g organic caster sugar
250ml organic double cream

Pour the milk into a heavy-bottomed pan. Add the vanilla seeds and pod. Beat the yolks in a heatproof bowl with the sugar.

Infuse the pan of milk over a moderate heat. Once simmering, pour the milk slowly on to the egg yolks and sugar, stirring all the while, and once mixed, pour back into the pan and return to a moderate heat. Stir continuously until the custard thickens. Pour in the cream, remove from the heat and strain into a wide bowl to cool quickly.

Pour into an ice cream machine and follow the maker's instructions. The ice cream will keep well in the freezer for 48 hours but is best within a few hours of churning.

Assembly of the profiteroles

Decant the chocolate sauce into a jug. Split the profiteroles. Spread a spoonful of confectioner's custard inside each, then add a scoop of vanilla ice cream on top of the custard. Replace the profiterole lid. Place three in a cluster on each plate and take swiftly to table with the jug of chocolate sauce. As an alternative to plating, build a mound of the filled pastries on a handsome dish and carefully though swiftly pour over the chocolate sauce in a steady fall.

St Emilion au chocolat

THIS WAS ON THE MENU AT BIBENDUM when I first started cooking there and has remained a constant companion ever since. The recipe remains pretty loyal to the original Elizabeth David version. St Emilion is known not just for wine but also for macarons, which here are steeped in cognac and set into both the top and bottom of an extraordinary cake that is the very essence of chocolate – rich, elegant and surprisingly light. I use Amaretti di Saronno macarons, dried fully, which I buy from the few surviving Italian shops in Soho such as I Camisa & Son and Lina Stores, or the Algerian Coffee Stores, or buy online, and with more than just a scent of bitter almonds from the kernels of apricots they are a perfect foil for cognac and chocolate.

PS: As a good-quality brandy or rum for that matter becomes more costly, a thought is to make use of amontillado, a sherry that delights with chocolate. The result is most pleasing.

Feeds 6

16 macarons or Italian amaretti biscuits
75–100ml sherry or cognac
55g unsalted butter, softened
115g organic caster sugar
1 organic egg yolk
200ml organic full-fat milk
225g dark bitter chocolate, at least 70% cocoa solids, chopped into small shards

Heap the macarons in a bowl and smash them into a coarse crumb. Strew two-thirds of the crumb in the bottom of a handsome dish. Put the remaining third to one side. Libate the coarsely crumbed macarons in the dish liberally with two-thirds of the sherry or cognac, putting to one side the remaining third.

Place the softened butter and sugar in a bowl and mix thoroughly until pale. Add the egg yolk and mix well.

Pour the milk into a pan, place over a moderate heat and bring to a simmer. Remove the pan from the heat, tip in the chocolate and stir until the chocolate has melted completely, becoming smooth. Pour this on to the beaten butter, sugar and egg yolk. Mix this all together

thoroughly. Decant the chocolate mixture on to the macarons drenched in cognac.

Strew the remaining macarons atop the chocolate, pour over the remaining cognac and press the macarons so very gently with your fingertips into the surface of the chocolate. Cover and refrigerate for at least 6 hours, or, better still, a few days in advance.

Chocolate and almond prunes

WE NEEDED A CHOCOLATE TO SERVE WITH COFFEE at Quo Vadis. My favourite chocolate bars are made with dried fruits and nuts. So we made a marzipan, stoned and stuffed a prune, then dipped the prune in chocolate, placing an almond on top.

PS: To make full use of the vanilla pod (and prune stones), wash the pod well and dry, and crack the prune stones to get the elusive bitter almond flavour. Place both in a jar of vodka (you can keep adding vanilla pods and stones to this over time, as well as libations from brandy or Armagnac bottles) and cover the jar. This makes a delicious essence to add to recipes for cakes, custards and creams.

Makes 20

150g whole almonds, blanched and peeled
20 Agen prunes, partially dried fruits or 'mi-cuit' as they are known in France
65g organic caster sugar
juice of 1 medium orange
300g bitter chocolate, at least 70% cocoa solids
12 whole almonds, roasted golden brown in an oven set at 150°C

Preheat the oven to 180°C. Put the 150g of almonds on a roasting tray and bake for 5–6 minutes. Remove and put aside to cool. Make a small incision in the prunes and pop out the stones.

Finely grind the cooled, roasted almonds in a food processor, then add the sugar and orange juice, mixing very well. Divide the mixture into 12 rounds and insert one inside each prune. Smooth the prune around the almond marzipan.

Line a baking sheet with baking parchment. Place the chocolate in a heatproof bowl and sit this over a pan of simmering water. Leave the chocolate to melt while you find a large fork.

Use the fork to lift a prune and carefully dip it in the melted chocolate, letting the excess chocolate drip away. Sit the prune on the lined baking sheet and continue until all are coated, then place a whole roasted almond on top of each.

Place in the fridge to set, then transfer to a container lined with baking parchment and refrigerate. These can be kept in the fridge for at least a week.

Chocolate and cinnamon tart with Boodle's fool

PAIRING CHOCOLATE AND CINNAMON is as lovely as it is ancient. A tightly-rolled stick of papyrus-thin cinnamon bark releases an aroma and flavour more delicate and elegant than commercially ground cinnamons. Served with a spoonful of Boodle's fool (see page 102).

Feeds 6

sweet shortcrust pastry (see page 156), plus flour for dusting
270ml good double cream
180ml whole milk
1 stick of cinnamon
375g dark chocolate, 70% cocoa solids, broken into pieces
1 organic egg, plus 1 egg yolk
Boodle's fool (see page 102)

Heat the oven to 180°C. Roll out the pastry on a lightly floured surface. Line a 25cm x 4cm tart case with it and refrigerate for half an hour. Line the pastry with baking parchment and fill with baking beans or uncooked rice. Place in the oven, lower the temperature to 150°C and bake for 20 minutes. Lift the tart case from the oven and carefully remove the paper and beans. Return the tart case to the oven for 2 minutes, then remove to a rack.

Pour the cream and the milk into a pan and add the cinnamon stick. Place the pan over a moderate heat and bring to a simmer. Remove from the heat. Remove the cinnamon stick. Place the chocolate in a heatproof bowl, strain over the hot milk and stir well until smooth. Crack the egg into a cup, add the yolk and mix well, then add to the bowl and stir, mixing thoroughly.

Pour the chocolate mixture into the tart case and place in the oven to bake for 10–12 minutes, there still being a wobble in the tart. Remove from the oven and cool. Serve with Jersey cream or Boodle's fool (see below).

Boodle's fool

Boodle's fool is named for the gentlemen's club in St James's where I worked as an apprentice when I first came to London. (Boodle's was itself named after its head waiter, Edward Boodle, when it was founded in 1762.) My mother used to make a Boodle's cake, rich with raisins and spices, to take with us on picnics to the Western Isles during our summer holidays, and although the fool was much in evidence at Boodle's – an orange-flavoured cream with a kick of the good stuff to add vigour – I always wondered, where was the cake? There was never a sign of it and I didn't dare ask.

Feeds 6

grated zest and juice of 4 oranges and 2 lemons (all unwaxed)
4 soup spoons amontillado or manzanilla or other good sherry
75g caster sugar
500ml double cream

In a bowl, mix the zest and juice of the oranges and lemons and the sherry with the caster sugar and stir until the sugar has dissolved. Whisking continuously, pour in the cream and continue whisking until soft folds are achieved. Spoon into a handsome bowl or 6 pretty glasses. Cover and refrigerate for at least an hour or overnight. This looks very pleasing decorated with candied orange peel. A nice thought is to serve the fool with shortcake biscuits (see page 61).

EQUIPMENT

COOKING PARAPHERNALIA FROM SMALL TO LARGE

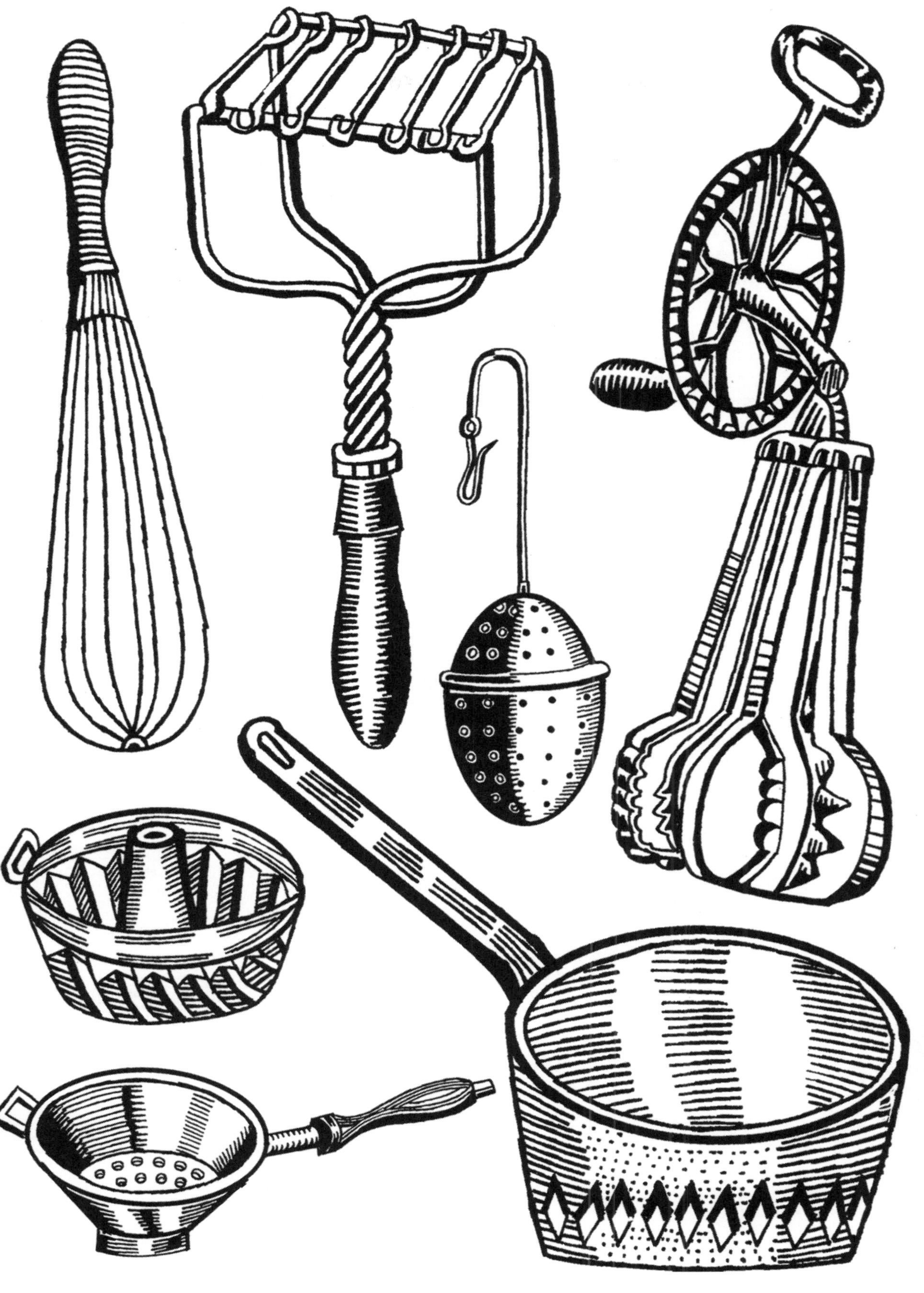

My parents were unable to resist a junk shop and were often found rummaging in Mr Pollington's most extraordinary antiques shop on the Perth Road in Dundee, acquiring another something they loved, which of course included kitchen paraphernalia, filling up a house already rammed to the gunnels with yet more stuff: a rummer or a bowl, a plate or a dish, a table or a chair.

I have inherited a great deal of my parents' kitchen finds, all manner of pottery and bowls and pots and pans, earthenware marmites, cast-iron this, stainless-steel that, acquired over decades since the fifties, which sit on shelves alongside the things I have found on my travels near and far. But despite this wealth of existing kitchen paraphernalia, it's still nigh on impossible for me to think of leaving a kitchen shop without at least a potato peeler, a wooden honey dipper or a bean slicer. In fact, the allure of a fine kitchen shop has become as great as that of a good junk shop – a little time spent out of the gale of life's furies to look at the work of craftsfolk and good things from times past.

A particular weakness for a pestle and mortar has led to a rather curious flock, all varying sizes, nationalities and types from marble to porcelain. Restaurant life usually involves an army of blenders and food processors whizzing away – they're always good friends to have to hand – but at home I like the pleasing business of rendering whole almonds or hazelnuts to a coarse crumb, the pounding and crushing of herbs and spices.

So here is a list of kitchen equipment I have found vital over the years, in both home and restaurant kitchens.

A FEW GOOD MEASURING JUGS AND SPOONS

Jugs with clear markings, measurements in litres/millilitres, are helpful. You need different sizes, and a good idea is to have separate jugs for oil, and for other liquids, available during cooking. A Tala measuring cone is also invaluable.

A pile of small bowls is useful for sitting on the scales to measure out quantities of liquid and dried goods.

I use soup spoons a lot at home for measuring (one soup spoon is the equivalent of one tablespoon) but it's also useful to have a good set of measuring spoons.

MARMITES *(stockpots with a lid)*

These tall terracotta pots, glazed inside, unglazed outside, are good for stocks, braises and pulses. On no account put these pots on the cooker, instead cover well and place directly in the oven. I have a 2–3-litre one for overnight stocks or braises, a 5-litre one for large gatherings. Stock benefits from being cooked in large quantities, giving depth to the flavour, and proves easier to skim off any impurities rising while simmering. Stainless steel or Le Creuset are good too – so long as the pot is sturdy and has a close-fitting lid.

A BREAD STONE

A ceramic disc, or a cast-iron griddle, is ideal for baking tarts and cakes and bread, especially flatbreads, or for giving the kiss of life to a stale loaf. Mine lives in the oven and has helped bake, braise, crisp and keep warm all manner of good things.

WOODEN CHOPPING BOARDS

Several wooden boards in varying sizes. Get rid of plastic and glass – these boards are treasures you love and respect. If you find a large one, buy it – you need plenty of room on your chopping board. Use small round or rectangular ones for slicing lemons for Martinis, or halving fruit for juicing, large for chopping onions and carrots for soup. Mine are mostly square or rectangular, occasionally round; one's a plank I bought in a junk shop. Boards for specific purposes are a wise precaution, e.g. one for meat, one for fish, one for herbs and so on. Using large boards gives a cook confidence when chopping. To clean, scrub boards with hot water and salt.

Restaurants have a rainbow of different-coloured plastic chopping boards for different tasks. It's quite an ask for the home cook, who may only have room for one or two boards. This is solved by the simple task of cleaning as you go, sound practice for the cook at home and in a restaurant alike.

A TERRINE

A rough size-guide to terrines: to feed 4–6 people, you'd need a 15–17cm diameter crock, 7–8cm deep. To feed 10–12 people you need a terrine 27–30cm in length, 10–11cm in width and 7–8cm in depth. Terrines, or crocks as they are better known in the British Isles, come in all shapes and sizes. I favour the small round ones for smaller terrines, be the meats chopped small or coarsely ground, and the long rectangular ones for larger terrines.

A PESTLE AND MORTAR

Use for grinding seeds and dried herbs together for braises and roasts. Marble is brilliant but heavy. I've got a nice cream ceramic one, not too heavy, that's good for pestos and pastes. A small cast-iron one is good for grinding herbs and spices (e.g. the Swedish Skeppshult version in which the pestle sits neatly in the mortar under a lid). John Julian pestles and mortars are sublime – flat in shape, a modern take on the old-fashioned bowl.

COLANDERS AND SIEVES

These are invaluable, and it is so worth having a few of these in different sizes, in aluminium, steel or enamel. When baking, use a drum sieve (you can buy them in multiples, sitting inside each other for easy storage). A few long-handled sieves are excellent too, particularly if one gets wet. They always seem to take an age to dry. A spider, a long-handled device with a hook at the end for hanging and a rounded drainer end for lifting out, is ideal for large batches of asparagus or spuds.

SEVERAL GOOD STAND-UP GRATERS

It's important that your grater can finely zest a lemon as well as grate a nutmeg, so a stand-up stainless-steel grater with numerous gauges is vital. Use the large gauge for cheese, smaller gauges for zest, horseradish, etc. A microblade is now part of daily kitchen life, and it is for the cook to decide which style is best suited for which task.

STAINLESS-STEEL, CAST-IRON OR ALUMINIUM BAKING SHEETS AND ROASTING TINS

Good quality – you don't want them to buckle or stain easily. Cast-iron ones from Netherton Foundry are brilliant. You need two to three roasting tins of different sizes, plus enamel or glazed terracotta for roasting small amounts. Cast-iron enamel dishes are excellent for roasting joints and baking pies and gratins.

A SKILLET

A wide, flat cast-iron skillet for cooking bannocks and farls, crêpes and pancakes (Netherton Foundry again: 35–45cm diameter is a good size for butterflied leg of lamb, pork or kid, or two birds, and useful for the recipes listed in Ashets). Plus a ridged one for grilling meats and vegetables and particularly whole mackerel and sardines.

A STEAMED PUDDING MOULD WITH A CLOSE-FITTING LID

Granny's and my parents' pudding basins remain in Scotland, so I've invested in Mason Cash lidded pudding basins, which are the business. Their classic pudding bowls, in different sizes, are splendid also – great for feeding large numbers. To feed 4–6, use a 15cm-diameter, 10cm-deep pudding mould. To make a steak and kidney pudding to feed 8–10, use a pudding mould 30cm in diameter, 15–20cm deep.

A PRESERVING PAN

Or jelly pan, as Mum used to call hers. It's good to have a correct implement for a ritual like preserving or making marmalade. Small batches of jam can be done in a saucepan big enough to hold a kilo of fruit.

Modern pans are stainless steel and very good. Bear in mind second-hand copper preserving pans which can be found reasonably priced online.

GADGETS

Electric lemon juicer: for blood oranges, lemons, pomegranates.

A spice/coffee/salt and pepper grinder: an electric grinder is useful for grinding whole spices in large quantities, but ideally you'd also have a little hand-operated one as well. Peugeot make prized grinders for both coarse sea salt and pepper.

Digital scales (free-standing).

Food processor: Magimix or KitchenAid.

Stand mixer: KitchenAid (KitchenAid also have a good attachment for grinding spices and a very good ice-cream churner).

Hand-held beater: a little Kenwood.

A blender: with the most powerful motor you can get, e.g. KitchenAid or Waring.

A stick blender: is good for all sorts, from soup to vinaigrette and mayonnaise.

POTS AND PANS

How I would love to have shopped at Cadec, the long-gone kitchen shop in Soho. And for that matter at Elizabeth David, where shelves were heaped with all manner of cooking implements.

Buying pans is not dissimilar to buying knives, their cost often the cause of a raised eyebrow or two. It is best to buy a superb one every now and again, to slowly build a good choice of sizes. And ensure pans come with tight-fitting lids, so necessary for cooking generally. There is little pleasure in waiting for an unlidded pot to boil. Good kitchen shops – and here I would cite casting an eye over the David Mellor catalogue, or, should the chance to walk past the door present itself, popping in for a browse – are never a bad idea, as they always have a fine collection. Buying stainless steel is preferable as it is good for all manner of cooking, where aluminium can taint.

The internet is awash with a bewildering choice and pleases not half as much as finding independent kitchen shops with good websites. Very sturdy, heavy-bottomed pans, in stainless steel, plus cast iron and enamelled cast iron for braising. Two small (15cm diameter x 8cm deep), two medium (20cm diameter x 10cm deep), two large (25cm diameter x 13cm deep). A big wide pan, 25cm diameter x 8cm deep, is good for a risotto. I also have two non-stick frying pans, one small, 20cm x 5cm deep, one large, 28cm x 4cm deep, plus one small egg-frying pan (12cm diameter). Much is made, and rightly so, of what is good quality, durable and does not chip and flake over time, so it is wise to keep abreast of findings and new technology. A 20cm diameter x 8cm deep pan, double-handed, is ideal for steaming. A pan 28cm x 15–17cm deep is good for stock. Good pan brands to explore include French, Italian and Danish heavy-bottomed, stainless-steel pans such as Le Creuset, Le Pentole, Iittala and Scanpan, but if the prices are daunting, investigate small hardware shops and big shops like John Lewis, or a vast Ikea. It is worth considering having pans that are compatible with electric and induction hobs.

I love cast-iron frying pans and flit happily between those such as Bourgeat in France, to be found in Nisbets, and those made in Britain by the estimable Netherton Foundry, to be found in some kitchen shops or on an excellent website.

A GOOD COLLECTION OF BOWLS

You can't have enough bowls in a kitchen, to my mind. They're incredibly useful when preparing ingredients. Have them in all sizes, in ceramic, pottery, glass and stainless steel.

TART CASES

My mum had a stack of different-sized and shaped tart cases and cake tins, square, rectangular, round, etc., and I find it hard to resist buying just one more myself. These days I buy aluminium, or non-stick. There is a brilliant tart tin called Perfobake, peppered with holes to facilitate a crisper pastry, removing the need for blind baking (try Lakeland, John Lewis or your local kitchen shop). To feed 6, you need a 20cm x 3cm tart case; to feed 10–12, you'll need a case 28cm x 3cm. For deeper tarts, use a 20cm x 5cm case. All tart cases should have removable bottoms.

A CHICKEN BRICK AND A DIABLE

I love these terracotta pots, primarily used for roasting chicken and vegetables. I have a fond memory of staying at a friend's house and putting a shoulder of lamb, plus accompanying veg and lentils, into a chicken brick with a splash of water. We left this in the oven while we went for an almighty walk, returning to a beautifully cooked lamb and lentil dish. (To make your own, put a shoulder of lamb, 2 handfuls of lentils, chopped onion, carrot and celery, a handful of chopped herbs and a splash of water, salt and pepper, into a chicken brick and leave in a low oven for 6–8 hours.) There are also vegetable bricks (diables) which are especially good for potatoes and beetroot. It is advisable to soak the two parts of the diable and the chicken brick for at least an hour or overnight before using – this generates the steam in order to cook.

A POT BRISTLING WITH WOODEN SPOONS, LADLES, WHISKS, ETC.

What's not to like? I have a pot of spoons that I used in my childhood, some of Mum's, from restaurants I cooked in when using wood was abolished, and picked up on travels near and far, plus another filled with tongs, 2 or 3 rubber spatulas, wooden rolling pins, 2 or 3 fine wire whisks. Have a variety of wooden spoons, small, medium, large, long and short-handled. A small pot of soup spoons or tablespoons for tasting as you go is also handy for the cook. A baker's dough scraper for scooping up chopped vegetables and herbs is a very good device to have at hand. Small, medium and large ladles, for different purposes – for example, a small ladle is very useful for adding small amounts of oil when emulsifying sauces, medium is very good for general kitchen use and large ladles are good for stocks and soups.

WEIGHING SCALES

I am devoted to a little set of digital scales on which I can put bowl after bowl to measure the contents (a good set should carry a good weight).

KNIVES

Chief among kitchen paraphernalia are cooks' knives, which, like pots and pans, come in a vast array of different sizes, makes and materials, with handles made with all manner of woods and finishes and often with a price tag to match. Eschewing French Sabatier knives made from carbon steel, as they discoloured so quickly, I fell instead for the beautiful stainless-steel Sabatier knives which I bought as a young apprentice chef. As I did for the superb knives made of German or Danish steel, such as those made by Henckels, Gustav Emil Ern or F. Dick. I then found the Japanese makers J. Coral, a neighbour to Global knives in Japan. I have them still.

There is an awe-inspiring array of knives for all manner of chopping and cutting in every shape and size imaginable made in China and Japan, and a fine array to be found in Chinatown or the Japanese Knife Store in Soho. As well as the more familiar tapering blade of the classically shaped knives ending in the sharpest points, there are cleavers. Made in different sizes, not just those more familiar in the hands of a butcher, cleavers are a revelation to the cook, proving always to be a swift and elegant tool, pleasingly lifting up what is chopped. There is also now in the UK an incredible new generation of knife-makers with their own forges, such as Clement Knives, Blenheim Forge and Savernake Knives.

Worth considering too are knives for opening oysters and the beautiful curved blades for cutting shards of Parmesan. And lest we forget, a small serrated knife is so useful for slicing oranges and lemons as well as tomatoes.

I must confess, having learned from experience and been in possession of a fair few knife rolls bristling with blades acquired over many years from shops at home and abroad, that I probably use only a fraction with any regularity. A few good knives of varying sizes are vital, the rest really acquired only because I loved them. On a daily basis, I find I need two small paring knives along with a medium and a large-sized cook's knife or cleaver. A long carving knife with a serrated blade ensures you can use the whole length of the blade for the clean slicing of bread or meat, using the whole arm, rather like the motion of a locomotive.

Knives must have a keen edge as this makes the task of chopping quicker, easier and curiously safer, a blunt edge quite simply dull in every way – so you might consider a whetting stone which comes in differing gauges measured in grit for smoothness (the higher and smoother the grit, the finer the edge on your knives) and a steel for maintaining that edge. Those with a grit count rising from the 1500 mark are the best for a keen-edged minimum marking.

To be sure, almost anything can be bought on the internet, but really, nothing beats actually finding a great knife merchant or shop and being guided by their sure knowledge. Good reading: *Knife* by Tim Hayward.

A PROJECT

To gradually replace single-use plastic in the kitchen with durable materials for storage as well as for food preparation.

FISH

Shiny darlings lifted from the deep

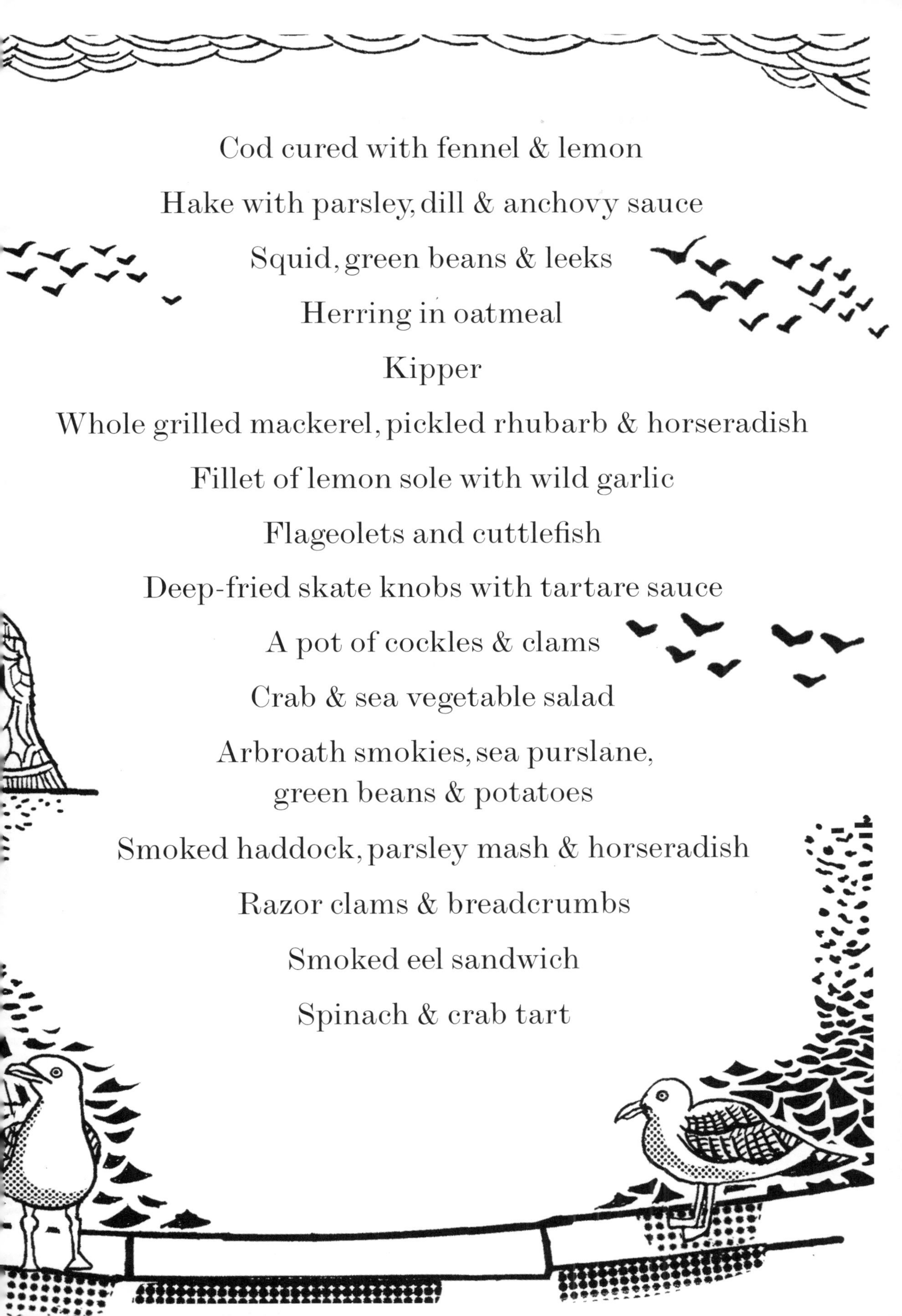

Cod cured with fennel & lemon

Hake with parsley, dill & anchovy sauce

Squid, green beans & leeks

Herring in oatmeal

Kipper

Whole grilled mackerel, pickled rhubarb & horseradish

Fillet of lemon sole with wild garlic

Flageolets and cuttlefish

Deep-fried skate knobs with tartare sauce

A pot of cockles & clams

Crab & sea vegetable salad

Arbroath smokies, sea purslane,
green beans & potatoes

Smoked haddock, parsley mash & horseradish

Razor clams & breadcrumbs

Smoked eel sandwich

Spinach & crab tart

While I was writing this book, Britain officially split from Europe on New Year's Day 2021, or, to be precise, at 23:00 hours on December 31st 2020. This while the whole of the British Isles was in the bitter grip of Covid-19, in the throes of a third lockdown.

There is much controversy over the effects of Brexit on the British Isles. There was word that paperwork for importing and exporting seemed to multiply at an alarming rate, but the loudest shout in January came from British fisheries. This is not surprising, as at least half the fish caught in UK waters is exported to Europe, and delays in transport were resulting in lorry-loads of fish waiting hours, and in some instances days, at the ports.

Add mounting concerns for global warming, the welfare of the planet and huge questions over sustainability, particularly of fish stocks in the oceans, and you have a perfect storm of impending trouble.

There is a school of thought that argues that a rise in sea temperature is as much a factor in the depletion of all types of fish as over-fishing. Cod, for instance, need the biting cold waters now shifting further north, closer to the Arctic and the Barents Sea.

But there is an upside: buying British fish from day boats has never had more appeal, or indeed more urgency, for not only is the quality unsurpassed, it is a way of life for many that demands respect and support. It is certainly notable that a call for good fish is on the rise, as more fishmongers and merchants appear, opening shops on land and online, selling fish of exceptional quality.

I recall the days prior to these turbulent times, in the late eighties and early nineties, when a few intrepid fishmongers such as William Black, Steve Bird and Steve Downey had begun supplying British fish to restaurants throughout the UK: Rowley Leigh at Kensington Place, the eponymous Alastair Little, and Simon Hopkinson at Bibendum, Ruth Rogers and Rose Gray at the River Café, as well as Joyce Molyneux at the Carved Angel in Dartmouth, Rick Stein in Cornwall and Shaun Hill at Gidleigh Park. It helped trigger a great change in British restaurants, which now began to demand good-quality local produce to match a fresh approach to food – creating simple dishes with the best ingredients. It was a new kind of cooking best summed up by dishes such as a whole grilled sea bass or sardines dressed only with a superb olive oil and lemon.

A young Ben Woodcraft was another of these suppliers who brought fish, landed that morning and sorted at his shed on Mersea Island near Colchester on the Essex coast, directly to London restaurants. I first met Ben, who was also supplying the River Café, when I cooked with Alastair Little in Soho. He would phone at the start of every day to list that morning's catch. I have spoken with Ben most mornings ever since, for a natter and to make an order for the day's fish.

It is a pleasure that never diminishes – ordering sea bass or cod, hake or a variety of sole, such as Dover, lemon, witch or megrim, mackerel or herring, squid or cuttlefish. Smoked fish, too: kippers, bloaters, buckling; sprats, nets of mussels, tubs of clams, bundles of razor clams, samphire and bags of seaweed to pile on plates for serving oysters. There are also crabs and lobsters, though I look to the south coast at Portland for the huge cock crabs that have great flakes of the sweetest meat.

But it is not just for the quality of his fish that I admire this quiet, gentle, unassuming man. Throughout the many storms, both literal and metaphorical, concerning questions of supply and sustainability that plague the fishing industry, Ben has made sure that we continue to get fresh fish. He sent us hake and the varieties of skate that were plentiful when the shocking facts were revealed about the absence of cod in British coastal waters through the nineties. Many other fish were in similar straits – the days of dancing over the North Sea on the backs of silver darlings are long gone.

When I asked what he thought the far-reaching results of Brexit and the full impact of restrictions imposed through the lockdown periods of Covid-19 might mean, the telling silence at the other end of the phone spoke volumes. Then he said, 'Well, as you are on the phone, would you like anything? I have some lovely mackerel…' Ben would do what he always did, getting on with the business of being a fish merchant, a purveyor of excellent quality fish from the business he had grown in a sea port on the east coast.

And that is the sort of spirit that has informed and fuelled dishes, vittled the kitchens I have worked in and now fills the pages of this book.

Many of these recipes are interchangeable with other fish, timings to be changed accordingly. It is worth checking which fish are plentiful, in season and caught close to shore before fully deciding which to cook.

Cod cured with fennel and lemon

THE SEEDS AND FRONDS OF FENNEL lend the cod a delicate fragrance. Once you've cooked the cod, sit it on a spoonful of mash made with olive oil, stirring in a handful of peppery rocket leaves just before serving. This will give the dish a wonderfully wild, unkempt look as the leaves yield to the comforting warmth of the mashed potatoes.

The cure for the cod is the very lightest, requiring just a few hours of refrigeration overnight, a mere dusting of sea salt mixed with lemon zest, chopped fennel fronds and whole fennel seeds ground fine with a few peppercorns. A pinch of dried chilli flakes is a pleasing addition.

It is worth considering other fish such as hake, coley and pollock for this dish.

Feeds 6

For the cured cod

1 soup spoon fennel seeds
½ teaspoon black peppercorns
grated zest of 1 unwaxed lemon
1 soup spoon sea salt flakes
a pinch of dried chilli flakes
4 small fennel bulbs

1.2kg cod fillet, cut into 6 equal-sized pieces
750g mashing potatoes, such as Maris Piper
125ml extra virgin olive oil
2 whole red chillies
12 black peppercorns
6 bay leaves
1 small branch of rosemary
3 large handfuls of rocket leaves, if possible the large foppish-leaved variety, picked, washed and dried
1–2 soup spoons double cream (optional)
4 soup spoons flour
4 soup spoons light vegetable oil, e.g. sunflower

Grind the fennel seeds and peppercorns finely, then mix with the lemon zest, sea salt and chilli flakes in a bowl. Finely slice the stalk

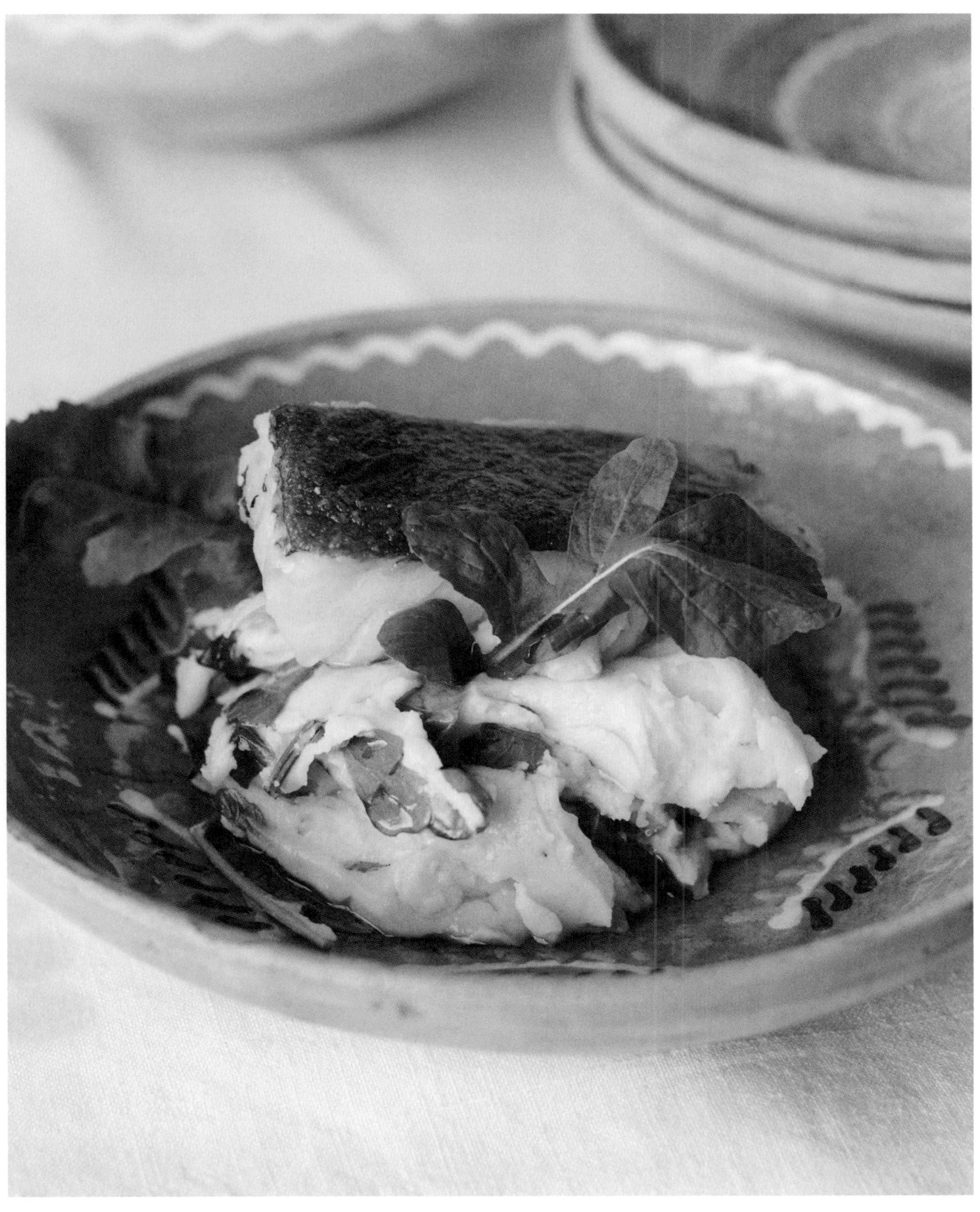

and fronds of the fennel and scatter over the fish. Rub the result into the cod. Place the fish in a deep dish, cover and refrigerate overnight.

Peel the potatoes and chop into equal-sized pieces, washing them well in cold water. Place in a pan of water with a pinch of salt and cook until tender. Drain the potatoes well and mash.

Pour the olive oil into a pan and add the chillies, peppercorns, bay leaves and rosemary. Place the pan over the gentlest heat for the oil to warm lightly and infuse. Strain the oil into the mash, season and beat until smooth. Stir in the rocket and keep warm. A spoonful or two of cream is most welcome.

Preheat the oven to 200°C. Put the flour into a flat dish and season with salt and pepper. Heat a large roasting tin and add the 4 soup spoons of light vegetable oil. Lightly dip the skin side of the cod fillets into the flour and place each piece skin side down in the hot oil, as far apart as possible. Place in the preheated oven for 12–15 minutes. Put a spoonful of the mash on a warmed plate, place a fillet of cod on top and serve.

Hake with parsley, dill and anchovy sauce

A STRIKING DISH WITH THE PALE GREEN LIMPID SAUCE pooled in the plate, contrasting with the delicate silvered skin of the hake.

Feeds 6

3 small shallots
1 clove of garlic
6 anchovy fillets
7 soup spoons olive oil
200ml double cream
150g picked flat-leaf parsley leaves
30g picked dill leaves
6 fillets of hake, roughly 1kg in total

Preheat the oven to 200°C. Peel and finely chop the shallots and garlic. Place in a pan with the anchovies and olive oil. Sit this upon the gentlest heat and warm until the shallots have softened and the anchovies have melted. Pour in the cream. Bring to a simmer, then pour into a blender packed with the picked herbs. Render smooth and pour this through a fine sieve. Cool swiftly and refrigerate until required.

Place the fillets of hake in a deep ovenproof dish, lightly season with salt and white pepper and lightly dress with a soup spoon of olive oil. Pour in enough cold water to cover the bottom of the dish. Cover the dish and bake in a hot oven until done, say 15–20 minutes. Remove from the oven and keep warm. Any residual juices left in the dish can be added to the sauce.

Warm the sauce and pour on to a dish. Place the fillets of hake on the sauce and serve swiftly. Heaven with the first crop of new potatoes.

Squid, green beans and leeks

DEPENDING ON THE TIME OF YEAR AND AVAILABILITY, the cook might consider adding some or all of these to this salad: samphire, monksbeard (barba di frate), bitter leaves such as puntarelle, as well as peas, pea shoots and broad beans.

Feeds 6

500g green leaves, e.g. dandelion leaves, watercress, leafy rocket, flat-leaf parsley
600g squid
1 unwaxed lemon and juice of 1 more
200g green beans
2 firm, bright leeks, green parts attached
a bunch of spring onions (or Tropea onions or small leeks if found)
75g flat-leaf parsley
1 soup spoon salted capers, soaked for 30 minutes in cold water
3 soup spoons extra virgin olive oil

Pick, wash and dry the leaves.

Ask your fishmonger to clean the squid, or do it yourself: holding the sac in one hand, with the other hand gently pull out the tentacles. With a sharp knife, cut above the eyes, discarding all else but the tentacles. Squeeze gently to remove the small bony beak. Pull the transparent quill-like bone from the sac. With a sharp knife cut along the length of the sac, then lay the squid flat and peel away any skin and matter, rinsing under cold water. Separate the tentacles with a knife, then slice the body into 5mm-wide strips. Rinse once more and keep in the fridge until needed.

In a pan of water, simmer the whole lemon for 25 minutes, until softened. Cut the lemon into quarters, despatching the pulp within. Slice the peel into the thinnest strips.

Top and tail the green beans. Wash them thoroughly, then boil in well-salted water until tender. Drain. Slice the leeks into rounds, wash well and cook in boiling water until tender (about a minute or two). Slice the spring onions thinly. Pick, wash, dry and chop the 75g of parsley.

Dress the tentacles and sliced squid with the lemon juice, sliced lemon peel and 2 soup spoons of the extra virgin olive oil. Season with salt and pepper and mix well.

Heat a wide frying pan. Tumble the squid onto the hot pan and cook undisturbed for 3 minutes, then toss in the pan for 1 further minute. Remove from the heat and tip into a large bowl. Add the beans, leeks, drained capers, spring onions and chopped parsley to the bowl. Check the seasoning and mix well.

Heap the salad on a big dish with a final flourish of the last soup spoon of olive oil and top with the contents of the bowl.

Herring in oatmeal

ACCOMPANY WITH BACON, OR FRIED EGGS, cabbages and leeks and boiled potatoes strewn with chopped curly parsley.

Feeds 6

6 freshest herring, scaled, gutted and filleted or butterflied
8 soup spoons milk
150g (roughly) milled pinhead oatmeal
50g unsalted butter

Remove any lingering bones in the herring fillets. Rinse quickly under cold water. Put the milk into a dish and the oats on a plate. Dip each fillet in the milk, then lay flat in the oatmeal, pressing lightly to ensure an even cover.

Put the grill on a high heat. Place the herring fillets on a baking tray, dot with the butter and place under the heated grill. Cook for 3–4 minutes, then turn the fillets, cooking for a further 3–4 minutes.

Kipper

Allow one kipper each

A kippered herring, when split and smoked, is the most familiar, not to mention the most beloved, of dishes made with herring. Be fastidious in your choice of kipper – they're best when larger and not overly smoked, resulting in plump, delicious fillets. Dot with butter and bake in the oven for 5 minutes or so until bronzed. Delicious eaten as is with plenty of bread and butter, or accompany with rashers of streaky bacon, a fried egg and perhaps a spoonful of potato salad too.

Another method is to jug the kipper. Lay the kipper flat in a heatproof dish and pour over boiling water. Cover the dish and leave for 5 minutes. The appeal of this dish is the revelatory delicacy of the flesh.

Whole grilled mackerel, pickled rhubarb and horseradish

CONSIDERING THE WEALTH OF PRODUCE in the British Isles, it is curious how few have protected designation of origin status, or PDO as it's known. The laudable list is easily found on the government website and makes for fascinating if somewhat brief reading.

There, nestled between cheese, perry, Bramley apples, Ayrshire earlies and Fenland celery, is rhubarb, grown specifically in the Rhubarb Triangle of Yorkshire between Bradford, Leeds and Wakefield. The methods used must be traditional, which means grown in long, dark, low-ceilinged buildings, illuminated solely by candlelight, to ensure only the stalks grow and the leaf remains a charming flicker at the top of the stem. Hearing the heads of rhubarb pop as they grow in the dim light is otherworldly. Rhubarb is pretty much a perennial, but the forced pink rhubarb is a ray of joy in the winter months. There are many recipes for rhubarb but I am fond of this pretty pickle, which tempers a fiery horseradish accompaniment and eats so well with grilled mackerel.

Make the pickled rhubarb in advance, a few days even, as it's happy to sit in the fridge (it's sensible to make more than required, too, as this pickle goes with many grilled foods). Here, all that is needed is a mackerel, whole or filleted, lightly oiled and salted.

To keep the pretty pink pickle count high, along with the horseradish cream you might consider borrowing the red onion pickle recipe that accompanies the smoked eel sandwich (page 144).

Pickle the rhubarb and red onions the day before. Horseradish cream is best made on the day (see page 146). As rhubarb can be very young and may cook quickly, baking the pieces side by side in a single layer is one way to ensure it does not collapse. It is worth noting that the pickle is delicious whole or otherwise. If there is a surfeit of pickle when all has been eaten, use any remainder for another batch and enliven with a strip or two of orange peel.

For each person

1 whole freshest mackerel, gutted, cleaned and trimmed
1 teaspoon light vegetable oil
pickled rhubarb (see below)
horseradish cream (see page 146)
red onion pickle (see page 146)
1 lemon, halved, to serve

Heat a ridged grill pan, or make embers in a fire or put the oven or grill on a moderate heat.

Lightly oil the fish and season liberally with sea salt. Place on the grill and leave undisturbed until blistered and lightly charred with a good crust, say 7–8 minutes, then turn the fish and cook for a further 6 minutes or so. Serve the grilled fish on a plate, with the lemon halves and bowls of pickled rhubarb, horseradish cream and red onion pickle.

Pickled rhubarb

Makes enough for 6

400g pink rhubarb
200ml organic cider vinegar
120g caster sugar
50g fresh ginger, peeled and thinly sliced
1 soup spoon black peppercorns
1 teaspoon sea salt

Heat the oven to 180°C. Trim the ends of the rhubarb and cut away any blemishes. Cut the stalks into 2cm lengths, and lay the pieces side by side in the widest ovenproof pan.

Put the cider vinegar, sugar, sliced ginger, peppercorns and sea salt into a pot and bring to the boil. Lower the heat and simmer for 10 minutes. Strain over the rhubarb.

Cover with foil and place in the oven for 12–15 minutes, until just tender when tested with the tip of a knife.

Fillet of lemon sole with wild garlic

A WHOLE LEMON SOLE OR A WHOLE PLAICE heaped with the thinnest slices of spring onion and chopped wild garlic has a gentle restorative quality. A steamer is excellent for this, or an oven dish or baking tray. This recipe is good for all white fish. Either cook the fish whole or use fillets.

For each person

a whole lemon sole or a whole small plaice, roughly 300g of fish per person
3 or 4 wild garlic leaves, coarsely chopped
1 spring onion, thinly sliced
1 teaspoon extra virgin olive oil

Preheat the oven to 200°C. Place the fish in a dish that will suit both oven-cooking and serving. Scatter the chopped wild garlic and spring onion over the fish. Season with salt and black pepper. Evenly distribute a teaspoon of oil over the fish and garlic and spring onion and add 2 soup spoons of water. Cover the dish with a lid or foil, then place in the oven and cook for 15–20 minutes, having a care not to overcook.

Lift the dish in its entirety to the table as soon as the fish is cooked. This is lovely with fresh peas simply boiled and dressed with a dot of butter, along with new potatoes dressed in olive oil and chopped wild garlic wilted at the last moment.

Flageolets and cuttlefish

BRINDISA, THE COMPANY SELLING IMPORTED SPANISH FOODS, is always a most inspiring source of beans. Monika Linton, its founder, tirelessly seeks out new producers and growers. Among her many finds over the years is an heirloom variety of green bean called verdina, similar to flageolets, coloured the palest green and superb with all manner of fish. In this recipe, cuttlefish are braised with the beans until tender.

As with all dried beans, these benefit from cooking the day before, which also allows for any mischievous beans slow to cook to soften.

PS: Chickpeas are also very good in this recipe.

Feeds 6

1 small onion
3 sticks of celery
1 bulb of fennel
5 cloves of garlic
450g cuttlefish, cleaned
4 soup spoons olive oil
500g dried flageolet or verdina beans, soaked overnight
6 bay leaves
a small posy of thyme

Peel, trim and coarsely chop the onion, celery and fennel. Peel and slice the garlic. Cut the cuttlefish into 5mm-thick slices.

Place a heavy-bottomed pot over a moderate heat and pour in the olive oil. Tip in the cuttlefish and cook for 2 minutes undisturbed, then stir. Add the chopped vegetables and sliced garlic. Place a lid atop, lower the heat and let cook gently until the vegetables soften, say 15 minutes or so.

Rinse the beans, place in a pot and cover with plenty of cold water, roughly 3 litres. Bring to the boil, drain and lightly rinse and add to the cuttlefish and vegetables. Pour in enough water to cover. Add the bay leaves and the posy of thyme to the pot. Leaving the lid slightly askew, let the beans and cuttlefish simmer very gently for 2 hours or so, until tender.

Deep-fried skate knobs with tartare sauce

THESE ARE A VERY GOOD REASON for having a conversation with a fishmonger. All too often despatched with the rest of the fish after filleting, these toothsome bites, cheeks from the head of the skate, are worth seeking out. As with all fish, freshness is vital. By all means consider cod cheeks too, or slices of monkfish cheek, for this recipe.

Feeds 6

roughly 6 skate knobs each or 150g, depending on appetite
2 organic eggs, beaten
3 heaped soup spoons plain flour, seasoned
fresh white breadcrumbs, roughly 3 large handfuls
2 litres sunflower oil
a bunch of curly parsley, leaves picked
1 batch of tartare sauce (see opposite), made earlier in the day

Leaving them whole, trim the skate knobs of any extraneous membrane, rinse well and pat dry.

Have ready side by side a large bowl containing the beaten eggs, a tray of seasoned flour, a tray of breadcrumbs and a tray for the breaded cheeks. Lay the skate knobs in the seasoned flour. Dip each in the beaten egg, then roll in the breadcrumbs until evenly coated. Place on the waiting tray.

Place kitchen paper on a plate, ready. Heat the oil either in a deep-fat fryer, following the maker's instructions, or heat 2 litres of sunflower oil in a deep pan (roughly 25cm wide x 12cm deep) to 180°C. Deep-fry the skate knobs in small batches for 5–7 minutes, then remove them from the fryer and lay on the kitchen paper to drain.

Fry the parsley in the hot oil for 1 minute, and drain on kitchen paper. Pile the skate knobs on a dish and scatter over the parsley. Decant the tartare sauce into a bowl, then take all to table.

Tartare sauce

This I like lots so always make lots… A dear friend always laughs when I stay, as the fridge usually ends up with much mayonnaise and other unguents. It's very good with many things.

Makes enough for 6

2 organic egg yolks
1 soup spoon Dijon mustard
1 soup spoon organic cider vinegar
1 soup spoon lemon juice
350ml light oil, such as peanut or sunflower
2 soup spoons olive oil
1 soup spoon salted capers, soaked for 30 minutes in cold water
2 soup spoons gherkins
3 hard-boiled organic eggs, peeled
1 heaped soup spoon finely chopped flat-leaf parsley
1 teaspoon finely chopped tarragon
1 teaspoon finely chopped chervil
6 shakes of Tabasco

Put the yolks into a bowl and add the mustard, vinegar and lemon juice. Beating continuously, slowly add the oil until a thickened mayonnaise results. Finish with the olive oil.

Coarsely chop the drained capers, gherkins and hard-boiled eggs. Mix these gently with the mayonnaise, along with the chopped herbs, and season with salt and black pepper and a few drops of Tabasco. Cover and refrigerate.

A pot of cockles and clams

THIS LIGHT, BRIGHT DISH WITH A SOOTHING BROTH delights in the addition of cream, although this is entirely at the cook's discretion. Depending on the time of year, add chopped wild garlic, cooked peas, broad beans, asparagus or spring onions to the pot. This is equally as good as a pan of mussels.

Feeds 6

450g cockles
400g clams
1 small onion, peeled
4 sticks of celery
1 small bulb or ½ a large bulb of fennel
3 soup spoons extra virgin olive oil
3 bay leaves
a small bundle of thyme and summer savory
2 leeks, green parts still attached
125ml white wine
200ml double cream
120g flat-leaf parsley, leaves picked and chopped

Rinse the cockles and clams well in several changes of cold water, for it is a shame after such efforts to have a mote of grit spoil the brew.

Chop the onion, celery and fennel into small pieces. Heat the olive oil in a large pot over a moderate heat, and add the onion, celery, fennel, bay leaves, thyme and savory. Cover the pot and cook until softened, about 20 minutes, stirring from time to time. Slice the leeks into pieces roughly 1cm wide, wash thoroughly and add them to the pot and cook for a further 5 minutes. Add the white wine, cockles and clams, cover and boil vigorously over a high heat until all the shellfish open (discard any that don't open).

Pour in the cream, add the chopped parsley, shake the pan gently, return to the boil and serve.

Crab and sea vegetable salad

A FAVOURITE DISH THAT ILLUSTRATES the satisfying business of making the effort to cook and pick your own crab. A very good, simple, bright and briny salad that features often on our menu. We love the beautiful great cock crabs from Portland but happily suggest a dressed crab or three. To kill and cook crabs is, to quote chef Rowley Leigh, 'a very messy business' but pays a great dividend. The prize here is the great flakes – that texture so often lost in bought prepared crab meat. One exception to this rule is an unadorned, unpasteurised, dressed crab bought from a good fishmonger.

Feeds 6

2 big handfuls of sea vegetables, picked and rinsed (e.g. samphire and sea purslane, sea beet and sea aster, or seaweed such as dulse)
50ml natural yoghurt
1 teaspoon Dijon mustard
50ml extra virgin olive oil
juice of ½ a lemon
400g picked white and brown meat mixed, from 2 large cock crabs or 3 dressed crabs

Bring a wide pan of water to the boil. Plunge in the sea vegetables and let cook briefly, just 30 seconds or so. Tip the vegetables into a colander and lightly cool with cold water from the tap. Let drain.

Whisk the yoghurt, mustard, olive oil, lemon juice and some salt and black pepper in a bowl until smooth.

When ready, tumble the sea vegetables, crab and dressing into a bowl. Mix lightly and thoroughly. Taste for seasoning. Serve swiftly.

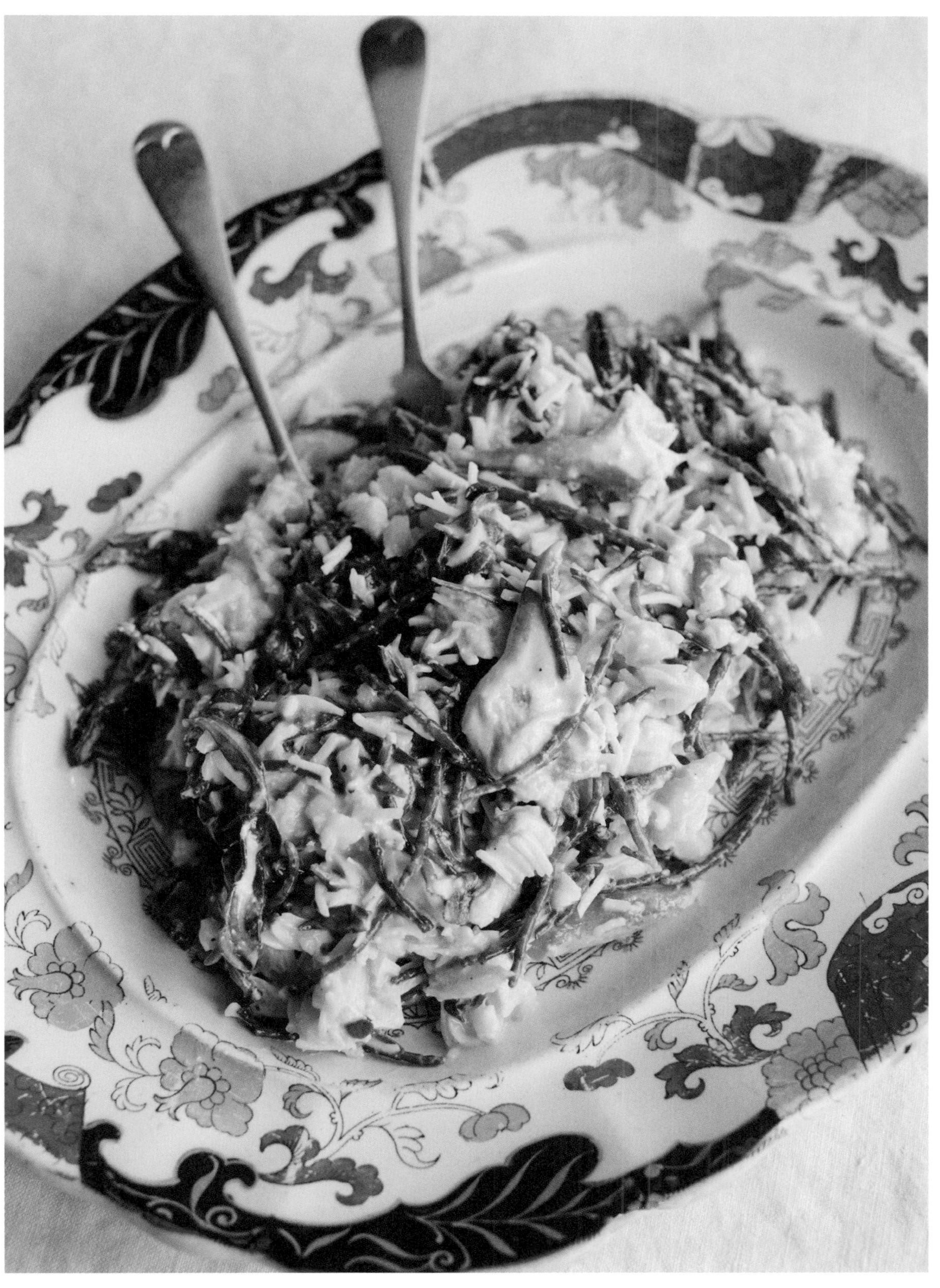

Arbroath smokies, sea purslane, green beans and potatoes

ARBROATH SMOKIES, ALSO A PROTECTED FOOD, are delicately smoked haddock from the eponymous town just up the east coast of Scotland from Dundee. The Spink family, Arbroath fish merchants, have made Arbroath smokies their own, so much so that Spinks appear at fairs and fêtes to smoke the fish on site. It is quite a show seeing a pit covered in jute sacks while the haddock smoke within. The resulting fish are wonderful eaten hot from the smoker with bread and butter.

Away from this happy scene in eastern Scotland, the smokies are stiffened by refrigeration and their delicacy somewhat diminished, for haddock is not an oily fish like herring. They are best warmed slightly and served with a salad. Removing the skin and bones is a simpler affair than with herring, and when warmed gently in a little water and butter, the smokies' qualities are reawakened. Cooked potato and beans are added with leaves of sea purslane, mixed lightly, then served. Consider, too, samphire, monksbeard, peas or a mix of young spinach and watercress for this salad. Should a smokie prove difficult to find, by all means use smoked haddock of the palest hue.

Feeds 6

4 Arbroath smokies (or 600g smoked haddock)
40g unsalted butter
750g cooked new potatoes, such as Jersey, Ayrshire or Cornish
300g green beans, cooked
10–15g sea purslane

Remove the skin from the fish. Carefully lift away the smoked flesh, and remove any bones. Place the flakes of haddock in a wide-bottomed pan with 100ml of water and the butter. Lightly season with salt and pepper. Cover the pan and place over a gentle heat to warm through, with only the gentlest movement to keep the haddock from breaking up.

Cut the potatoes into 6–8mm-thick slices and lay them on the fish in the pan. Add the cooked beans. Strew with the picked sea purslane leaves. Cover and simmer a further 2–3 minutes. Serve in bowls.

Smoked haddock, parsley mash and horseradish

THOUGHTS MIGHT ALSO WANDER TO COD OR HAKE for this delightfully simple dish.

Feeds 6

1.2kg best mashing potatoes, such as King Edward
80g unsalted butter
750g smoked haddock fillet
2 handfuls of curly parsley, leaves picked and finely chopped, stalks reserved (the mineral tang of curly-leaf parsley, as opposed to the softer taste of flat-leaf parsley, suits this dish very well)
100ml whole milk
200g horseradish cream (see 146)

Preheat the oven to 180°C.

Peel and chop the potatoes, simmer in salted boiling water until tender, then drain and mash. Beat in the butter and keep warm.

Cut the smoked haddock into pieces for 6 folks. Lay these in a roasting tin, skin side up, strew with the parsley stalks, pour on the milk, cover well and cook in the oven for 8–10 minutes. Remove the tin from the oven and lift the haddock carefully on to a plate. Remove the skin if so wished.

Drain the hot milk into the mash, add the chopped parsley leaves, season with salt and black pepper and beat until smooth. Serve the smoked haddock upon a spoonful of mash, with a spoonful of horseradish cream on top.

Razor clams and breadcrumbs

Razor clams, or 'spoots' as they are known in the Orkney and Shetland islands, were rare, and on occasion Dad would come home with a 'wee baggie', usually a bundle wrapped in white paper, steam them in salted water and eat them with bread, butter and a big grin. This is a favoured recipe, enjoyed often at the bar of Le Caprice when the kitchen was under the command of Mark Hix. This simple dish partnered with an excellent Bloody Mary is most winning.

Feeds 2, for a light lunch or a starter

6 razor clams
a splash of white wine, roughly 50ml
2 soup spoons olive oil
2 heaped soup spoons parsley crumbs (see page 73)

Turn on a grill to a high heat. Wash the razor clams throroughly of any grit. Place the clams in a pan with the wine. Cover and place over a high heat. Cook thus for 30 seconds. Lift out the clams. Add the olive oil and some ground black pepper to the pan and simmer this until only 2 spoonfuls of the resulting liquor remain.

Remove the clams from the shells and place the shells in an ovenproof dish. Cut away the small grey sac from the meat of the clam and chop the meat into large pieces. Return the meat to the clam shells, strew with the parsley crumbs and place under the grill for 1 minute, until just coloured. Lift the clams on to a serving dish, pour over the juices remaining in the bottom of the pan and serve at once.

Smoked eel sandwich

SMOKED EEL IS A TRUE DELICACY with a flavour the equal of its antiquity. Those I use were originally from Mr Beale's Eels in Lincolnshire, which over time became the Dutch Eel Company, which in turn became the Devon Eel Company. When bought whole and cut from the bone they are peerless. Wild eel are fiercely protected. So we use farmed, smoked eel, which is scrupulously monitored. Buying from an accredited sustainable source is vital.

It is hard to remember a time when sourdough bread was a rarity and the legendary loaves from the Poilâne bakery in Paris were a luxury, sought to serve toasted with terrines, rillettes and for becoming the foundation for this sandwich. I have tried endless sourdoughs since, but the structure of the bread made in the bakery founded by Mr Poilâne and now run by his daughter, Apollonia, remains true for this dish.

The remains of the smoked eel once prepared make a formidable stock, and when cooked with potatoes, leeks and mussels and the remaining pieces of smoked eel, an estimable soup.

Feeds 1

75g smoked eel fillet
1 slice of sourdough bread, ideally Poilâne
unsalted butter, softened
1 soup spoon horseradish cream (see page 146)
1 soup spoon mustard cream (see page 288)
1 soup spoon red onion pickle (see page 146)

Cut the eel into 4 pieces. Cut the bread into 2 pieces. Butter the bread sparingly. In a pan, fry the bread lightly, butter sides down, until crisp and golden. Place the bread on a board, crisp side up. Put a spoonful of horseradish cream on one slice. Do not spread, as gravity will do the work for you. Secure the eel in the horseradish cream. Place a spoon of mustard cream atop and the remaining slice of bread on top of that. Return the sandwich to the pan and cook swiftly until crisp and golden. Turn the sandwich and repeat, then lift on to a plate and serve with a small tangle of red onion pickle.

Horseradish cream

Makes 200g

300g fresh horseradish
50g caster sugar
55ml organic cider vinegar
100ml double cream

Peel and finely grate the horseradish. Dissolve the sugar in the vinegar by whisking the two together in a bowl. Stir in the horseradish and avert your eyes and nose, covering the bowl quickly. Let sit for 15 minutes, then remove the covering, don't inhale, stir in the cream, decant into a bowl, cover and refrigerate.

The fresher you use this, the better, but it will keep in a sealed jar in the fridge for 2–3 days.

Red onion pickle

Serves 6

85g caster sugar
220g organic cider vinegar
125g red onions

Dissolve the sugar in the vinegar by whisking them together in a bowl. Peel the onions, halve them through the root and cut into thin slices with the sharpest knife. Stir the slices into the brine and cover. Let sit for at least 45 minutes.

Spinach and crab tart

THIS IS A LUXURIOUS TART, but surprisingly light. I particularly like pastry for unsweetened tarts to include lard, as it gives the pastry a delicate crumb. Serve a green salad alongside, including, when around, samphire, monksbeard, or any of the other wild sea vegetables.

Feeds 6

shortcrust pastry with lard (see page 252)
300g picked spinach leaves, well washed and stalks removed
2 whole organic eggs, plus 3 egg yolks
300ml whipping cream
150g crab meat (any brown is welcome), or a handsome dressed crab

Roll out the pastry to fit a 25cm wide x 2cm deep tart tin with a removable bottom, then line the tin with it. Let rest in the fridge for half an hour. Heat the oven to 150°C and put a baking sheet inside to help crisp the pastry. Cover the pastry with baking parchment and fill with uncooked dried beans or rice. Bake for 25 minutes. Remove the parchment and beans with care.

Wilt the spinach in a wide pan over a brisk heat with just the water adhering to the leaves after washing and draining. Remove the pan from the heat and spread the cooked spinach in a wide dish to cool very quickly. Once cooled, squeeze thoroughly into a ball or two and chop into very small pieces.

Mix the eggs, egg yolks and cream in a bowl with some salt and pepper, then stir in the spinach and the crab meat. Pour all this into the blind-baked tart case. Place in the oven on the preheated sheet and bake until golden and set, about 30–40 minutes. The tart is best served just warm.

FRANGIPANI

THERE'S SOMETHING ABOUT ALMONDS

Almond tart

Chocolate, almond & marmalade tart

Sweet shortcrust pastry

I THINK OFTEN OF AN ALMOND AND RASPBERRY SLICE from Fisher & Donaldson, or a slice of frangipane tart from J. S. Doig, and all the other Dundee bakers (alas, mostly gone now) and their windows and shelves with a few good things made with almonds. Not least, of course, a famous fruit cake studded with whole almonds which is excellent with a cup of tea, whereas for pudding, this recipe delights in requiring considerably more of the costly tear-shaped nut.

There are variations of this recipe that have fruits and preserves baked within the tart and others with fruit, cooked or not depending on the season, heaped upon the tart, tumbling into a flurry of cream and a pool of custard.

Almond tart

AN ALMOND TART IS A TESTAMENT to *faites simple* – a recipe requiring simple ingredients of superb quality. In this case, almonds, eggs, butter and sugar mixed with care. Over the years I've tasted, and made, many almond tarts but the best were made by Mum. She scoured books galore for different pastries, some plain, all made with butter and, on occasion, a scrape of vanilla seeds, a grating or two of lemon zest, ground almonds or walnuts or hazelnuts.

Different recipes were tried for the filling but the frangipanes we loved best were those with little or no flour, so different to those more cake-like in texture, made with almonds already ground. Mum always blanched, peeled and ground the almonds to bake because they were so good, giving lightness to a yielding texture, and I have followed suit ever since.

When the tarts were assembled, Mum would set to with whichever fruit was to bake within or spoon upon it – apricots or greengages, plums, prunes or apples or, a great favourite then and now, a pear and almond tart studded with shards of crystallised stem ginger.

I can map the course of the year through the fruits that grace an almond tart, from the first forced pink rhubarb of January to the damsons, medlars, quinces and sloes of autumn – a succession of fruit advancing with the seasons.

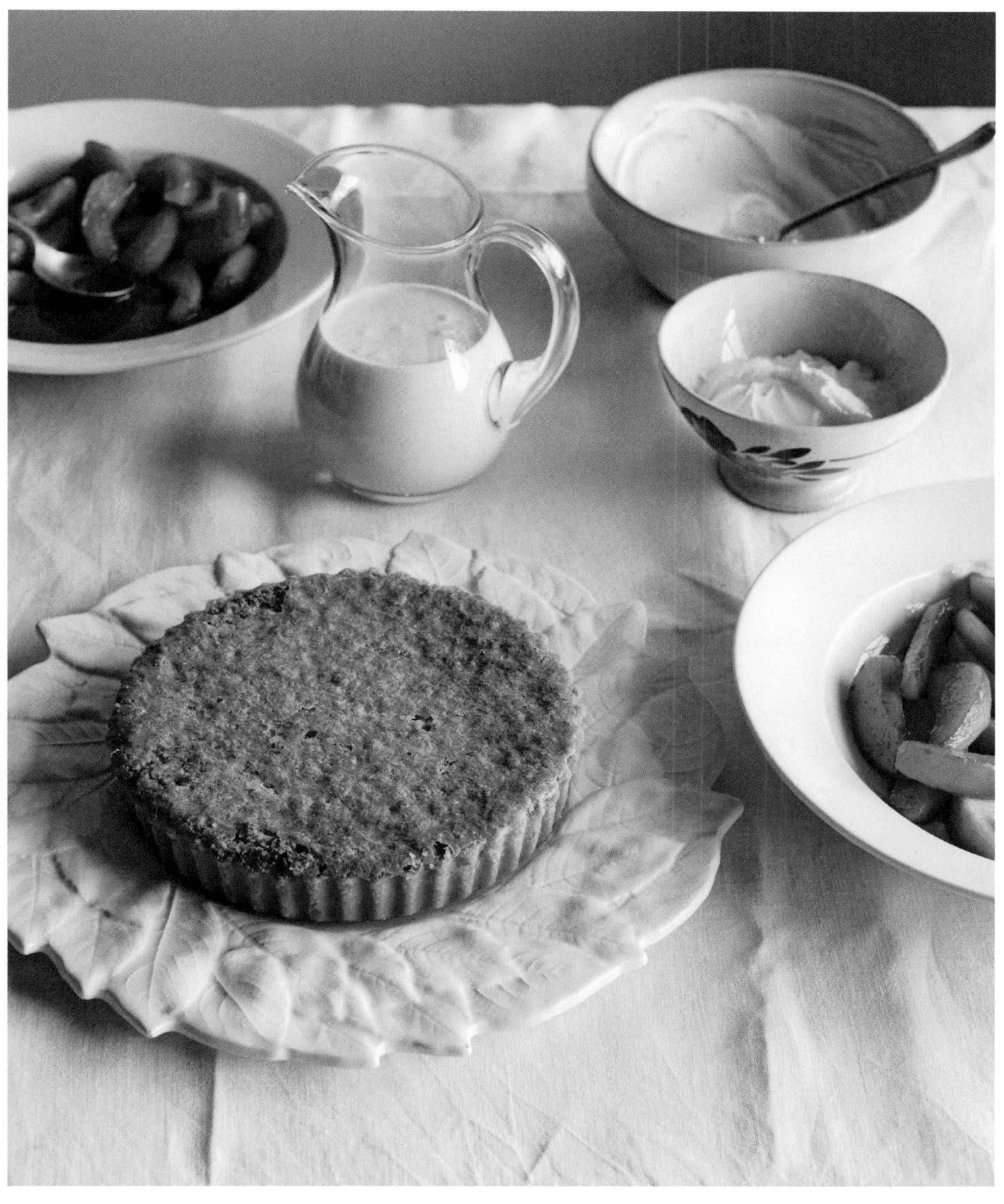

Arriving at Bibendum, years later, I was overjoyed to discover that Simon Hopkinson had an ace almond tart as a permanent fixture on the menu. At Alastair Little it was an exemplary prune and almond tart, the prunes steeped in Armagnac for days. (They were equally excellent in ice cream, which was often how they were served up too.)

I think it worth noting that it is a long time since I bought almonds already ground, preferring by far the resulting coarse crumb from grinding whole almonds myself. I favour the whole blanched Marcona almonds from Spain, where the almond is almost a religion. If the almonds are unpeeled it is not such a chore to steep them in boiling water to loosen the skins to facilitate peeling. The difference is remarkable. But almonds are not only for confectionery and puddings, creams and ices; they are also good company in compounds redolent of a pesto – leaves and nuts and cheese ground with olive oil.

Make the frangipane and the pastry for this tart the day before for best results. See opposite for seasonal variations on this tart.

Feeds 6

sweet shortcrust pastry (see page 156), plus a little flour for dusting

For the frangipane

250g whole blanched almonds
250g unsalted butter, softened
200g caster sugar
2 freshest organic eggs

Grind the almonds whole in a food processor to a fine crumb. In a separate bowl, beat the butter and sugar together. Beat the eggs, pour slowly into the butter and sugar and stir in until all is just mixed. Add the ground almonds. Cover and refrigerate overnight.

Get ready a 20cm wide x 3cm deep tart tin with a removable bottom. On a lightly floured surface roll out the pastry thinly, wide enough to line the tart tin with an overhang. Place the lined tin in the fridge for half an hour.

Preheat the oven to 180°C and place a tray beneath the rack on which the tart will be cooked to catch any dripping butter. Remove the lined tart tin from the fridge and spoon the frangipane in clumps (do not smooth it out!) over the pastry. Place on a rack above the baking tray, then turn down the oven to 150°C and bake for 1 hour. Bake for up to 20 minutes longer at 120°C if uncertain whether the base of the tart is cooked fully.

The company required for almond tart, mostly inspired by my dad, it must be said, is a jug of custard, warm or chilled, Jersey cream, whipped cream and ice cream.

For a winter tart

Remove the tart from its case and place on a handsome dish. Heap caramelised apples or pears (see page 335) on the tart, strew with slivered almonds and dust lightly with icing sugar.

For a spring tart

Substitute baked rhubarb (see page 338) for the apples.

For a summer tart

Remove the tart to a plate. Beat the grated zest of 1 orange, the juice of 1 lemon, 1 soup spoon of extra virgin olive oil and a big pinch of freshly ground pepper into 250g of ricotta and spread over the tart. Hull and slice 300g of ripe strawberries, slice and dress with freshly squeezed lemon juice and a grind or three from a pepper mill, tumble over the ricotta mix and lightly dust with icing sugar.

For an autumn tart

Remove the tart to a plate. Beat 250g of confectioner's custard (see page 93) into 250g of mascarpone and spread randomly over the tart. Slice 6–8 figs and arrange over the top. Evenly dot the figs with 1 soup spoon of clear, floral honey and squeeze over the juice of ½ a lemon. Strew with 25g of shelled pistachios and a light dusting of icing sugar.

Chocolate, almond and marmalade tart

THIS IS A GOOD USE OF HOMEMADE MARMALADE. At the restaurant, we like to spread the marmalade on a tart case, dot with frangipane, then strew with chocolate and bake. Served with cream, ice cream and custard, this is very good in those last days of winter when a great treat is often much needed. A thought for the cook is to prepare it the day before, as frangipane cooks best when refrigerated.

PS: Any leftover tart can be sliced thinly, laid on a baking sheet and baked in a low oven until crisp and lightly coloured, making rather wonderful biscuits.

Feeds 6

sweet shortcrust pastry (see page 156), plus a little flour for dusting
4 soup spoons marmalade
125g best dark chocolate, at least 70% cocoa solids, cut into small pieces

For the frangipane

250g unsalted butter, softened
200g caster sugar
2 organic eggs
250g whole blanched almonds, coarsely ground

Beat the butter and sugar together in a bowl until mixed. Crack the eggs into a jug and beat lightly. Pour into the beaten butter and sugar. Stir in the ground almonds. Mix all together thoroughly and refrigerate, preferably overnight.

On a lightly floured surface, roll out the pastry large enough to line a tart case 25cm wide x 2.5cm deep, with a removable bottom. Pop this into the fridge until required.

When ready to bake, preheat the oven to 150°C. Spoon the marmalade over the bottom of the tart case. Heap the frangipane in little clods over the marmalade. Strew the chocolate over the frangipane.

Place the tart on a wire rack over a tray to catch any butter that may fall from the tart while baking. Bake in the oven for 1 hour. At the end of the hour, lower the temperature to 120°C and bake for a further 20 minutes, until golden and crusted. Remove from the oven and let the tart sit on a rack for at least an hour before serving. It is very good when served just warm.

Sweet shortcrust pastry

MAKING PASTRY IS SO WORTH THE EFFORT. Knowing the quality and freshness of ingredients used cannot but add to the cook's pleasure and confidence in cooking, not to mention the superb result. The bold cook may halve the ball of pastry to roll a thinner tart case and form 2 discs, putting one, carefully wrapped, in the freezer for a few weeks hence. Swiftly defrosted in an hour or so, or overnight if remembered, the pastry can be rolled out, lifted on to a baking sheet and layered with fruits, the edges lifted gently in small folds to form a galette, baked roughly in the same time as a tart.

150g cold butter
250g 00 flour, plus extra for dusting
75g icing sugar
a pinch of salt
1 organic egg
1 teaspoon cold water

Put the cold butter, the flour, sugar and a pinch of salt into the bowl of a food processor and render to a fine crumb. Add the egg beaten with the water and pulse until a dough forms. Place the dough on a lightly floured work surface and knead deftly into a drum shape. Cut the dough in half, then gently press down to form a disc. Wrap each disc, and freeze one for another time. Refrigerate the one you are using for at least 30 minutes. Each will fit a 20–25cm x 4–5cm tart case.

GARLIC
THE REMARKABLE QUALITIES
OF A BULB

Whole garlic with grilled bread, black olive and broad bean condiments and goat's cheese

IN THE RESTAURANT we cook whole heads of wet garlic (new season's garlic) in olive oil for an entire day, which produces rich, sweet and beautifully softened garlic that you can smash on to toast and eat. For the home cook, a more modest approach that does not use up all your olive oil in one pot is to bake the garlic in the oven. The sheer beauty of a handsome roasting dish holding whole heads of garlic, herbs such as thyme, summer savory and bay leaves, along with cracked black peppercorns, is reason alone to make this dish.

This recipe seems lengthy, but is mostly about allowing the whole heads of garlic to cook very slowly in a gentle heat. Baked thus, the garlic softens and becomes almost sweet, its feisty character mellowed.

I used to make this dish with Tymsboro, a beautiful goat's cheese shaped in a pyramid. A cheese as lamented as the uniquely brilliant Mary Holbrook at Sleight Farm near Bath, all of whose cheeses were touched by hand to gauge their ripeness. Seeking out the creamiest and most flavoursome goat's cheese now involves many merry tastings. Current favourites include Innes Log or St Tola.

Early crop garlic with a bulbous head streaked with crimsons and pinks is most suited to this dish. There is little point in trying this dish with the small mummified heads of garlic with paper-like skins packaged in little string nets found in supermarkets.

At the restaurant, we serve this dish individually plated. At home, a happy thought is to place the dish of garlic in its entirety on the table, the goat's cheese on a board, the condiments of broad beans and black olives in bowls and grilled or toasted bread heaped in a basket for all to pile into – a joyous, messy affair.

Whole garlic with grilled bread, black olive and broad bean condiments and goat's cheese

FOR THE BEST RESULT, start early in the day and have the garlic cooking gently on a very low temperature until quite softened. If the amount of oil used here seems excessive, you can use the oil again in other dishes, e.g. for cooking fennel bulbs in a similar style, in mashed potato or, indeed, for more garlic.

Feeds 6

6 plump newish heads of garlic
3 sprigs of thyme
3 sprigs of summer savory
3 bay leaves
15 black peppercorns, cracked
200ml olive oil
6 slices of sourdough bread
125g tapenade of black olives (see page 163)
250g broad bean condiment (see page 163)
1 whole goat's cheese, such as Blackmount or Innes Log
6 soup spoons black olive crumbs (see page 73)

Preheat the oven to 140°C.

Put the whole heads of garlic snugly side by side in a deep, lidded enamel or earthenware dish. Bury the herbs and peppercorns among the garlic heads and pour over the olive oil. Cover and bake for an hour, until the garlic heads are soft; older heads of garlic will take up to 2 hours. Grill the bread slices and pile on a plate. Put the garlic, grilled bread, tapenade, broad bean condiment and cheese on the table and encourage your guests to smash the garlic heads on to the bread with the tapenade and broad bean condiment, and top with the black olive crumbs.

It is worth noting that the garlic keeps remarkably well stored under the olive oil in the fridge (new season's garlic will store like this for 2 to 3 weeks; if older, up to a week), to be heated gently when required.

A tapenade of black olives

Feeds 6

1 soup spoon salted capers, soaked in cold water for 30 minutes
6 anchovy fillets
125g black olives, pitted
1 clove of garlic, peeled
2 soup spoons extra virgin olive oil
a pinch of freshly ground black pepper

Drain the capers, then grind everything together in a pestle and mortar, or chop by hand, or blend in a food processor until a coarse paste forms.

A condiment of broad beans

Feeds 6

250g broad beans, podded, blanched and peeled
50ml extra virgin olive oil
50g Parmesan, freshly grated

Grind everything together in a pestle and mortar, or chop by hand, or put into a food processor, until a coarse paste forms.

IMPROMPTU SUPPERS

Off-the-cuff cooking

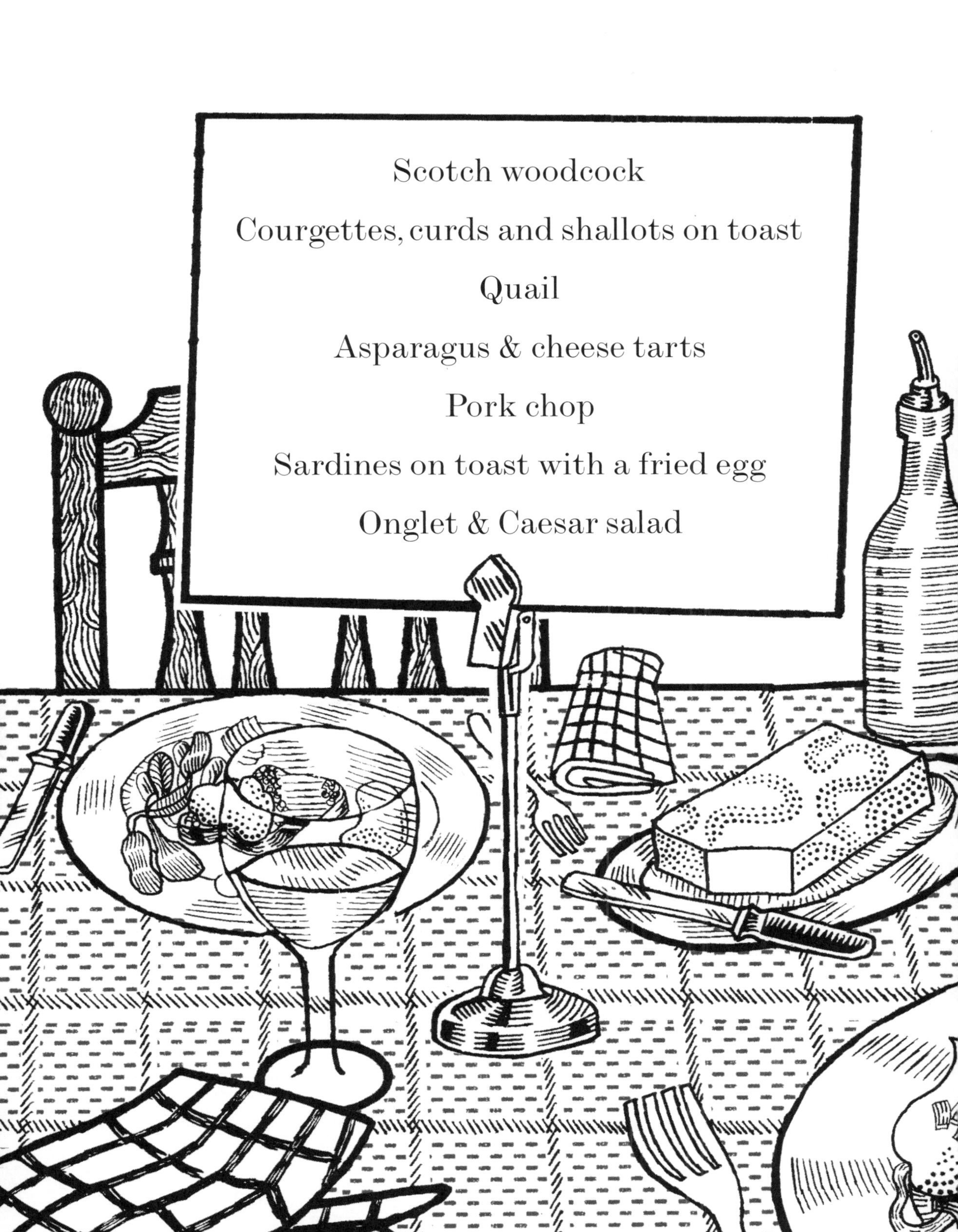
Scotch woodcock
Courgettes, curds and shallots on toast
Quail
Asparagus & cheese tarts
Pork chop
Sardines on toast with a fried egg
Onglet & Caesar salad

Often, simple and swift being the priorities, cooking at home alone is an excuse to feast on sardines, scrambled eggs, or cheese on toast. And these are tasty things to eat, as well as being easy to produce, with a kitchen well provisioned with a few good things such as a block of Cheddar, a piece of Parmesan, bread, butter and eggs. A pan of soup is always pleasing, too, be it a long-simmered lentil soup or a swiftly cooked pot of asparagus or spinach. Any leftovers can be frozen for emergency rations for other times.

As most of my days are spent either cooking in a restaurant, eating in a restaurant, at friends' or away, simple fare is usually the order of the day whenever I cook for myself at home. The opposite end of the spectrum is putting every pan, bowl, wooden spoon and mixer to work cooking for a crew of chums. It was not until lockdown, the plug pulled on those days always filled with much to do, that I remembered the quiet satisfaction of having a well-vittled kitchen while on your tod.

I will look back on the strange days of Covid-19, home alone in the kitchen, with a curious sense of nostalgia. Mornings were spent sitting at the table, a coffee pot on the stove, a pile of books at hand, plotting what to eat in the days to come, scribbling in a jotter what fruit, vegetables, herbs and leaves to buy and from where, what olive oils, vinegars, beans, chickpeas, rice and lentils I needed to order online. And as I was bound to cook the days away on my own, I wanted the good stuff: a duck from Coombeshead Farm, a choice of lamb and pork chops, a strip of onglet, a box of different varieties of potato from farms and suppliers around the country who revved up home delivery for all of those in the same boat.

Often a film would be playing on the laptop while I cooked, usually with food involved, background scenes of Robert Donat, in *The 39 Steps*, offering Finnan haddock to a woman in dire straits, or of Cary Grant tucking into quiche Lorraine in *To Catch a Thief*, or the severe kitchen envy induced by Ang Lee's *Eat Drink Man Woman*.

The recipes here are a modest collection of dishes that are good for one person and a laptop, but are also simple to scale up for company.

Scotch woodcock

HAVING A BOX OF EGGS AT HOME has saved me from the tragedy of an empty fridge on more occasions than I care to count. So long as you also have a loaf of bread and a packet of best butter, the presence of the eggs means a plate of scrambled eggs on toast. Lay on this a few plump fillets of anchovy, a few capers and you have that estimable savoury of old, Scotch woodcock. Substitute asparagus spears for the anchovies, and you have something equally wonderful.

For each person
1 or 2 slices of bread
a nut of unsalted butter
3 best organic eggs, beaten
4 plump anchovy fillets
6 salted capers, soaked in cold water for 30 minutes

Toast the bread, spread with butter and keep warm. Melt the remainder of the butter in a pan over a moderate heat, pour in the eggs and scramble gently to soft curds. Spoon the eggs on the toast. Season and lay the anchovies and drained capers over the top.

Or boil asparagus spears until tender and sit them upon the scrambled eggs instead.

Courgettes, curds and shallots on toast

SLICED BREAD GRILLED OR BAKED CRISP IN THE OVEN, piled with goat's, sheep's or cow's curd with herbs and vegetables. With all at hand, it takes no time at all.

For each person

1–2 thin slices of bread
2–3 soup spoons extra virgin olive oil
1–2 medium courgettes
1 shallot, finely chopped
1 clove of garlic, peeled and thinly sliced
a pinch of dried chilli flakes
1 teaspoon lemon juice
30–35g curds or ricotta
finely grated zest of ½ an unwaxed lemon
1 teaspoon chopped flat-leaf parsley
1 teaspoon coarsely chopped or torn mint

Preheat the oven to 200°C. Lightly brush the bread with olive oil and bake until golden and crisp. Let cool.

Warm a frying pan over a moderate heat. Add 1 soup spoon of olive oil. Slice the courgettes thinly, add to the pan and cook gently for 8–10 minutes, until lightly coloured. Add the chopped shallot and slices of garlic and let cook for 3–4 minutes until softened, longer if the courgettes are larger. Add the chilli flakes and lemon juice. Mix well. Taste for seasoning.

Beat the chosen curd (or ricotta) with the lemon zest, chopped parsley and mint, the remaining olive oil, and some salt and black pepper. Spread generously on the toasts and spoon the courgettes and shallots over the top.

These are very good with a few black olives too, or slices of grilled artichoke or onion.

Quail

HOW MANY QUAIL CAN YOU EAT? One certainly, two usually and when ravenous… three. Ask your butcher to cut away the backbone and snip the wishbone, which was once known as the 'merry thought'.

These are very good eaten with boiled potatoes dressed with wild garlic, walnut and almond pesto (see page 377).

For each person

1 or 2 quail, spatchcocked
2 sage leaves
5 sprigs of rosemary, leaves picked
1 small sprig of thyme, leaves picked
1 clove of garlic, peeled and thinly sliced
1 teaspoon olive oil
½ teaspoon red wine vinegar

Preheat the oven to 200°C.

Push down on the birds to flatten them. Cover with the sage, rosemary and thyme leaves and the slices of garlic. Liberally season with black pepper, then add the olive oil. Rub the seasonings all over the bird.

Lightly salt the quail and lay them in a roasting tin, spaced apart, cut side facing upwards. Place in the oven and cook for 8–10 minutes, then remove and add a few lightest drops of vinegar. Carefully turn the quail and let rest for 5 minutes. Serve.

PS: Should the birds not colour, heat the grill, place the tin beneath and watch over for a minute or two until the birds take on a golden hue.

Asparagus and cheese tarts

MUM WAS VERY GOOD AT MAKING a batch or two of puff or rough puff pastry, wrapping it well, placing in a sealed container and freezing. This was always the best frozen puff pastry, the commercial varieties all too often falling short of the mark, unless French and sold mostly in large blocks or rolls intended for restaurants. There are exceptions, such as one named for the county in which it is made, Dorset Pastry, which is very good.

Rolled thin and laid upon a baking sheet, topped with blanched asparagus in close formation with the thinnest slices of a washed-rind cheese such as Rollright or Riseley or Wigmore (a ewe's milk cheese, but almost any gorgeous runny cheese will do) makes a very fine tart. If cooking for more people, either make individual tarts for each person, or, to make one large tart, multiply the ingredients accordingly, e.g. for 4 people use 400g pastry, 20 spears of asparagus, 300g Wigmore cheese.

Add an accompanying salad made from herbs and leaves such as flat-leaf parsley, chickweed, chervil, lamb's lettuce, purslane, dressed with olives, lemon zest, olive oil and capers, and you have dinner.

I love the random-shaped thinness acquired when rolling out pastry without exact measuring. Keeping a bread stone or a baking sheet in the oven should ensure a crisp bottom to the pastry. You can also make this tart with young leeks instead of asparagus.

For each person

100g rough puff pastry (see page 251), plus a little flour for dusting
4–5 spears of asparagus
75g Wigmore, Stinking Bishop, or another favourite runny cheese

Heat the oven to 200°C.

On a floured surface, roll out the pastry thinly and lay upon a baking sheet. Refrigerate. Trim the asparagus, then plunge into boiling water for 1 minute. Lay the asparagus spears side by side on the pastry. Slice or, indeed, spoon the cheese as thin as can be and lay over the asparagus. Place in the hot oven and bake for 15–20 minutes, until puffed and golden, the cheese melted fully and pooled around the asparagus as if a sauce. Add a few grinds of pepper and eat swiftly.

Pork chop

For each person

300–400g pork chop, preferably on the bone
1 teaspoon light vegetable oil
½ a clove of garlic, peeled and finely chopped
zest of ½ an unwaxed lemon
a pinch of thyme leaves
2–3 sprigs of picked rosemary
a pinch each of fennel seeds and celery seeds
1 teaspoon very good red wine vinegar, e.g. Banyuls (see page 198)

Heat a cast-iron frying pan over a moderate heat. Liberally and evenly pepper the pork chop on both sides and lightly season with sea salt. Put the oil into the cast-iron pan, lay the pork chop on top and let cook undisturbed until deep mahogany in colour, roughly 8–10 minutes.

While the pork chop is cooking, grind the garlic, lemon zest, thyme and rosemary, with the fennel and celery seeds, in a pestle and mortar and set aside. Turn the pork chop and cook for a further 2–3 minutes. Remove the pan from the heat and spoon the contents of the mortar on to the chop. Discard any excess fat from the pan, pour the red wine vinegar on to the chop, and turn it a few times to make sure it's evenly coated. Cover and set aside to rest in the pan for at least 3–4 minutes. Gently warm the pan to heat up any juices gathered, to pour over the pork chop before serving. The chop goes wonderfully with so much, from olive oil mash or potato and celeriac gratin to green beans, asparagus, peas, courgettes, Jerusalem artichokes or chicory.

Sardines on toast with a fried egg

WORTH CONSIDERING TOO FOR THIS CHARMING DISH are mackerel and herring, cooked similarly.

For each person

3 spring onions, trimmed
1 slice of bread
butter
1 teaspoon olive oil
3 fresh sardines, butterflied, i.e. split and flattened
1 organic egg

Heat a griddle or frying pan over a high heat. Lay the spring onions on the hot pan to blister, turning after 3–4 minutes to blister the other side. Toast the bread and chop the spring onions finely. Butter the toast and spread with the chopped spring onion.

Lightly oil and season the skin side of the sardines, then lay them in the onion pan, skin side down, and cook undisturbed for 3 to 4 minutes, until the flesh turns pale, then flip and cook for no more than 1 minute on the other side. Heat a small frying pan and gently fry the egg. Carefully lift the sardines and turn them, set them skin side up on the onion, then place the egg on the sardines – et voilà.

Onglet and Caesar salad

WE OFTEN SERVE ONGLET WITH a trinity of pickled walnuts, horseradish cream and watercress. But every now and again I get a hankering for this favourite cut of beef, crusted with pepper, cooked in a frying pan, served alongside a plate of Caesar salad. This was a dish that featured on the menus at Alastair Little in Soho and always came with the exclamation from Juliet Peston, as incredulous as impressed, that *From Julia Child's Kitchen* devoted not one but three pages to Caesar salad.

It is indeed remarkable how a salad of such simplicity took the world by storm, and Caesar salads made today remain pretty much faithful to Caesar Cardini's original, except perhaps for the instance of using raw egg rather than coddled eggs, eggs boiled for just a minute, which are defeated by a blender, and the addition of anchovies, nowadays almost mandatory instead of a few drops of Worcestershire sauce, as originally used by the salad's eponymous creator.

PS: The anchovy dressing has many virtues and keeps remarkably well. Delicious on crostini, for dressing green beans and potatoes, to serve with veal, pork or guinea fowl or simply with a bowl of radishes to dip into.

For each person

1 onglet, roughly 400g, trimmed
1 soup spoon light oil (sunflower or vegetable)
Caesar salad (see below)

Lightly brush the onglet with a little of the oil, season evenly all over with first black pepper then sea salt (sea salt prevents the pepper from sticking), and lightly press the seasonings into the meat.

Heat a large frying pan over a moderate heat. Add the rest of the oil and the seasoned onglet and cook undisturbed for 6 minutes on one side, tilting and turning the pan for an even crust on the meat. Turn and cook for a further 2 minutes, then remove the pan from the heat, leaving the onglet to rest for at least 8 minutes. This will give the meat an excellent crust and a sanguine interior. Reduce the cooking time by a few minutes for a rarer steak and a few minutes more for beef well done.

Slice the onglet and serve alongside the Caesar salad.

Caesar salad

heart of 1 Romaine lettuce (the outer leaves are excellent in chopped or leaf salad)
4 slices of baguette, or a slice of sourdough, sliced and roughly cut into 1cm squares
1 teaspoon extra virgin olive oil
1 soup spoon anchovy dressing (see below)
20g Parmesan, grated

Preheat the oven to 180°C.

Pull apart the Romaine heart, then wash, drain and dry the leaves.

Lay the squares of bread evenly on a baking tray and dot with extra virgin olive oil and a pinch of sea salt. Place in the oven for 15 minutes until golden and crisp. Remove from the oven and leave to cool.

Tear, or perhaps leave whole, the leaves of Romaine and place in a large dish. Spoon over the anchovy dressing and half the grated Parmesan. Season with black pepper and a pinch of sea salt. Mix deftly, then lift on to a handsome dish or bowl. Scatter the croutons atop and strew with the rest of the grated Parmesan.

Anchovy dressing

Makes 2 x 150g jars (this keeps well in the fridge for at least 5 days in a sealed container).

100g anchovy fillets
2 cloves of garlic, peeled and halved
2 organic egg yolks
1 lemon, halved and juiced
8 drops of Tabasco
200ml extra virgin olive oil

Place all but the olive oil in a food processor or blender and blend until smooth. Slowly add the olive oil in drops over the back of a spoon, which keeps splatter to minimum and allows the oil to drip in slowly. Once made, add a soup spoon of cold water. Taste for seasoning.

OFFAL

THE HEART OF THE MATTER

Griddled chicken livers, bacon & sage

Lamb's sweetbreads, peas, almonds & herbs

A dish I would like to call 'fechoulette'

Devilled kidneys

Fegato alla Veneziana

NOURISHING, DELICIOUS, CHEAP AND PLENTIFUL, whether grilled, fried, braised, made into pâté and terrines, the most important rule when debating the preparation of offal is freshness and quality. While we wish for meat to be aged well, we want offal as fresh as can be, for the simple fact that when clean and bright, such qualities are reflected in the flavour.

Perhaps there's still a lingering hangover from badly cooked liver, and rationing in the past. I find it curious that I rarely, if ever, ate offal growing up in Scotland, not even at my grandmother's. I was never really aware of offal at the butcher, while standing beside Mum and Dad, my eyes wandering to the extraordinary sight of two sides of beef hanging in the window. It was not until coming to London that I encountered most of the dishes made with liver, kidneys and sweetbreads, and those mostly through talking to butchers and the ever-growing number of farmers rearing rare breeds of cattle, sheep and pigs who would supply the offal with cuts or a whole side of an animal.

I learned that onglet, the French term for the curiously named cut, 'body', in the *Meat Buyer's Guide*, going by hanger steak in the USA, was also called the butcher's cut. So the story goes, butchers made their money with the prime cuts like fillet, famed for being tender but famously lacking in flavour, while taking home an onglet – that superbly flavoured cut of beef, categorised as offal, but which, when generously seasoned with salt and black pepper and cooked until a rich crust forms, and then rested, is considered a fine steak.

It's a cut I have continued to cook often. Other dishes followed. Lamb's sweetbreads, fried crisp with almonds, garlic, peas, fragrant with mint and pepper, is an excellent pan of good things. Simple dishes made with the livers of chickens, ducks, pork, kid, venison or rabbit, chopped and fried, a little sliced shallot added, with a few herbs and a jigger or two of a fine vinegar shaken over a few leaves to make a pleasing salad, or chopped and set in a pot or rendered smooth for a pâté.

All of these are eminently doable at home, providing you clear the decks, and have a good-sized chopping board and a knife with a clean blade. A simple, excellent dish is thinly sliced liver threaded on to skewers with a leaf of sage and strip of pancetta. The skewers only need to sizzle on a grill for a few minutes to colour, before seasoning with a drop or two of sherry vinegar.

A real change in approach to, and quality of, offal came about with the emergence of farmers' markets and a resurgence of interest in rare breeds of pig, goats, sheep and cattle; quality, flavour, environment, sustainability and welfare are of the utmost importance. It is now no longer enough for meat to be just 'Scotch Beef' or 'English lamb'. Butchers must know from which part of the country, which county, which farm and which breed their meat has come. Is it Blackface lamb? Dexter beef? Tamworth, Gloucester Old Spot or Middle White pork?

When James Whetlor founded Cabrito Goat Meat Ltd and began selling kid, we were graced not only with superb meat but with offal so fresh the livers were wine-dark and magnificent. They have become the benchmark for great offal ever since. We trimmed the pluck and lights, most famously known in the making of haggis, and which beyond the borders of Scotland are but the lungs and heart. These are chopped fine to make a dish that Jonathan Meades told me was called 'fechoulette', a ragù of offal cooked tender, rich, bright and fresh with wine and herbs.

In the eighties, like other farmers, Richard Vaughan at Huntsham Court Farm in Herefordshire began selling Middle White pork, Ryeland lamb and Hereford beef directly to restaurants and swiftly built up business delivering once a week; now, like so many producers, he has a very good website for ordering online. As prized as the meat are the kidneys, liver and other parts of the fifth quarter (aka offal).

The quality of the meat and fat of the Middle White pig is especially good for roasts, but this breed is also excellent in a terrine of chopped or ground meats and offal generously flavoured with spice, herbs, wine and perhaps sherry or Madeira. It's important to check the seasoning for a terrine, for 'tis a pity for the effort of making it to be undone for want of a pinch of salt and a grating of nutmeg. A good way of doing this is to take a spoonful of the finished mix, cook it quickly in a small pan, taste, and then season the rest as necessary.

A cook, at home or in a restaurant, should become adept at using all the bits and bobs that cooking throws their way, not least because you'll be getting much greater value from expensive cuts of meat if you can use any leftover offal in a terrine or a ragù, to make cecils or polpette (see page 78). The result will be very good, simple dishes as satisfying to cook as they are to eat.

Griddled chicken livers, bacon and sage

THESE ARE AS PLEASING AS THEY ARE SIMPLE. Two each will serve well for a bite, or buy and make more for a more substantial dish. Made earlier in the day and refrigerated, they are a treat cooked swiftly on a grill, heaped on a dish and taken piping hot to the table.

When buying chicken livers, ensure they are dark in colour, firm and, above all, fresh. Wooden skewers are best here, and soak them for 20 minutes before using.

PS: I have enjoyed this dish with rabbit livers and with the kidneys and heart too when buying rabbit whole. If buying from a supplier of rare breeds and game it is worth asking about the livers of, say, a Blackface or Ryeland lamb or a Middle White pig, or venison, all of notable quality.

Feeds 6

150g freshest chicken livers
12 rashers of streaky smoked bacon
24 sage leaves
2 soup spoons olive oil
½ teaspoon red wine vinegar

First off, clear the decks. Trim the livers of all and any trace of gall, easily recognised by its green colour.

Cut the rashers of bacon in half. Lay these flat on a chopping board or baking tray. Lay a small sage leaf on each piece. Lay a piece of liver on top of each leaf. Thread the skewer securely through the bacon, liver and sage. Cover and refrigerate until required.

Place a skillet or griddle on a high heat. When ready to cook, have a dish beside you. Lay the skewers on the skillet or grill, season well with a pinch each of salt and black pepper, then let cook until a fine-sounding sizzle is achieved after a minute or so. Turn the skewers and cook for a further minute or two. Remove to the waiting dish, then mix together the oil and vinegar and lightly brush the meat. Serve swiftly.

Lamb's sweetbreads, peas, almonds and herbs

THE SCENT OF SWEETBREADS TURNING GOLDEN and crisp in a pan, with almonds ground with garlic and pepper, with peas, chopped mint and parsley, makes this an estimable dish. Once the preparations have been completed, all happily done in advance, keeping well in the fridge, the actual cooking of the dish is pleasingly straightforward.

Feeds 6

300g freshest lamb's sweetbreads
900g peas in the pod, resulting in roughly 300g shelled weight
3 cloves of garlic
150g whole blanched almonds
1 level teaspoon freshly ground black pepper
3 soup spoons plain flour
2–3 soup spoons sunflower oil
30g unsalted butter
50g picked mint leaves, chopped
50g picked flat-leaf parsley leaves, chopped
juice of ½ a lemon

To begin, a few simple preparations which can all be done beforehand. Soak the sweetbreads in a large pan of cold water for as long as possible but at least half an hour, then drain and rinse in several changes of cold water.

Place a pan of water on to boil. Drain the sweetbreads of any excess water and plunge them into the boiling water. Return the pan to the boil, simmer for a minute, then drain through a sieve. Line a plate with a cloth and lay on the sweetbreads, then cover with a plate weighted with a heavy tin for half an hour. Remove the fat and membrane. Cover and refrigerate until required.

Pod the peas and cook in boiling water until tender, at least 2–3 minutes. Once cooked, carefully tip the peas into a wide dish to cool quickly, then refrigerate until required. They miraculously keep their colour.

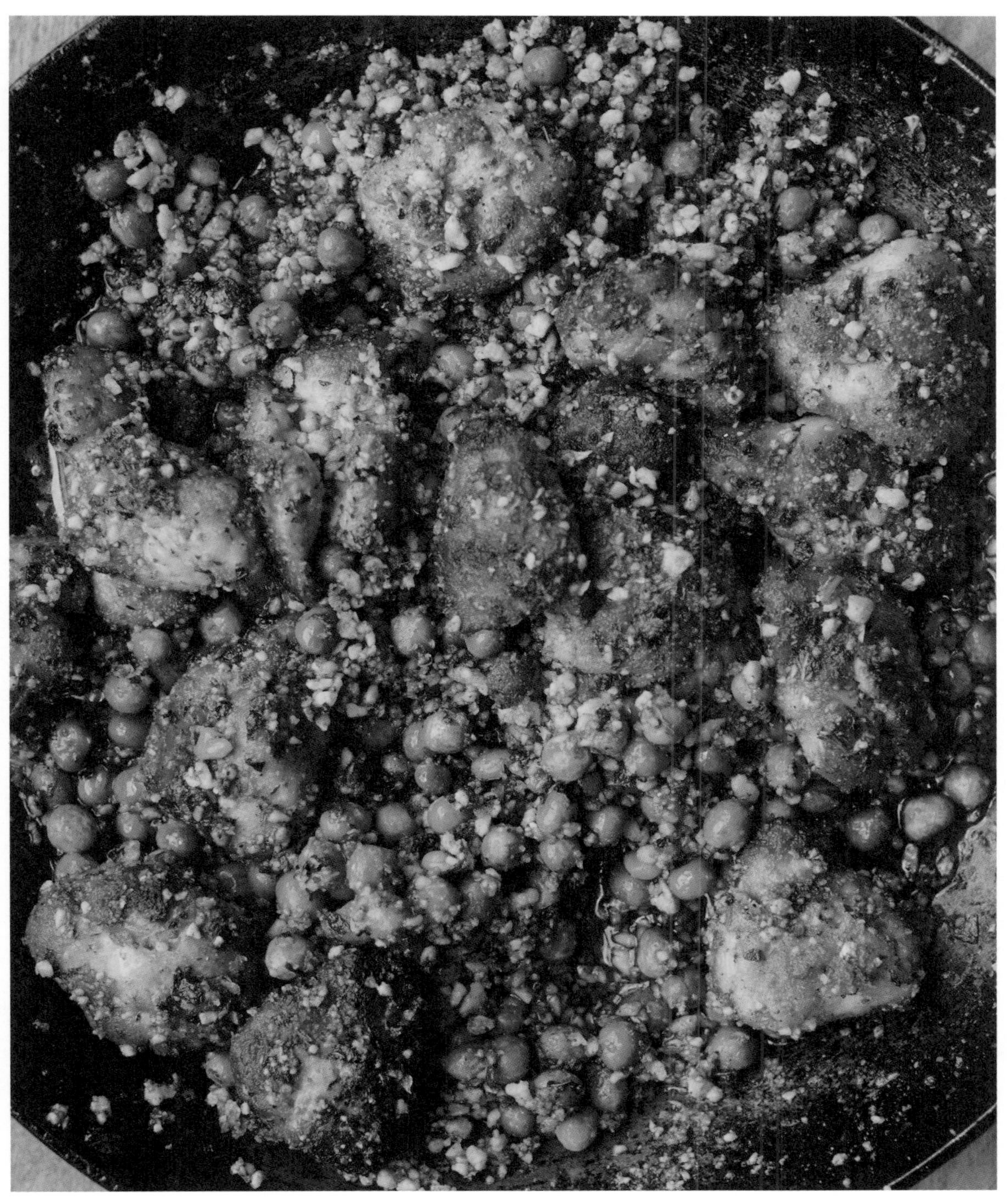

Peel and finely chop the garlic. Put the whole almonds, the garlic and the ground pepper into a food processor and whizz to a coarse crumb.

Put the flour on a plate and lightly season, then dust the sweetbreads in the seasoned flour. Despatch any excess flour, for it will scorch in the pan in an unseemly manner. Warm a wide frying pan and heat the oil within. Gently lay in the sweetbreads and let cook undisturbed over a modest heat until the edges turn golden, about 3–4 minutes. Turn the sweetbreads and cook for another 3–4 minutes. Add the butter, then the almond, garlic and pepper mix – this will colour swiftly, so stir often. Once coloured, add the peas, mint, parsley and a teaspoon of lemon juice, mixing all together very well. Take the pan sizzling to the table, or spoon onto a great dish and serve swiftly.

A dish I would like to call 'fechoulette'

I WAS MUCH INTRIGUED when Jonathan Meades gave me the name of a dish while having dinner one night at Quo Vadis. We had taken delivery of a whole kid including the lights and pluck, not just the heart, liver and kidney but the lungs too, all in attendance. It was not something we had prepared often, rarely if ever before with lung, as freshness is vital and hard to find, usually used for making pies or faggots. But the quality of the offal was outstanding, wine-dark and fresh, and the intention this time had been to produce a simpler dish, akin to a ragù. We served this to Jonathan, who tasted it, and looking away, then turning back his head pronounced – 'Fechoulette!'

I cannot swear to the provenance or the name of the dish, but its origins appear to be a dish made with lamb, mostly; recipes for lamb as a rule suit kid. The ragout has a warming richness that eats well with just a bowl of mashed potatoes or indeed can be added to a braise (see page 246) to put into a pie or steamed suet pudding. As long as the offal is as bright and fresh as can be, it can be ox, calf, pork, venison or lamb.

Feeds 6

250g liver
150g heart
200g kidney
6 soup spoons olive oil, plus a little extra

6 rashers of streaky bacon, cut into small strips
2 small onions, peeled, chopped into small pieces
2 sticks of celery, finely chopped
1 clove of garlic, finely chopped
350ml red wine
300ml chicken stock
1 small bundle of thyme

To start, clear the decks to make as much elbow room as required for preparing and chopping. Peel and trim the liver (carefully cutting away all trace of ducts as you go), heart and kidney (remove all trace of fat and sinew from the kidneys, then split them lengthways and remove the fat round the kidney) and chop finely. The best way to do this is to slice thinly lengthways, then slice into strips and the strips into small pieces. Put the chopped offal on to a plate or dish.

Heat a wide, heavy-bottomed pot and add the olive oil. Add the bacon and fry for a minute, then add the chopped onions, celery and garlic and cook gently for 10–15 minutes.

Heat a wide frying pan and add a little oil. Season the chopped offal with plenty of salt and pepper and fry, on a moderate heat, in small batches until very lightly brown, adding each to the onions. Deglaze the pan with a splash of the red wine and pour into the pot with the rest of the wine. Add the stock and the thyme, place a lid atop, then bring to a simmer and cook over a gentle heat, stirring from time to time, for 2 hours.

The simplicity of a bowl of potatoes strewn with chopped curly parsley alongside a bowl of greens is all that is needed to serve with this dish.

Devilled kidneys

THE FRESHEST KIDNEYS HAVE A BRIGHT, shiny appearance, so avoid those with a dull pallor. It is worth noting, too, that the suet surrounding the kidney is of the highest quality and can be trimmed and minced for suet pastry. Ironically, the devil's 'fire', or mustard, is diminished by contact with heat, hence the seemingly high seasoning which is vital to give the necessary zip that defines this timeless dish.

Always having loved this dish, I was often rather bothered by slices of kidney cooking unevenly, bubbling and toughening in a great gloop of marinade. Laid on hot buttered toast, the kidneys passed a sort of muster. Then, during an idle reading one afternoon, when turning the pages of *Mastering the Art of French Cooking* by Julia Child, Louisette Bertholle and Simone Beck, eureka, a recipe for kidneys. I read that it is better by far to trim and cook the kidney whole, then rest, slice and reheat in the devilled sauce. So simple. So good.

Feeds 6

6 soup spoons olive oil
2 soup spoons sherry vinegar
2 soup spoons Dijon mustard
1 teaspoon Colman's English mustard powder
2 soup spoons Worcestershire sauce
½ teaspoon ground black pepper
a pinch of dried chilli flakes
500g kidneys of ox, calf, pork, venison or kid
8 drops of Tabasco
50g unsalted butter
2 shallots, peeled and finely chopped
200ml white wine

In a bowl, mix the olive oil, sherry vinegar, Dijon mustard, mustard powder, Worcestershire sauce, pepper, chilli flakes and Tabasco until smooth, then put aside.

Remove all trace of fat and membrane from the kidneys. Melt the butter in a high-sided pan over a moderate heat, and add the kidneys. Turn them after a few minutes, and continue thus for 10 minutes, turning and browning the outside of the kidneys while the sides cook to a rosy blush. Remove them from the pan to a dish and cover.

Return the pan to a moderate heat, add in the shallots, stir and cook gently for 1 minute. Add the white wine and bring to a simmer, stirring well to lift up any goodness adhering to the pot, and continue to cook until only 2 soup spoons remain. Stir in the devil from the bowl and warm. Cut the kidneys into 1cm-thick slices, evenly seasoning with salt and black pepper, then lay in the warmed devil, turning carefully and cooking gently for just a minute before serving. They are ideally served on hot buttered toast.

Fegato alla Veneziana

THERE ARE MANY RECIPES FOR THIS MOST SIMPLE and unassuming dish. This one owes much to Elizabeth David's recipe in her book *Italian Food*, likening the cut liver to scraps of tissue paper. Cooking the onions in advance is vital, even the day before.

PS: A happy thought is to cook more than you need here and then make a pissaladière, that marvel of pastry, onions and anchovy, with the remaining onions.

PPS: Consider frying chicken livers whole for 'Fegatini alla Veneziana', using the same method.

Feeds 6

25g butter for the onions, plus a further 25g butter for the liver
3 medium onions, peeled and thinly sliced
4 bay leaves
600–700g or so best liver, from kid, pork, lamb, calf or venison
2 soup spoons olive oil
12 sage leaves

Melt 25g of the butter in a heavy-bottomed pot, tip in the sliced onions, then add the bay leaves and season. Once the steam is rising, stir well, cover with a lid and cook gently for approximately 1 hour, longer if required. Once the onions have softened completely, remove the lid and up the heat to boil away any remaining liquid, and when this is done, put the onions into a bowl and leave to one side.

While the onions cook, prepare the liver. Lay it on a board and remove the thin membrane adhering to it with your fingers. With a sharp knife, cut the liver into thin slices and in turn cut the slices into pieces the size of a thumbnail. Place the pieces on a tray, cover and refrigerate until ready to cook.

Once all is ready, heat a frying pan over a high heat and add a spoonful of the olive oil. Add half the liver, half the cooked onion, half the sage leaves and half the remaining butter. Liberally season with salt and black pepper and let cook undisturbed for a minute, then mix well, cook for a further minute, stir well, cook a minute more and decant on to a waiting dish. Repeat the process with the remaining liver and serve swiftly. Mashed potato is a perfect accompaniment.

PANTRY PAGES

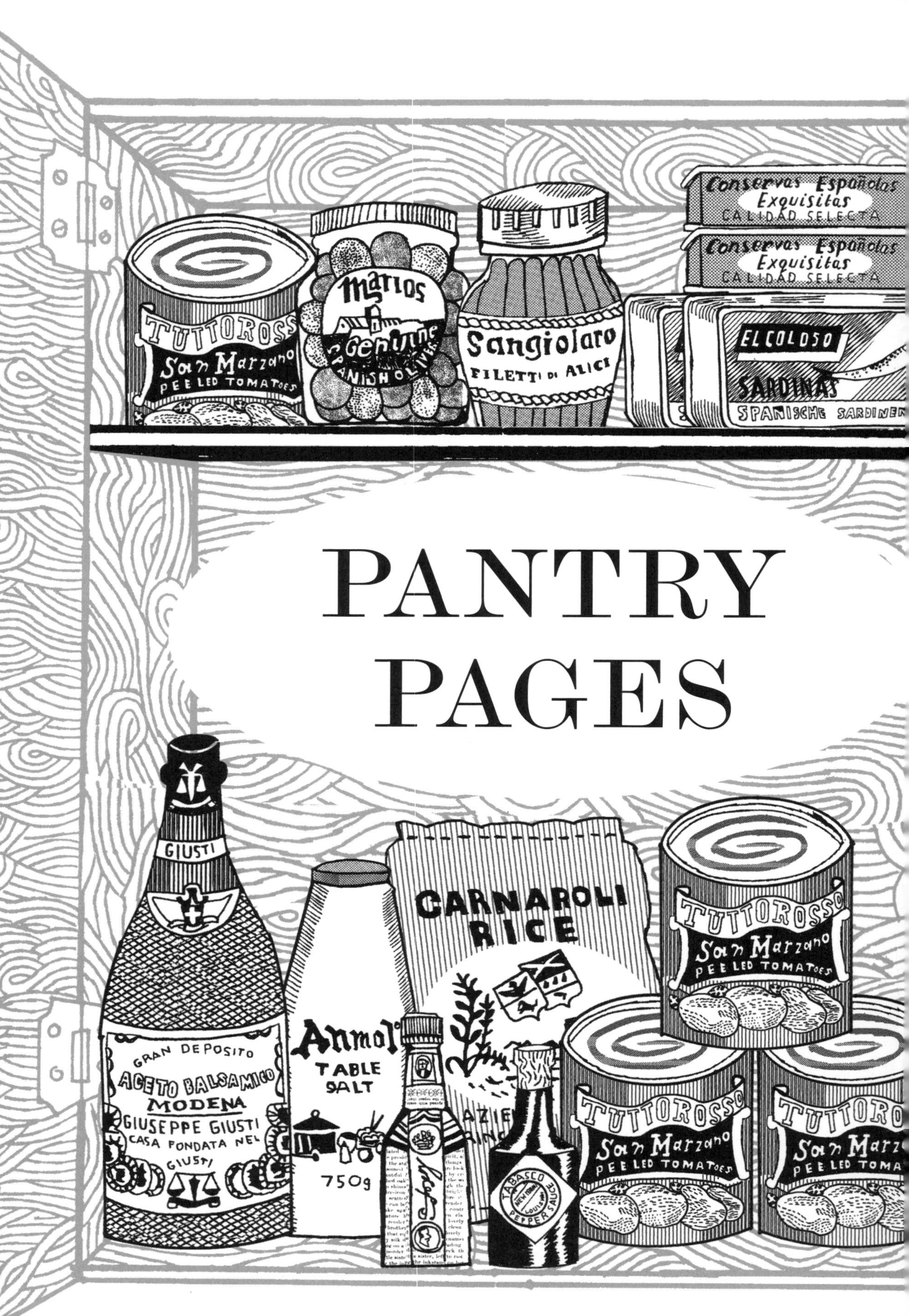

Veg/fruit
Jars, tins, packets, bottles
Cupboard
Soda bread
Of stoppered jars full of beans
Chicken stock
Vegetable stock
Fridge
Marmalade

It's that smell you get. I remember it as a kid when Mum and Dad shopped at Mr Armatruda's, a tiny Italian deli in Lochee where we would stop on our way back home to Auchterhouse. My memories are of shelves packed with pasta and tinned tomatoes but there must have been hams and salami and a tub of olives for that distinctive smell of a great deli – the mingling scents of cured meats, coffee, spices, garlic and herbs, artichokes, cheese, bunches of basil and baskets of tomatoes on the counter.

I think of that tiny shop in Dundee now when I walk into I Camisa & Son on Old Compton Street in Soho, somehow so reassuring and ace, just as an old pal should be. When I was a child, there were still two Scots grocers on the Perth Road: Mr Galloway's and Mr Aikens. We shopped there every week and the smell was completely different from an Italian deli, but equally seductive: Cheddar cheese, smoked ham and bacon. On the rare occasions when Mum and Dad announced a trip to Edinburgh, our visits were always concluded with a pilgrimage to Valvona & Crolla in Leith, a deli packed to the roof with wonders of every kind – and that distinctive Italian smell. Mum and Dad would ponder and taste olive oils and cheese while we four wandered about the shop, marvelling at its glorious abundance.

Once home from these adventures, I would hand Dad the bottles, tins, jars and packets from the boxes and bags brought in from the car. It then became my job, helping Dad keep the cupboard in order. There was always lots – often too much – and on occasion, a cracking good sell-by date, on a tin or jar pulled from the shadows, going back years beyond its expiry. 'I'll bet you it's still good,' Dad would say when I queried it. 'Just think of the archaeologists. They threw old tins at the rocks and ate the ones that didn't explode . . .'

My childhood job taught me a simple rule: buy well, to cook well to eat well. It's a rule that has stood me in good stead ever since I started cooking in restaurants as an apprentice. One of the many chores heaped on the newbie was taking in the deliveries, unpacking them and stowing them. I was rather good at this, too good in fact, as no one else ever did it. I love still to walk into a kitchen where order reigns and all is as it should be. In a restaurant it is law.

At home, my storecupboard is a wall-mounted cabinet with two doors and just the one shelf upon which are the few vitals I could not live without (listed on page 203).

As concerns about the environment mount and calls grow louder for action to help protect it, we should, wherever possible, search out the many growers, farmers and producers who have put sustainability and the welfare of their livestock first and buy organic produce, free of chemicals. Look for reduced or, better still, no packaging; buy the freshest produce grown in clean soil and air; eat fish caught and sold locally, farmhouse cheese and dairy. Try to ensure that chocolate, coffee, tea, spices, oils, vinegars, grains, pulses, charcuterie and all imports are impeccably sourced, from excellent suppliers and merchants.

Veg/fruit

Lemons, oranges and limes

No cook should ever be without a lemon in arm's reach – for juice, salads, dressings, roast chicken, fish. A squeeze of lemon is a cook's best friend. The winter months are the best time for citrus. Of particular note are the oranges and blood oranges from Sicily and lemons from the Amalfi coast. Buy unwaxed, untreated and organic fruits. The oils contained in the zest of such fruits are prized for all manner of sauces, baking, infusing syrups for poaching, pickling, custards, ice creams and sorbet. Sliced and segmented, oranges are superb in salads made with winter tomatoes, thinly sliced fennel and celery and, of course, for peerless juice.

It is worth noting that citrus fruits in the summer months tend to be thin and sharp-tasting – a judicious use of vinegar might be considered a more pleasing thought.

Onions, garlic

Always have a few good brown and pink onions, keeping an eye out for different varieties (e.g. Breme, Tropea, pink Roscoff, yellow Vidalia) which are becoming more available, and are all good for cooking and slicing or chopping fine for salads and pickles. I tend to favour small, tightly packed brown onions for cooking – large ones often collapse and release an alarming amount of liquid. White-bulbed fresh onions (spring onions) should be valued for their fresh green stalks, which can be chopped and used in salads, etc. A half-dozen shallots are invaluable, as they cook swiftly when time is of the essence, or when a pan of mushrooms or courgettes requires a scatter of finely chopped shallot and garlic to finish.

Look for larger heads of garlic, tinged with pink, rather than the often tiny little heads found in supermarkets, or white new-season garlic with a tinge of green to it. If there are a lot of green germ shoots poking through, avoid as this may make the garlic taste bitter. The huge-toothed variety of garlic going by the name of Elephant is worth seeking out for its sweet, mild flavour.

Horseradish

My preference for always using freshly grated horseradish, impervious to the tears which are only of joy, means keeping a stick of horseradish in the fridge. Wrapped tightly, horseradish keeps remarkably well. A jar of Tracklements horseradish cream is an excellent standby.

Jars, tins, packets, bottles

Peppercorns

Good seasoning plays a significant role in cooking. The magic of a perfumed heat that imbues a distinct flavour never fades, quite the contrary in fact. Always grind pepper as you need it. Peppercorns are highly volatile and once ground lose their flavour quickly.

I usually have a tub of white as well as black peppercorns at home, with a pepper mill for each. The white peppercorn is notable for the pleasant benefit of not flecking pale soups and sauces. The French have a term for equal parts black and white peppercorns ground together: 'mignonette' – good for all manner of cooking. All peppercorns, apart from pink, are from the same plant in different stages of ripening.

On occasion I find a new pepper such as voatsiperifery, a wild red pepper from Indonesia, malabar, a white pepper, and mlamala, black pepper – all beautifully fragrant. A pestle and mortar is excellent for grinding only the few peppercorns required.

Olive oil

More? But I just bought some the other day? It is always a surprise when I'm told we need to order more olive oil at the restaurant. What on earth do you do with it, I ask, and the response is always the same, with a big grin: just have a look at the menu. And it's true; since salads are something of a must with us, olive oil is a mighty factor in our kitchen.

In the summer months, we crave the peppery bite of an extra virgin olive oil from Provence, Liguria, Sicily or Tuscany. These are costly but are only used in small amounts. Much effort, care and money goes into the making of olive oil, from growing to harvesting and bottling. The colour of the oil, ranging from hues of deepest green to the palest yellow, depends on variety and locale. As with all good things, olive oil should be tasted, as colour is not always the best gauge of a good oil and many are pasteurised and blended and, in some instances, coloured.

PS: New-season olive oil, harvested in the autumn, is bright, green, with all the exuberance of youth, perfect for spooning over the thinnest slices of fennel and orange, on grilled bread and perhaps the freshest mozzarella or ricotta. These oils are rare and expensive, but so worth it if you can find one.

PPS: For cooking, use a light oil such as sunflower, grapeseed and peanut. Rapeseed oil, golden in colour, requires tasting. If it lacks punch, or seems too bland, give it some zip by mixing in a measure of extra virgin olive oil: 5 soup spoons rapeseed oil to 1 soup spoon olive oil.

Good olive oils are as varied and complex as a good wine – the best come from Provence and Italy. Spanish oil, e.g. Brindisa's Arbequina, is good for everyday cooking. Experiment with different oils. Here are a few suggestions for good olive oils to try:

Capezzana – Tuscany

Badia a Coltibuono – Tuscany

Colonna – Molise

Ravida – Sicily

Walnut oil

See page 374.

Vinegar

Look out for really good red wine or cider vinegar for cooking and pickling. The choice of vinegars can be bewildering, but finding excellent suppliers despatches doubts. It is remarkable how judicious use of a sherry, wine or a beautiful fruit vinegar can elevate dishes. Conversely, poor-quality vinegar can be so sharp that it dramatically alters the nature of a dish.

For cooking and pickling: use cider vinegar, e.g. Aspall, but look out for small producers at farmers' markets.

For vinaigrettes: experiment with different flavours, from plum, lemon and orange to quince, pear and prune (e.g. a fennel and orange salad could be dressed with a few drops of clementine vinegar). Magnificent sherry or those made with a single grape variety, such as Vieux Banyuls, Cabernet Sauvignon, Merlot, vermouth, Pineau des Charentes, Muscat, Chardonnay or Moscatel vinegars, are now coming more and more to the fore and can be used equally in cooking as well as for dressing salads.

Saba or a good-quality balsamic vinegar is very good on rich meats such as game and beef – a loin of venison cooked in a pan and finished with a few drops of Saba is sublime. Use judiciously, for the genuine article is costly and only two or three drops are needed.

There are vinegars infused with all manner of herbs and leaves, such as tarragon, lovage, marjoram and wild garlic.

Worth considering is verjus, an ancient style of vinegar made from pressing unripe grapes. You can even make it from crab apples. Use as an alternative to vinegar, lemon or citrus.

Dried herbs

A few small jars or tins of herbs, firmly sealed to maintain their fragrance, are a boon to the cook when a little lift and a memory of sunshine are needed in the kitchen. Though we use armfuls of fresh herbs in the restaurant, particularly parsley, both flat-leaf and curly, dill and chives, some herbs are particularly good dried: e.g. rue, marjoram, borage, rosemary, sage and oregano, fennel flower, thyme and savory, both winter and summer, not dissimilar to thyme but gentle in flavour.

Use judicious pinches of a few of these to add to finely chopped lemon peel, shallot, garlic and olive oil to spoon over grilled vegetables, fish and meat. Add pinches of ground dill, fennel and celery seed – also excellent. Quality is all. Quantities are best kept small so they can be used within months rather than years, thus avoiding that shaming long-since-expired sell-by date. Oops.

Merchants who sell good oil and vinegar usually carry a good supply of dried herbs too. When grinding spices such as pepper, coriander and fennel seeds to season meats, add a pinch of dried herbs, though remember, dried herbs have a powerful presence. Lamb chops dusted with dried borage and thyme with a drop of olive oil and a drop of good vinegar are delicious.

Whole spices

As with dried herbs, spices are best bought in small quantities and whole so their fragrance does not diminish. Buying spices in small quantities should help ensure their use within a few months. Whole spices, e.g. coriander, cumin, turmeric, fennel seed, dill seed, mustard seed, celery seed, cinnamon sticks, allspice, nutmeg, should be ground as needed for braises, baking, preserves, chutneys, both fresh and cooked. It is worth keeping an eye out for unusual spices such as whole dried rhizomes of ginger which are free of that metallic flavour so often found in ginger bought already ground. The difference is remarkable.

Salt and other finds …

Use beautifully made, fine-quality unadulterated salts such as Halen Môn, Cornish sea salt, sel gris and sel de Guérande. Grind crystals in a pestle and mortar. It's worth buying salt to bring home every time you go abroad, as is the case with much else besides – chocolate and cocoa, tins and jars of anchovies and sardines, tins of cooked flageolet beans. It is also worth finding local honey and herbal teas, local olive and walnut oils and vinegars, tins and jars of duck and goose fat from farms. To such finds might be added dried fruit such as prunes, currants, sultanas, mulberries, red and blackcurrants, figs and apricots. (See entry for Cheese on page 344–5). Keep a beady eye out for vanilla pods and pure vanilla extract and bitter orange oil for cooking, as well as newly harvested hazelnuts and walnuts, more and more often found shelled, roasted and ready for cooking (see entry on Nuts on page 203).

Sugar

Seek out organic, less refined, less processed sugar. And try reducing the sugar quantities in all aspects of cooking. Our almond tart recipe was once a classic recipe of equal amounts of almonds, butter and sugar. Halving the sugar seemed not to alter the recipe so much; if anything the almonds are more pronounced.

Refined white sugar is vital for a more delicate school of baking but where possible try muscovado sugar, both dark and light, and demerara. Muscovado sugars will dry into clods so should be stored in tightly sealed containers.

Tinned or jarred anchovies

The British Isles are curiously shy of salted fish, preferring smoked or pickled fish. This also applies to salted anchovies which have become increasingly difficult to find except in a few specialist shops. Most anchovies are tinned or jarred in oil, and in this case the rule is the pinker the better. The pinker the fillet, the milder and more delicate the flavour of the anchovy. As with all fish, sustainability and quality are paramount, hence their cost. The good news is that you do not need many, unless you are like me and can eat them straight from the tin or jar.

Good-quality anchovies, lightly rinsed, melt beautifully when warmed with a few spoonfuls of extra virgin olive oil, finely chopped garlic and a little chopped chilli to make a sauce that does not overwhelm vegetables such as sprouting broccoli, cardoons, artichokes, green beans and spinach. Anchovies have many uses in sauces, salads and for impromptu suppers involving Scotch woodcock, Caesar salad or anchoïade to serve with poached and grilled vegetables, fish and meats. There is, too, the estimable serving of a slice of a crusty loaf of bread spread with cold butter with an anchovy fillet laid atop.

Tinned tuna

Don't. There is only one exception to this rule: buying the best-quality tins from trusted suppliers for making 'porchetta tonnato', a mighty dish of pork, highly seasoned with pepper and herbs, roasted and cooled before slicing thinly, to be then spread with tuna ground smooth with anchovies, garlic, olive oil and lemon. Fillets of anchovy and capers are scattered over, to be finished with chopped parsley and pools of olive oil.

Tinned sardines

One of the most useful cupboard standbys: best-quality pilchards from Cornwall, Spain or Portugal. Mash them with chopped parsley, heap on toast and grill. I can't say I am wild about the sardines inventively tinned with spiced tomato sauce, preferring by far the tins filled with fish that are lightly salted and oiled only. To these can be added slices of tomato, capers and freshly squeezed lemon juice.

I always check the shelves for sardines and keep a dozen or so tins at home at all times. Sometimes, only sardines on toast will do, and sometimes with a fried egg on top with a few fillets of anchovy and capers. Elizabeth David wrote an essay about tinned sardines, comparing the different vintages of the tinned sardines in her cupboard (see *An Omelette and a Glass of Wine*). I like to make a homage to a salade Niçoise with tinned sardines and happily confess to a preference for the pilchard over tuna, as indeed does my conscience.

Olives

An olive is excellent company in a martini, a bowl or a salad. Olives come in all shapes, sizes and shades of green, purple and black. Their texture and flavour vary dramatically, and quite simply, only the best will do. Olives are best bought with their stones still in, and as with all ingredients in brine, require tasting for strength, for it is the flavour of the olive that matters – it should not be overwhelmed by an excessive brine.

There is always great discussion over olives, so tasting is as crucial as it is pleasing. Greece, Spain, France and Italy are famous for olives and the oils they make. Be they for cooking, eating or drinking, black or green, marinated in herbs, lemon and chilli, or not, all require due consideration. A favourite olive for eating is Petit Lucques, a beautifully structured green olive with a curious curve. Kalamata olives are generally most reliable, though the darkest black seem most often to be associated with Provence. The huge green Gordal olives of Spain are exceptional. If there are olives needing to be used up, grind them with breadcrumbs and bake crisp to sprinkle on salads (see page 74), particularly those with capers, anchovies, shallots, dried tomatoes, artichokes and thinly sliced shallot, or roast or grilled slices of red onions such as Breme, Roscoff or Tropea. They are ace, too, spooned atop slices of bread baked crisp, spread with curds, ricotta or mozzarella.

Capers

A caper is a fine thing. A bag of salted capers keeps remarkably well, once opened, in the fridge. There are different sizes of caper and though I like them all, I find the medium-sized best for bite and flavour, the large often too soft. Always buy capers in salt, and if possible those from Salina, an island near Sicily. Rinse well before soaking for 30 minutes or so, changing the water a few times. Capers are a vital part of sauces such as tartare, ravigote, gribiche and for a wing of skate with black butter, capers, parsley and lemon. Capers are needed for tapenades, regardless of which olives are used and are splendid in salads, particularly those made with squid and salt cod, and of course salade Niçoise and salmagundy (see page 31).

Best tinned tomatoes

A kitchen shelf without a few tins of tomatoes is unthinkable. Their presence in your larder confers comfort. They are vital for a swift sauce made with a tin of whole tomatoes, rinsed of excess gloop and coarsely chopped. Put them into a lidded pan, with the addition of a whole onion, peeled and roughly sliced, and a large knob of butter, cover and cook gently for half an hour over a low flame. Season to taste. Delicious as is, such a sauce can be added to with all manner of vegetables, braised beans and chickpeas to make a pretty good soup. Mutti San Marzano tomatoes are a good bet.

Cupboard

Rice

There is always a bag of Carnaroli rice at home ready for those times when you need a risotto. There are other rices too, such as Arborio or Vialone Nano, which cook very well. It is a happy thought to cook lots and with the leftovers to make 'suppli alla telefono' (see page 309), rice cakes formed round a nut of mozzarella. Traditionally, suppli are rolled in breadcrumbs and deep-fried. I prefer, risking the wrath of purists, making the cakes into small drums, dipping each end in beaten egg, then breadcrumbs, frying lightly, then warming through in the oven so the mozzarella melts, pulling like telephone wires when cut into, hence their name. Ace with a tumble of vegetables and a salad.

There are so many rices available, new labels appearing every year alongside favourites: vintage basmati and splendid long-grain rices, including a beautiful and flavoursome black rice from Piedmont stocked by Belazu, that is wonderful with roast or braised vegetables abundant with herbs and lemon.

My dad always made a sturdy rice pudding with Arborio rice that I remember fondly, eaten with a great deal of Mum's raspberry jam. My preference is for rice pudding made with Carnaroli scented with vanilla, lemon and marigold leaves, cooled and served with all manner of poached or baked fruits, such as rhubarb, apricots, gooseberries, apples, blackberries and plums. It's particularly good with cold custard and cream added, and for increased giddiness, strewn with slivers of pistachios, almonds, walnuts or hazelnuts.

Simply nuts for them

My admiration for the almond never dims. I have spent years roasting, baking and grinding them for all manner of salads, pastes both sweet and savoury, cakes, tarts and biscuits. The same is true for pistachios, walnuts and hazelnuts; I love them all equally.

Grinding nuts with salad leaves and herbs, garlic, perhaps some cheese, and olive oil makes a paste (or pesto) that delights in being spooned on fresh sheep's, cow's or goat's cheese spread on grilled bread, grilled polenta (so much better cooked than the instant, which has all the culinary charm of a tractor tyre) and grilled vegetables.

I bake an almond tart or cake most days of the year, if not all. One rule is absolute: grinding the nuts. Nuts, like spices, lose much vitality if left for any length of time after grinding, and they are often ground too fine, almost to a powder. A food processor makes short work of grinding nuts to a coarse crumb. Almost all nuts are sold out of the shell and peeled. Worth finding in particular are hazelnuts, shelled and roasted in tightly sealed packages, the best from Piedmont; so good for praline, ice cream, custard, tarts, biscuits, galettes and cakes. Marcona almonds from Spain are bought whole, blanched and ready to chop and grind for all manner of good things. Walnuts, ancient and venerable (the paler the better: a light-gold walnut is a good indication of quality and should have the longest shelf life). The newly harvested walnuts of autumn and winter are the best, as with hazelnuts.

Some intrepid greengrocers sell fresh almonds, covered in a pale green velvet with a milky nut within, that are a treat with wine, ham and bread, and perhaps a ripe peach, though often too early for figs, as a rule.

Dishes of grilled bread spread with ricotta beaten with black pepper, olive oil and lemon zest, with slices of peach or fig, and nuts ground with herbs spooned on top, make for delightful eating. They look rather good too.

Pine kernels should be youthful, for they diminish swiftly. They are delightful in pastes, pesto, on cakes, tarts and biscuits.

Chestnuts, so good with beans, pumpkin and bacon in soup, are often better bought roasted, peeled and tightly packaged. First encountered in Spain, I have relied on them ever since. Those from France and Italy are of equal quality.

Dried mushrooms

Buy really good dried mushrooms to make pies, braises and soups. Dried porcini, chanterelle and girolles are usually the best. If kept in the dark, they'll last at least a year, if not longer. Always rinse the mushrooms thoroughly for any stubbornly clinging grit. Have a care if tempted to add the water in which the mushrooms soaked – it will reduce while cooking and can prove overwhelming. I often pour the murky brew away, offering the water up as libation to the gods.

Judicious use is called for, as dried fungi have an unexpected potency. They are a wonderful alternative when mushrooms are rare, costly, or only buttons are to be had and a mushroom soup or risotto or a braise of venison or beef cries out for a mushroom or two. They are also wonderful for adding depth to a vegetable stock.

Lentils

Lentils, nothing if not versatile, pair with all manner of meats, fish and vegetables, herbs and cheeses. The ones I cook most and know best are grown in France, Italy and Spain, and are an essential staple of the kitchen. Wonderful with sausages, roasts, poached fish, a whole garden of greens and of course soup, and time willing, they braise beautifully. Rinsed, then placed in a pan with cold water, the lentils are brought swiftly to the boil, drained and rinsed and added to a pan of vegetables, with a little garlic, and simmered for an hour or so with a bundle of thyme and bay leaves. Adding bacon, cut in strips or left whole, is entirely at the cook's discretion. Lentils cooked thus are even better a day or two later, kept in the fridge in a sealed container, requiring little more than a splash of water then warmed through over a gentle heat.

The colours of lentils – as varied as pebbles on a beach – range from dark viridian greens through to earthy reds and browns. The green, red and brown lentils are esteemed for holding their shape, plumping slightly while cooking and keeping their form.

Orange lentils, yellow and green split peas cook quite differently, simmered gently until cooked almost to a purée, sometimes plain or made beguiling with spice.

Honey

Part of the weekly shop involved standing with Mum and Dad at the counter in Mr Braithwaite's tea and coffee shop in Dundee. While the coffee beans were ground, Mum would choose a jar each of clear and thick Angus heather and clover honey. This was often eaten on buttered bannocks and oatcakes, sometimes with cheese, or with poached rhubarb and plain yoghurt. The habit stuck. There are always jars of honey in my kitchen, bought from tables selling local produce on roadsides, markets and cheese shops abroad. Spread honey thick or drizzle clear honey over yoghurt. It's wonderful too in custards, ice cream, tarts, cakes and macaroons.

In sustainability terms, bees are as imperilled as the fish in the sea. Only buy honey from reputable sources such as merchants who pile their tables and stock their shelves with care and conscience.

Should a jar of honey crystallise, add some hot water, lemon juice, ginger wine and whiskey to make a hot toddy.

Tabasco, Worcestershire sauce, Angostura bitters

The realm of the condiment grows and grows. Jars and bottles of fermented vegetables and fruits appear in a dazzling array of colours as brilliant as the flavours. Alongside the stalwarts such as bottles of Tabasco and Worcestershire sauce are ferments, oils and sauces made from every kind of chilli found on the Scoville scale. Chutneys, pickles and piccalillies come in every form, and it's advisable to taste and try before buying. Needless to say, the general rule is the less commercial the better the quality.

Some of the best ferments to buy are to be found at the London Fermentary in Bermondsey (see stockists, page 390).

There is always a bottle of Angostura bitters in the house. A few drops on a scoop of vanilla ice cream makes a speedy, delicious pudding.

Dried fruit

Every two years, Bra, a small city in Piedmont in the north of Italy, birthplace and home to Slow Food and one of the most beautiful wine regions in Europe, organises a cheese festival. The streets are lined with myriad stalls and tents offering some of the world's finest cheese. For a few days, life begins and ends with cheese. The festival is always held in the autumn, coinciding with an abundance of grapes, rumours of early white truffles, wonderful vegetables (including a rare variety of leek called Lungo d'invierno, very good with tripe), peerless hazelnuts and honey.

Away from the streets thronged with cheesemakers there are wonderful shops selling coffee, dried fruits, spices, dried herbs and vanilla pods. Here can be bought superb dried apricots, mulberries, figs, currants, prunes, raisins and sultanas of all colours and sizes. I cannot resist, and only the tiresome thought of a baggage allowance keeps me in check, but the expense of getting them home is repaid tenfold when the time comes to bake an Eccles cake, make a steamed pudding or mincemeat for Christmas, or make a pickle to accompany a terrine or slices of a roast meat such as venison or pork, or simply to eat with cheese. Dried fruit keeps remarkably well in sealed jars in a cool, shady spot.

I always buy vanilla pods from Bra, as they seem more reasonably priced than at home. Steep dried fruit for a few days with split vanilla pods saved after poaching fresh fruits and infusing custards for ice cream and trifles.

There are, too, the most wonderful Spanish wheels of dates or prunes or marzipans pressed with walnuts and almonds to be had, as well as membrillo, which on occasion can be found studded with walnuts and almonds.

Vanilla

Vanilla beans rightly make a mockery of most of the commercial essences I have tried. Their considerable cost – and being an orchid and grown in Madagascar and Tahiti, they should be costly, like a great olive oil or rare wild pepper, a little going a long way – is more than compensated for by the glorious, unique flavour they bring to fruit compotes, poaching syrups, custards, caramels, chocolates, creams, baking of all sorts. And when the pod has been split, scraped clean of its seeds, infused and dried, if put into a tightly sealed, scrupulously clean jar with vodka, or rum, it makes a formidable essence that elevates all it flavours.

Vanilla beans should be bought when richly dark, plump and not in the least dried and twisted like seaweed on a beach. Good grocers like the Vinegar Shed, La Fromagerie and the splendidly named Zazou Emporium Vanilla (see pages 390–1) are but a few excellent sources. I dream still of a shop visited long ago in Italy, with a remarkable choice of dried fruits and spice. I bought several different types of mulberries, currants, prunes, figs and apricots, and beautiful vanilla beans that almost shone in the light of the shop. I steeped the lot in rum when I got home and added them to cream to make the most wonderful ice cream and cakes. There was no recipe, it was just one of those delightful moments that writer Laurie Colwin describes as a 'lost note', for just that moment. The inspiration remains, and a love for steeping fruits in vanilla is undiminished.

Flour

The practice of milling unrefined flour for baking is increasingly common. Mills such as Gilchesters sell bags of flour packed with nutrients. Varieties such as spelt, rye, emmer and einkorn flours are making a comeback. All of these are excellent for baking and general use. Keep in your storecupboard: bags of rye, white and one other such as emmer or einkorn. Best to buy as you need so that the nutrients are kept as fresh as possible.

PS: Soda bread is a miraculous loaf, swiftly made and so good just with butter, maybe jam, but best of all with smoked and pickled fish. There is an ancient variety of barley grown and milled on Orkney called beremeal that makes a splendid soda bread.

Soda bread

Makes a 20cm round loaf

115g self-raising flour
85g beremeal, plus extra for dusting (available from baronymill.com, or try buckwheat or pinhead milled oats)
¼ teaspoon sea salt
1 teaspoon baking powder
½ teaspoon bicarbonate of soda
30g black treacle
30g honey
45g unsalted butter, melted
150ml buttermilk

Heat the oven to 190°C and oil a baking sheet. Sift the dry ingredients into a mixing bowl.

Melt the treacle, honey and butter together in a pan, but do not boil, then pour into the dry ingredients. As deftly as possible, mix in the buttermilk to make a soft dropping consistency.

Scrape on to the middle of the baking sheet and dust with extra beremeal. Shape into a round and cut a deep cross in the top with a long-bladed knife.

Bake for 25 minutes until risen and firm. Cool on a wire tray. This is best eaten freshly baked.

To make your own self-raising flour: for every 100g of plain flour, add one teaspoon of baking powder. Keep a tin of baking powder, a tin of bicarbonate of soda and a tin of cream of tartar in your kitchen cupboard for impromptu baking or emergencies. A box of Allinson's dried yeast in easy-bake sachets is also very handy.

Very much for the grain

Small bags of barley, orzo, farro and spelt are very fine friends indeed. Rinsed well, a small handful of grain will bloom considerably when simmered very gently so as not to release any excessive starchiness. The resulting water, if not being used for a hearty broth, can be flavoured with the zest and juice of oranges, blood oranges, pink grapefruit, limes and lemons. This is particularly good in the wilds of winter when a jolt of sunshine in a glass precedes a comforting, soothing, nourishing soup or salad of grains with all manner of vegetables, fishes and meats.

Mustard

There must always be three jars of Grey Poupon Dijon or Maille mustard in the kitchen. One open in the fridge, one in readiness for when the first jar is emptied and one in reserve. I prefer the smooth to the grain mustard, for no other reason than it has a cleaner, brighter snap to it.

Mustard is vital for making mayonnaise, occasionally vinaigrette, as essential for roast meats as for smoked fish such as mackerel or eel. Beaten into natural yoghurt and olive oil, mustard makes a light, clean dressing for a chopped vegetable such as in a Cobb salad.

English mustard powder cannot go unmentioned. It's vital for Welsh rarebit, gratins of cauliflower and sprouting broccoli and, of course, dabbed on a pork pie. The powdered form not only lasts well in the cupboard but is quickly made when mixed with enough cold water for the desired consistency.

Of stoppered jars full of beans

Deliberating whether or not to use jarred or tinned legumes, or soak dried beans overnight, I more often than not choose the latter, as the taste and texture of a gently cooked bean, simmered slowly in a pot with a spoonful of olive oil, a few bay leaves and a sprig of thyme, is wonderful, particularly when the skin turns to silk.

I like the idea of cooking a pot of beans or pulses to make dishes later in the week, giving time for the braise to settle and the flavours to deepen, lifting out a few spoonfuls to add to soups and stews. Such culinary rituals are as old as the hills and a staple of regional cooking around the world: soothing, nourishing and good.

There are so many varieties of bean to choose from: beans in beguiling shades of ivory to black, or palest pink and the softest of greens with lovely markings in different hues of pink and purple. There are blues, too, that mysteriously vanish in cooking. Beans picked fresh in the summer and the autumn, such as borlotti and coco de Paimpol beans, require no soaking beforehand. They cook astonishingly quickly, a boon for the cook who forgot to soak a pan of pulses the night before.

Beans dressed with olive oil and perhaps a few chopped herbs are good company to all manner of vegetables, fish and shellfish, and lamb and pork in particular. A few good shots at cooking beans, chickpeas or lentils and the cook's confidence grows with each success. Any beans that misbehave in the pot usually require longer cooking, which I try to remember for the next time. And if there is the odd batch of beans that refuses to soften, or collapses rather alarmingly, it happens, tant pis! Just reach up for the jar sitting so patiently on the shelf. It makes me smile that even the humble bean is possessed of such human traits.

Beans from a jar are best decanted into a colander and the adhering cooking liquor gently rinsed away under a quiet stream of cold water from the tap. Placed in a pan, the rinsed beans are warmed gently with a soup spoon of water.

On the other hand, beans that have been dried, soaked and simmered for an hour or two or longer in a slow oven, drink up the flavours of all that simmers in the pot with them – vegetables and herbs, a piece of salted pork, sausages and perhaps preserved goose melting sublimely. When the beans are cooked gently with pumpkin and chestnuts for a soup to warm a winter night, the beans become almost silken while infusing with the vegetables, herbs and olive oil with which they were simmered.

Often to be found at shops such as Brindisa and the Ealing Grocer, which also have websites for online deliveries, heirloom varieties such as Judión or Tolosa, produced in tiny quantities by farmers working smallholdings in, say, Spain or Italy where such cooking is exalted, are exceptional when cooked and dressed with a few spoonfuls of extra virgin olive oil, or simmered with vegetables, a lamb shank, a piece of bacon or slowly cooked pork belly, sometimes sliced and cooked crisp in a pan. I never tire of preparing vegetables and beans for the pot, leaving them to cook gently on a quiet heat, a complete repast in one pot to take to table. Beans often make the best leftovers should there be any left at all.

A pot of lentils

BE THEY FRENCH, SPANISH, GREEK OR ITALIAN, lentils coloured in shades of darkest green to the palest sienna cook remarkably quickly and do not require soaking, an admirable quality for a cook short of time. Once simmering, lentils may only require half an hour or so, though it is worth bearing in mind that, left to cook gently for longer, to the pot can be added chopped vegetables or bacon or just olive oil scented with garlic and herbs, which will imbue them with a deepened flavour and the softest texture.

A pot of lentils cooked early in the week can be cooled and stored in the fridge to be warmed through when needed. To this can be added spoonfuls of chopped tomatoes, both red and green, shallots or red onions, fresh green onion tops sliced thin, herbs, anchovies, capers and garlic, to be served with poached fish, poached meats such as chicken or tongue, or roast belly of pork.

Feeds 6

5 rashers of smoked streaky bacon, should you wish
1 carrot
1 onion
1 heart of celery, leaves attached
4 cloves of garlic
4 soup spoons extra virgin olive oil
500g lentils
3 bay leaves

Cut the bacon into thin strips, if using. Peel and coarsely chop the vegetables and garlic. Place a pot on a moderate heat and add the oil. Add the strips of bacon and fry for a minute, then add the vegetables and garlic. Stir well, place a lid atop and lower the heat.

Rinse the lentils in cold water. Put them into a pot, cover with cold water, then place over a high heat and bring to the boil. Drain carefully, rinse swiftly and add to the pot of bacon and vegetables. Add the bay leaves and cover with cold water. Bring to the boil, then lower the heat and simmer for 30–40 minutes until all is softened. Cook for longer if required or, if time allows, a few hours on the gentlest heat.

A pot of beans for a pleasant summer's day

FOR COOLER TIMES, make this with kales, greens and cabbages.

Feeds 6

500g dried cannellini beans
120ml extra virgin olive oil
6 small courgettes
1 bulb of fennel
2 small onions
6 cloves of garlic
6 ripe tomatoes
a large bunch of basil
a large bunch of flat-leaf parsley
a small bunch of rocket
150–200g young spinach
dried chilli flakes (optional)

Soak the beans overnight, then rinse them and place in a pot with enough cold water to cover generously. Place the pot over a moderate heat and bring to a simmer. Spoon away any foam rising to the surface. Pour in the olive oil and let cook gently for an hour.

Peel and finely chop the courgettes, fennel and onions, then peel and slice the garlic. Add them to the pot of beans and let cook gently for a further 30–45 minutes, until tender.

Blanch the tomatoes in boiling water for 10–12 seconds, then remove and leave to cool. Once cool, peel and chop into small pieces.

Pick and tear the basil leaves. Pick the parsley leaves and chop finely. Chop the rocket and spinach. Stir all into the pot, bring to a simmer and cook gently for a few minutes longer. Tip in the chopped tomatoes. Remove from the heat and season liberally with sea salt, black pepper and perhaps, too, a pinch of dried chilli flakes.

This soup is best served just warm, with a small spoonful of a superb olive oil added when ladled into a bowl.

Stock

Generally speaking, it is worth making more stock, in a larger pot, than is immediately required, for stock benefits from being made in large quantities with enough space for the ingredients to be able to impart their properties gently without being jostled and crowded. Any remaining stock can be frozen for another time. Stock will last a good 6 months in the freezer, but obviously the sooner it is used the better. The ice-cube tray manoeuvre is welcome: freeze stock in ice-cube trays and bundle the cubes into a sealed container to use in small quantities if required.

A stock can be made with pigs' trotters, carcasses of birds such as guinea fowl, duck or wild duck, turkey or goose. In colder months, you might consider game such as venison and wild rabbit, or pheasant, which make wonderful deep, richly flavoured stocks.

Preparing a stock requires only a modest effort but enough time to cook. Wash and chop the vegetables, combine them in a large pot with herbs, a few cracked black peppercorns along with bones or a carcass and a glass of wine, to be then covered in water. Bring to a boil, then simmer over the lowest heat for a couple of hours, usually the duration of a film or two, I find.

The stockpot put on early can tick over quietly through the day. Spoon away any froths or foams, then leave the surface of the stock undisturbed as the crust that forms acts as a filter, leaving the stock below clear until the heat is turned off and the pot is removed from the stove.

It is always worth asking a butcher if there are any bones and trim going spare. And should a trip to the butcher prove bountiful, here is another thought. Put all the bones, with scraps and trim of pork and beef, and a pig's trotter or two, into a deep tray with vegetables, garlic, herbs and peppercorns. Cover the contents of the tray with water, adding a glass of wine if you wish. Place a sheet of baking parchment over the bones, then tightly seal the tray with foil. Place carefully in a low oven and leave for the rest of the day.

Whichever form the cook chooses, here are two simple stock recipes which can be added to and aggrandised as you wish.

Chicken stock

Makes about 1½ litres of stock

1 small carrot
1 small onion
1 stick of celery
2 cloves of garlic
3 bay leaves
a sprig of thyme
a sprig of summer savory (optional)
a small bunch of parsley stalks, finely chopped
12 black peppercorns, cracked
100ml white wine
1 chicken carcass
a bag of giblets (optional)

Wash and coarsely chop the vegetables and tip into a wide-bottomed deep pot. Add all the other ingredients. Top up with enough cold water to cover everything by at least 5cm, roughly 2 litres in total. Bring this to the boil, spoon away any foam arising and lower the heat until only an occasional bubble appears on the surface. Let this cook undisturbed, checking from time to time that the stock is not boiling or reducing, adding enough water to cover the contents of the pot.

Simmer the stock for 1.5–2 hours. Strain to remove all the vegetables, herbs and bones, return to the pot, bring back to the boil and skim away any fat and foam arising. Simmer gently for 5 minutes until clear, then cool and refrigerate or freeze. Stock keeps well in the fridge for 3–4 days or, if frozen as soon as possible, freezes well for 6 months.

Vegetable stock

ASPARAGUS PEELINGS, pea pods, dried and fresh mushrooms, chopped tomatoes, pumpkin rinds, sweetcorn husks and the stalks of picked herbs can all be added to this stock.

Makes roughly 1½ litres of stock

1 small celeriac
3 carrots
3 onions
6 sticks of celery
2 leeks
6 cloves of garlic
6 bay leaves
a small bundle of summer savory and thyme, or parsley
12 black peppercorns

Wash and chop all the vegetables to roughly the same size. Place in a pot with the herbs and peppercorns and pour in 2 litres of water. Bring this to the boil and simmer for 45 minutes.

Strain the stock to remove all the solids, herbs and peppercorns. Cool and refrigerate for no more than a couple of days. Vegetable stock does not freeze well.

Fridge

A few good cheeses

A good cheesemonger is as vital as a good butcher, fishmonger, greengrocer and all the other merchants necessary for a well-stocked kitchen. There are few things as irresistible as a magnificent array of cheese. It is quite something to stand at the counter in Neal's Yard Dairy and watch the flourish of the distinctive blue-capped servers extending slivers of cheese cut from the piece to the hands of customers tasting before deciding what to buy. The choice of farmhouse Cheddars alone is staggering. Old favourites sit side by side with the new, the air rich with the scent of cheese, newly cut in perfect condition. And that is just the British cheese – they also sell an ace feta, a great mozzarella and exceptional Comté.

The quality and breadth of farmhouse cheese made in Britain is superb.

Store in the fridge cheeses that keep well over time, e.g. a good chunk of Cheddar or a good chunk of Parmesan. Ideally buy cheese as you need it and always buy farmhouse. Bring cheese out of the fridge about an hour before you want to eat it. Keep an eye on the cheeses in your fridge: if they need using up, they can be turned into soufflés and salads, cheese straws and that eternal wonder, cheese on toast. Don't forget elevenses – a brilliant way of ensuring oatcakes, cheese and apples that might otherwise linger are consumed regularly. Goat's cheese, cow's curd, mozzarella, etc., should be bought fresh as needed. Leftovers make good grilled sandwiches.

Yoghurt

There are times, quite often, when a craving for yoghurt must be sated. The huge array of yoghurts available makes choosing a favourite nigh-on impossible. Seek out the most natural yoghurts made with the best milk from cows, sheep and goats reared with the utmost care and welfare. I return time and again to the Greek-style yoghurt sold by Neal's Yard Dairy for that light, bright, creamy tang that is as good with a spoonful of honey or a fruit compote as it is mixed with handfuls of chopped parsley, mint and coriander. You can also spice it lightly with roast ground cumin, chilli and coriander to serve with griddled squid, spinach rendered smooth and a purée of pumpkin seasoned with nutmeg, lemon and pepper scooped up with feuilles de brick baked crisp.

Butter

Buy organic salted butter from Ireland, the UK and France for spreading on toast or the best bread. For baking, and cooking, I rely on pale, lighter unsalted butter.

Milk and cream

Always bought fresh and from a dairy with the welfare of cows, sheep and goats in mind.

Not such a frozen wasteland

All too often I pause before a stall with boxes of peas and broad beans and ponder their age. As there are no sell-by dates for fresh vegetables, on occasion I've inadvertently bought peas that refuse to cook until tender, remaining stubborn and quite firm, or worse mealy, a most unsatisfactory return for the time spent podding and shelling. A useful standby for times such as these are bags of frozen broad beans and peas. They can be a boon to the cook for use in soups and braises and rice and pasta, or for mashing with herbs and ricotta on toast.

PS: Frozen peas are loved by all and are an ace standby when fresh peas prove troublesome to source, but should be used wisely, using less. Frozen broad beans, on the other hand, are excellent. The table will always be divided regarding peeling broad beans. The business is usually settled by biting through the pods – if sweet, gentle and fresh, they require no podding, if toothsome and thick-skinned, then a swift dip in boiling water and peeling after removes a jarring note to the finished dish.

Marmalade

MARMALADE-MAKING WAS AN ALMIGHTY PERFORMANCE played out in the kitchen by our parents. The morning was spent cutting Seville oranges, lemons and grapefruit in half, then scooping all the flesh into a pan, covering it with water and setting it to simmer on the stove until it became, in Dad's words, a gloop. While the gloop glooped, Mum and Dad sat and cut the empty halves of the fruits into strips of peel.

It was quite a sight, us watching from the sidelines as Mum held a large muslin bag stuffed full of boiled Seville orange, lemon and grapefruit pulp over a jelly pan while Dad, applying every ounce of strength, squeezed all the juice that could be squeezed out, affirming constantly this was the secret to 'yer mither's marvellous marmalade' – and my father was an erudite man who rarely spoke with a strong east coast accent except when making marmalade.

Mum's recipe was almost certainly one torn from a newspaper, so thanks must go out to the original author. It is vital that the peels are cooked until tender. Should they remain firm, the rinds will, if anything, toughen while simmering in the sugar.

Makes 5 or 6 x 450g jars
1.5 kg Sevilles
750g blood oranges
750g navel oranges
2 pink grapefruit
2 lemons
2.5kg caster or preserving sugar, approximately

Traditionally, marmalade was made with 2kg sugar for each kilogram of cooked peel and pulp. If you find this overly sweet, use only half the sugar, which requires scrupulously clean jars, placing in a cool place and checking from time to time against the presence of mould, a potential with all preserves. Making marmalade in small batches is preferred.

Cut all the fruit in half. Squeeze the fruits thoroughly, removing as much pith along with the seeds and juice as possible.

Slice the peels thinly, roughly 2-3 mm in thickness. The strips will naturally vary in length.

Place the peels in one pan, the pulp and seeds in another. Cover both with plenty of cold water, roughly 1 litre in the pulp and 3–4 litres onto the peels. The quantity of water at this stage is roughly measured, most importantly the peel having plenty of water to ensure an even softening while simmering in a plentiful amount of water infused with the flavour of the fruit, any excess being boiled away during the making of marmalade. Bring both pans to a simmer. Cook the peels gently for 2–3 hours, longer if required, until fully softened, stirring occasionally. This is vital as the peels will toughen if not fully softened through cooking, and once simmered with sugar, it cannot be corrected. Simmer the pulp for an hour and a half, stirring from time to time, lifting away any foam arising. Pour this through a sieve into a bowl. Push a ladle through the pulp to extract as much gloop as possible. Put to one side.

When the peels are fully softened, let cool. A thought here is to cover both pots and leave overnight, making the cooked fruit much easier to handle. Add the sieved goop and weigh the peels and the infused liquid in two batches, then place in a preserving pan. To each

marmalade '22
marmalade '22
marmalade '22

kilogram add 1 kilogram of sugar. This will lightly set the marmalade and result in a less-sweet conserve.

Place the pot on a high heat and bring to a boil. Spoon away any froth arising. Continue thus for 20–30 minutes until a syrup thickens. There is a joyful moment seeing the peels, somewhat limp after softening in a liquid infused with the spirit of the fruit, begin to seize and take on the form of candied peel in the sugar and dance in the syrup, the colour deepening and the air imbued with the unique scent of marmalade. As the conserve bubbles in the pan, testing for a setting point is best done in the time-honoured tradition of lifting out a teaspoon of preserve onto a plate that when cooled will tell the degree of setting reached.

There are always all sorts of jars on a shelf or two gathered over the years which are gratefully lifted down when the time comes for potting preserves. The jars need to be scrupulously cleaned in hot water and dried carefully, perhaps on a tray in a warm oven heated to 100°C.

To make a marmalade with a greater depth of colour and flavour there is a thought to use an unrefined raw cane sugar called panela; the one I used I was introduced to at Leila's shop, who delighted in in its journey from Colombia to the British Isles in a sailing ship. The best result is using raw cane sugar and caster sugar in equal measure.

PEAS

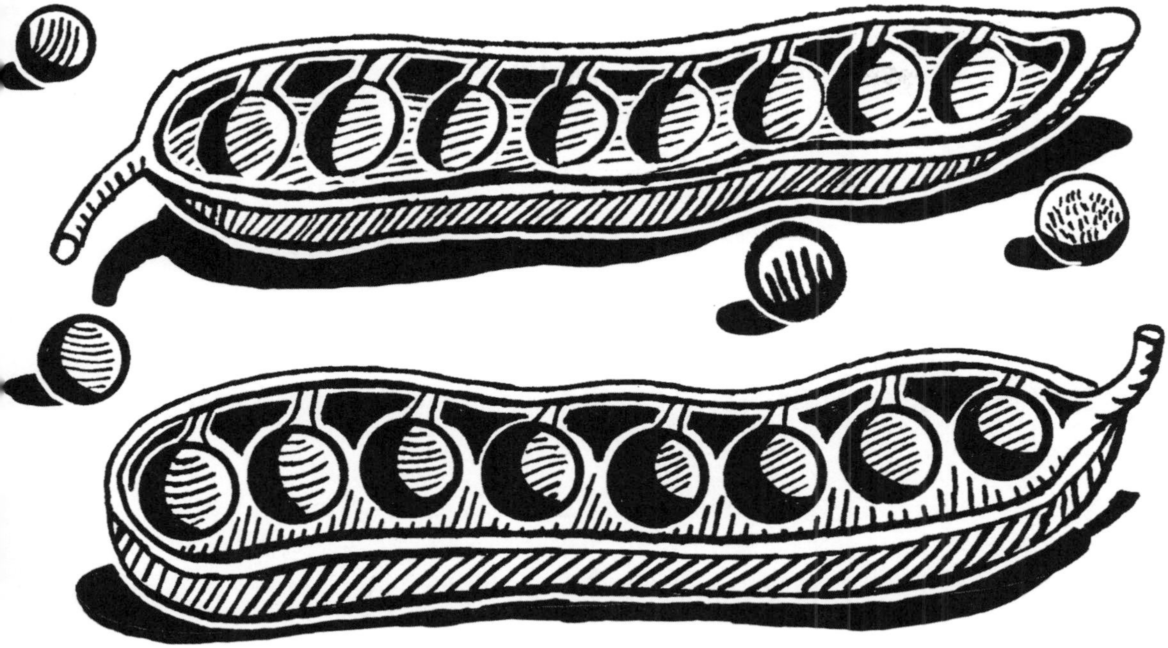

A BUSHEL AND A PECK

Pea & almond pesto with Parmesan biscuits

Duck, pea & cabbage hash

Peas, lettuce & herbs

Pea, broad bean & lettuce salad

There are few dishes I can think of that do not benefit from being eaten with peas. Whether raw, or barely cooked, or boiled for an unseemly length of time due to age, peas mightily brighten and cheer a dish. Early peas are eagerly awaited, among the first of the great harvest of green vegetables that announces the arrival of summer in the British Isles.

It's hard to resist a great heap of peas in the pod and a slab of sheep's cheese set in the middle of a table, encouraging all to pop peas from the pod and eat them with small shards of the cheese. A few young, tender broad beans are a welcome addition here. Add to this pretty scene a dish of radishes, a bowl of sea salt and a generous pat of butter, and there is a fanfare to a summer's repast as elegant and delightful as it is pleasing to eat.

The fresher the pea, the younger it is picked, the sooner it is podded and cooked, the better the eating. Boiled simply and served with a dod of butter, a young garden pea has no equal. But age catches up with us all and so it is with a pea, and should the pods have been parted from their tendrils for even a few days then a starchy toughness forms, in which case they need more cooking, or braising for that matter. One way to tell if peas are past their best is to see if the pods are a bright, fresh-looking green or of a darker hue, with markings on pods full to bursting.

Pea and almond pesto with Parmesan biscuits

Peas coarsely ground with almonds and parsley, mixed with Parmesan and olive oil, are scooped up by a thin crisp biscuit made with feuilles de brick. You can also use this pesto on steamed fish and steamed vegetables, or on grilled bread spread with goat's curd and ricotta. The 'leaves' are best eaten when newly baked.

Feeds 6

250g Parmesan (50g for the biscuits, the rest for the pesto)
50g unsalted butter
10 leaves of feuilles de brick
100g whole blanched almonds
2 cloves of garlic, peeled and chopped
50g picked flat-leaf parsley leaves
125ml extra virgin olive oil
400g peas in their pod, shelled and cooked, or 250–300g cooked weight

Preheat the oven to 180°C and put a baking sheet into the oven.

Grate the cheese, then melt the butter. Unwrap the feuilles de brick, brush each sheet with melted butter and strew with grated Parmesan. Season lightly with sea salt and freshly ground black pepper. Cut each circular brick in half, then fold in four, formed into a fan-shaped leaf. Continue thus until all are done. Refrigerate until required.

Place the almonds, chopped garlic and parsley in a food processor. Add half the oil and grind until coarse. Add the peas to the bowl. Scraping the sides, grind once more until a coarse paste forms. Decant this into a handsome bowl. Check for seasoning, adding salt and pepper.

With care, place the fan-shaped leaves, spaced out, on the hot baking sheet. Bake for 2–3 minutes, then carefully turn them and continue baking for another 2–3 minutes until golden brown. Lift from the tray and continue until all are done. Heap the leaves around the bowl of pesto and serve.

Duck, pea and cabbage hash

PAIRING DUCK WITH PEAS IS A GREAT TRADITION. There is even a play called *Duck with Peas*, and a copy of the script published with beautiful engravings by Thomas Crawshall. But blessed is the kitchen that has leftover duck to make this venerable hash, the supreme leftovers dish. Quantities are really at the cook's discretion.

Any shortfall in meat can be made up with eggs, bacon or vegetables, in this instance peas, perhaps adding a few pea shoots to the mix. A great pan of hash taken to the table generally elicits a happy hum. This can be used for leftover roast meats in general. Trenchermen might need 2 eggs each.

PS: Buying a few duck legs to roast with this dish in mind is a good ploy. Heat the oven to 180°C. Lightly oil an ovenproof pan, season the duck skin with sea salt and lay skin side down in the pan. Place in the oven and turn the heat to 150°C. Roast gently for 45 minutes, then check that it's ready by inserting a sharp knife. If there is no resistance, the leg is done, but leave for longer if required and let rest before they are served.

Feeds 6

3 soup spoons olive oil
2 onions, peeled and chopped small
6 rashers of streaky smoked bacon, cut into small strips
250g cooked peeled potato, chopped into thirds
200–300g cooked duck, coarsely chopped
a small Savoy cabbage, chopped and cooked until tender
200g (approximately) cooked peas
6 organic eggs
2 soup spoons chopped parsley

Heat a large pan over a moderate heat. Pour on a film of the oil to just cover the base of the pan. Add the onions and bacon and fry, stirring regularly, until lightly coloured and translucent. Add the potato and fry gently for a few minutes, then add the duck, cabbage and peas. Fry all together, lifting up and turning until the hash begins to colour, having a care to let the hash cook long enough on the heat, 10–12 minutes, until a light colour and crust forms, before turning. Warm a frying pan and fry the eggs separately in a vegetable or olive oil. Serve together on a big dish, with the eggs sitting on top, and strew with chopped parsley.

Peas, lettuce and herbs

BLESSED WITH SUNSHINE, France and Italy have a wealth of knowledge, cooking and recipes for vegetables and their many varieties that have inspired gardeners and cooks alike for centuries. When I started cooking, English peas with onion and lettuce were known as 'petits pois à la Française'. A simpler name is peas with lettuce – a prosaic title for a dish that for me sums up everything that is wonderful about local regional cooking. Add bacon and it becomes the dish that all Italians love – Roman peas, or 'piselli alla Romana'. Marvellous with many things, such as cecils (page 79), roast chicken or lamb, and all manner of fish such as roast cod, hake, sole or plaice. Instead of a small round onion, the cook might consider using Tropea onions or small leeks, or both.

Feeds 6

1 small onion
100g unsalted butter
750g peas in their pods (300g unpodded)
12 spring onions
lettuce, a soft green one such as butterhead or little gem or both
a small bunch of mint, leaves picked and torn
a small bunch of flat-leaf parsley, leaves picked

Peel and finely chop the onion. Place a wide-bottomed pan over a moderate heat and melt the butter. Add the onion and cover. Cook gently for 20 minutes or so until softened.

Add the podded peas and a glass of water, then replace the lid. Cook these gently for another 20 minutes or so, shaking the pan from time to time to agitate the peas and ensure they are not sticking to the pan.

Slice the spring onions thinly. Separate the leaves from the lettuces and chop coarsely.

Add the sliced spring onions and chopped lettuce to the peas. Season with salt and black pepper. Stir all this well and cover. Cook for 10–12 minutes, stirring now and again, then add the chopped mint and parsley and take to table.

Pea, broad bean and lettuce salad

IN ARABELLA BOXER'S ESTIMABLE BOOK *English Food* are many recipes with great charm, one of which inspired this delightful salad.

Feeds 6

1 cucumber
750g peas in the pod (or 250g frozen)
1 round lettuce, a soft-leaved variety
200g waxy potatoes (Jersey Royals when in season), scrubbed and boiled until tender
500g broad beans in the pod (250g unpodded), blanched and peeled
a handful of mint leaves, chopped
a small bunch of flat-leaf parsley, chopped

For the dressing

1 soup spoon organic cider vinegar
1 soup spoon Dijon mustard
4 soup spoons natural yoghurt
3 soup spoons extra virgin olive oil

Peel the cucumber, split it lengthways and remove the seeds, then slice into pieces roughly 1cm thick and salt very lightly. Put into a colander or a sieve and let drain over a bowl. Cook the peas in boiling water until tender. Leave in the water and set to one side.

Make the dressing: beat together a good pinch each of sea salt and freshly ground black pepper with the vinegar, add the mustard, then the yoghurt and the olive oil. Cover and refrigerate.

Lay the clean lettuce leaves flat on a large dish. Slice the potatoes in half if large, or leave whole. Put the potatoes, peas, cucumber and broad beans into a bowl with the chopped mint and parsley. Add the dressing, mix well and taste for seasoning. Tumble over the lettuce leaves.

PIES

Even the planet must have a crust

PROOF THAT COOKING AT HOME is a worthwhile endeavour lies in a pie. The wisps of steam emanating from, say, chicken, leek and tarragon fused with the aroma of a finely crusted pie baked golden will have noses twitching the second the oven door is open. And pies are also a boon to the home cook because not only do they come in an impressive array of guises, but all the preparation and cooking can be done the day before – benefiting both the pie and the cook equally.

Once those preparations are done, assembling a pie is a straightforward affair of decanting the braise into a handsome dish, perhaps inserting a chimney – a marrow bone as mighty as a smoke stack – then placing in the oven.

And then there are steamed suet pudding recipes, like the one here for kid pudding, inspired by the mighty steak and kidney pudding unique to the British Isles. Requiring less time to steam, a pleasing alternative is to make a braise, say, with kid, which improves with cooking the day before. Line the basin with rolled-out suet pastry then ladle in the braise. Place a layer of pastry atop, trim the edges and seal with a lid or with a sheet each of greaseproof paper then tin foil, to be tied tightly with string, prior to steaming in a pan. Furthering the enjoyment of the theatre of a suet pudding, I like to serve these puddings, removed from the pan, with a large napkin tied round prior to taking to table.

There are of course lighter pies requiring less cooking. Shepherd's pie, for instance, makes excellent use of any leftovers from serving a roast or a braise. And vegetable pies are made with spinach or chard, or both, leaves and stalks piled with cheese and onions, and herbs both dried and fresh depending on what is at hand.

There is a lovely French pie that I much enjoy making – flamiche. Leeks encased in puff pastry, or shortcrust perhaps (an old Scots version of this is leeks encased in suet crust and steamed). Not too distant a relation is a jalousie, a pie formed from a sheet of puff pastry heaped with mushrooms or pumpkin, then laid upon this is another sheet of pastry cut through many times, to emulate the Venetian blinds that give the pie its name. I baked a lot of these when I cooked for Duff & Trotter, a catering firm, sadly long gone. Baked crisp and then left to cool until just warm, cut into slices, jalousies are estimable. Make them in miniature and they become excellent company for drinks.

Pies layered with filo pastry are always worth considering. They make excellent use of all manner of vegetables, such as courgettes, artichokes, peas, asparagus and broad beans, as well as the more familiar spinach and chard. Between the layers of filo are spread the vegetables, with chopped herbs, chopped nuts such as almonds or pistachios, and perhaps some cheese such as ricotta or Parmesan, or indeed both, a whisper of garlic and a grating or two of nutmeg.

PS: Any leftover pastry can be fashioned into kickshaws, a favourite of my mum's – small geegaws or dainties made from scraps of pastry rolled out thinly, cut into roughly shaped triangles, each stuffed with a nut-sized spoonful of the pie filling chopped fine. Once the edges are sealed, the kickshaw looks like a small pyramid. These are then refrigerated until needed, when they are deep-fried and served piping hot. Particular favourites were made from lifting a few spoonfuls of chicken or mushroom jalousie filling (see below).

Mushroom jalousie

THE JALOUSIE HAS MANY INCISIONS made in the pastry to let the steam out, so the pastry can crisp. A large version of this old-fashioned pie is very good, but when made smaller, cooked crisp, cooled then sliced, it makes excellent bites with drinks.

Feeds 6

25g dried porcini
3 or 4 shallots
3 cloves of garlic
50g unsalted butter (or use 2 soup spoons of olive oil instead)
1kg large flat mushrooms, peeled and halved then blitzed fine in a food processor
75ml white wine
1 small finger-sized bundle of thyme and summer savory
1 handful chopped parsley
125g freshly grated Parmesan
500g puff pastry or rough puff (see page 251)
1 organic egg, beaten with a teaspoon of cream to make a glaze

Soak the porcini in water for 30 minutes. Peel and finely chop the shallots and the garlic, then cook in the butter (or oil) in a pan. Drain the soaked porcini, chop, add to the shallots and cook gently for 10 minutes, then add the flat mushrooms. Cook until the mushrooms are bubbling away. Add the wine, thyme and summer savory, season with salt and black pepper and cook for a further 5–10 minutes, until no trace of liquid remains. Remove from the heat, take out the thyme and add the parsley and Parmesan. Spread the mushrooms on a flat tray and let cool. (This can be made the day before, very much to its benefit, I find.)

Preheat the oven to 200°C.

Roll half the pastry out quite thin and cut into two long strips, 5cm wide, 30cm long. Lay these on a baking sheet lined with baking parchment. Roll out another two lengths with the other half, 1cm wider. Fold these in half lengthways and make incisions every 2mm along the length of the pastry except for 1cm at each end.

Form the mushroom mixture into the shape of a rod and lay along the middle of the pastry (the strips on the baking parchment) from one end to the other, leaving a 1cm border each side. Lightly brush the edges with egg wash. Take the lengths of cut pastry and lay them over the mushroom filling, pressing lightly round the edges until aligned, trimming the edges to neaten if necessary. Egg wash the surface and fully press down the edges with the tines of a fork. Refrigerate for at least 30 minutes. (These can be made the day before.)

Place the tray in the heated oven and lower the heat to 180°C. Bake for 30 minutes, until well coloured and crisp. Remove from the oven and cool before slicing and serving.

These are best eaten just warm. A flourish of freshly grated Parmesan atop is a happy consideration.

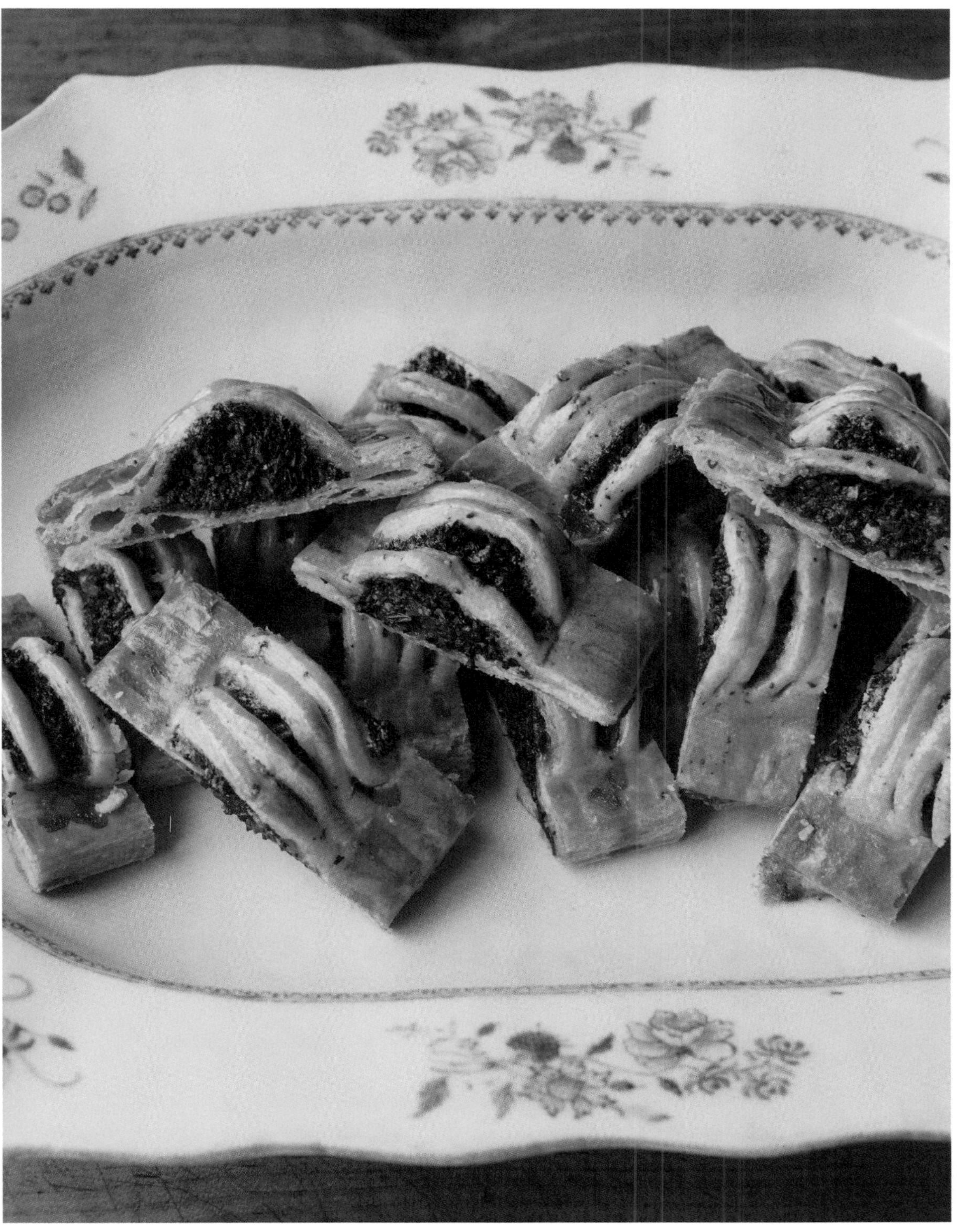

Artichoke and ricotta pie

THIS IS A PAIRING OF A CURIOUS PASTRY made with ricotta, with the softness of the artichokes, which has much charm.

Feeds 6

ricotta pastry (see page 253)

For the filling

4 large globe artichokes, or 8 to 9 small ones
juice and grated zest of 1 unwaxed lemon
2 medium onions
1 clove of garlic
the heart and leaves from half a head of celery
3 soup spoons olive oil
5 bay leaves
300g very good ricotta
a very big handful of flat-leaf parsley, chopped
75g freshly grated Parmesan
1 egg yolk
1 soup spoon double cream

Exerting some force, snap the stalks from the heads of the artichoke, thus ensuring all the fibrous stalks are pulled from the heart. Pull away each leaf from the heart until the tip of the heart is exposed. Cut the rest of the leaves away. Use a very sharp little knife to cut away any green upon the heart and neaten the sides. Remove the fibrous choke inside the heart. Repeat until all are done. Toss each heart in the lemon juice. Set aside.

Peel the onions and garlic and chop small along with the celery. Warm a wide, shallow pan, heat 2 soup spoons of the olive oil and cook the celery, onions, garlic and bay leaves gently until softened though uncoloured. Slice the artichokes very, very thinly and add to the pot with the lemon juice, stirring well to coat completely. Pour on enough water to barely cover the vegetables, adding a little salt and black pepper. Simmer for 20–30 minutes, until the slices are fully cooked and any residual liquid has been boiled away. Set aside to cool.

Preheat the oven to 180°C. When the artichokes have cooled, remove the bay leaves, stir in the ricotta, the remaining 1 soup spoon of olive oil, the lemon zest, chopped parsley and Parmesan, with some more salt and pepper. Line a 23cm x 4cm tart tin with the larger round of dough, crimping and then trimming the edges, and fill the pie. Roll the smaller piece to fit the surface and trim away any excess. Cut a small hole in the centre. Beat the egg yolk and double cream well, then brush evenly over the pastry lid. Bake the pie until beautifully coloured, say roughly 60 minutes. Turn down the heat and cover if it's colouring too quickly. Best served just warm.

Leek pie

IN FLANDERS, LEEK PIE IS POETICALLY NAMED 'FLAMICHE', Flemish for gâteau, as much revered as its not too distant cousin quiche Lorraine. I like the Presbyterian forthrightness of leek pie.

Feeds 6

250g shortcrust pastry (see page 252), plus flour for dusting
1kg leeks, both green and white parts
1 small onion
1 stick of celery
30g unsalted butter
2 whole organic eggs, plus 1 yolk
1 small teaspoon Dijon mustard
60ml double cream, plus a teaspoon for the egg wash
a big pinch of thyme or summer savory
1 heaped soup spoon chopped flat-leaf parsley

Make a batch of shortcrust pastry or use frozen. Cut the dough into 2 pieces, roughly one-third and two-thirds. Roll the larger piece into a disc on a lightly floured surface and use it to line a 23cm tart case. Roll out the other piece of dough to make a smaller disc just large enough to cover the tart case. Refrigerate both.

Chop the leeks and wash well, then drain thoroughly. Peel and chop the onion and celery, place in a wide heavy-bottomed pot with the butter, then cover and cook gently for 20 minutes or so until softened completely. Season with salt and black pepper, stirring from time to time over a moderate heat, covered, until just cooked. Add the leeks and stir well. Return the lid and cook for about 15 minutes until softened. Drain and cool.

Preheat the oven to 200°C. Beat together the 2 eggs, mustard and cream in a large bowl. Add the leek, onion and celery mixture, stir in the thyme and parsley, and mix well. Ladle the leeks and egg into the lined tart shell. Brush the edges lightly with egg wash made with the single egg yolk mixed with a teaspoon of double cream, and lay on the pastry lid. Seal the edges, pressing down with your thumb. Brush the pastry with the rest of the egg wash. Cut a small hole in the centre, and bake in the middle of the oven for 40 minutes until golden and crisp. Best when served just warm.

Cottage pie

LEFTOVERS ALWAYS MAKE THE BEST COTTAGE PIES, and this one is made from the remains of a pan of braised oxtail. So, to attain the genuine article, make a large pan of braised oxtail and the leftovers will then form next day's cottage pie. Lamb, beef or mutton can replace the oxtail, braised to the same recipe.

Feeds 6

For the braised oxtail

4 soup spoons light oil, such as sunflower oil
3 oxtails, roughly 1.5–2kg (or 1.5kg of lamb, beef or mutton)
200g piece of unsmoked streaky bacon, cut into small strips
2 bottles of full-bodied red wine
3 onions
4 large carrots
7 stalks of celery, the heart and the leaves
2 cloves of garlic, peeled and thinly sliced
a small bundle of thyme
7 bay leaves
1.5kg mashing potatoes, such as Maris Piper
a whole head of savoy cabbage
a head of spring greens

Heat a large ovenproof pot and pour in enough oil to just cover the bottom. Add enough pieces of oxtail to just cover, and let cook undisturbed until browned. Turn the oxtail over and colour, then turn on to its sides until crusted all over. Repeat until all the pieces are done. Lift the oxtail out into a waiting colander set over a bowl. Fry the bacon in the same pot, add to the oxtail in the colander, discard the fat from the pot, then pour in 200ml of red wine and bring to a boil, stirring with a wooden spoon, adding more wine if required, to aid the loosening of any goodness adhering to the bottom of the pan. Pour the result through a fine sieve into a waiting pan and reserve.

Preheat the oven to 180°C. Peel the vegetables and chop into large pieces. Add a little clean oil to the pot, tip in the vegetables and let brown, then stir, add the garlic, and continue thus until the vegetables are browned all over. To this add the bacon and the set-aside contents of the deglazed pan. Pour in the rest of the red wine and boil for 5 minutes. Return the oxtail to the pot with all the herbs tied together, plus a pinch each of sea salt and black pepper. Top up with water if necessary, to ensure the oxtail is covered, then bring to the boil, seal tightly with a lid, place in the oven and cook gently for 4 hours until tender.

To serve the braise, with cottage pie in mind, make a large pan of mashed potato to ensure plenty of leftovers. Similarly with spring greens and cabbage, cook a lot more than is required for serving.

Pick the meat from the leftover oxtail bones and lay in a wide, deep, ovenproof dish. Strew with the leftover greens. Lay mashed potato atop and spread using the tines of a fork. Bake in a hot oven for 50 minutes or so, until piping hot and browned.

Courgette, green bean, ricotta, feta and filo pie

DEBORAH MADISON'S EXCELLENT *THE GREENS COOKBOOK* inspired this recipe. Curiously, filo pastry seems to appear very rarely now, which is a great shame.

Serves 6

125g pine nuts or blanched almonds
2 small onions
3 cloves of garlic
1 mild green chilli pepper
1 unwaxed lemon
2 soup spoons olive oil
500g courgettes, cut into 1cm-thick slices
200g green beans, topped and tailed
300g spinach, leaves picked and washed
75g Parmesan, finely grated
a pinch of dried chilli flakes
150g mild feta or ricotta
125g melted butter or olive oil, plus extra melted butter for brushing
½ a packet of filo pastry (refreeze the other half if not using)

Heat the oven to 180°C. Place the pine nuts or almonds on a tray and bake in the oven until golden, 3–5 minutes only. Peel and finely chop the onions and garlic. Finely chop the green chilli pepper, having a care for any excessive heat in the seeds – this is best judged with a seed placed on the tip of the tongue. A dab of sugar to the tongue will resolve any surprise. Finely grate the lemon zest.

Heat a wide-bottomed pan and add the olive oil, then add the onions and garlic and cook gently under a lid over a moderate heat. After 5 minutes, add the sliced courgettes and the chopped green chilli, stir well, return the lid and let cook gently while preparing the remainder of the filling. Cook the green beans in a pan of boiling lightly salted water. Once cooked, lift the beans from the pan with a pair of tongs and cool under cold running water. Cook the spinach for a minute or two, until wilted, in the same water as the beans. Drain the spinach and cool quickly in cold water. Once cooled, lift out the spinach, squeeze dry and chop coarsely.

In a large bowl place the cooked courgettes, green beans, spinach, pine nuts, grated lemon zest, Parmesan, chilli flakes and the feta or ricotta, and season with salt and pepper. Mix quickly and deftly.

Brush the inside of a dish roughly 30cm x 20cm x 5cm with the melted butter. Lightly brush the first sheet of filo pastry and lay in the dish with 2–3cm hanging over the edge. Continue until 2 layers have lined the dish. Spoon half the vegetable and cheese mixture evenly over the pastry. There is no need to smooth. Sparingly, butter enough filo to just cover the mixture, then spoon over the remainder. Fold over the overhanging pastry. Lightly butter the remaining sheets and let them fall in folds over the pie until well covered. Distribute any remaining butter over the pastry. Bake for 35–40 minutes, until golden brown.

Chicken, leek and tarragon pie

THE BETTER THE CHICKEN THE BETTER THE PIE – so seeking out a dry-plucked chicken from a good supplier is worth the effort.

Feeds 6

1 whole chicken
1 onion
1 carrot
1 leek
2 sticks of celery
5 rashers of unsmoked streaky bacon
a small bunch of thyme or summer savory
5 bay leaves
300ml white wine
4 leeks, firm and fresh, with greens attached preferably
100ml double cream, plus a teaspoon for the glaze
a soup spoon Dijon mustard
a soup spoon picked chopped tarragon leaves
a small bunch of flat-leaf parsley, leaves picked and chopped
flaky shortcrust pastry with lard (see page 253)
1 organic egg, beaten, to glaze

Place the chicken in a close-fitting pot. Peel the vegetables, chop them into smallish pieces, cut the bacon into small strips, and place all around the chicken. Tie the herbs into a small bundle and add to the pot. Season, then add the white wine and 100ml of water. Bring to the boil, simmer for 30 minutes, then turn off the heat and let cool with the lid still in place.

Slice the leeks and wash well. Plunge them into a pan of boiling salted water and cook for a few minutes until tender. Drain the leeks and spread on a flat tray to cool.

Heat the oven to 180°C. Lift the chicken from the pot and pick the meat. Lift the vegetables and bacon from the pot and discard the herbs. Bring the stock back to the boil, spooning away any foam rising to the surface. Add the cream and boil for a few minutes. Mix together the chicken meat, mustard, leeks, vegetables, bacon, tarragon and parsley, then spoon into a deep, wide pie dish roughly 30cm x 4–5cm. A pie chimney of sorts is helpful here.

Roll out the pastry on a floured surface and lay atop, letting it drape slightly down the sides. Tidy the edges. Beat the egg yolk and double cream well, then brush evenly over the pastry lid. Make an incision in the middle if not using a chimney and bake for 45–50 minutes, until browned and piping hot.

Steamed kid pudding

YOU CAN SUBSTITUTE LAMB OR PORK IN THIS DISH. The braise is ideally done the day before.

Feeds 6

For the braise

1kg kid, leg and shoulder meat
150g unsmoked streaky bacon
2 onions
2 carrots
2 sticks of celery
2 cloves of garlic
a sprig each of thyme and summer savory
4 bay leaves
4 soup spoons sunflower oil
500ml red wine
suet pastry (see page 253)

Trim and chop the kid and bacon into pieces roughly 2cm across. Season with sea salt and black pepper. Peel and chop the vegetables and garlic into small pieces. Tie the herbs into a small bundle. Heat half the sunflower oil in a wide heavy-bottomed frying pan over a brisk heat and fry the kid in small batches until crusted brown all over. Lift the meat from the pan into a colander set over a bowl. Fry the strips of bacon and then set aside. Add the rest of the oil, then tip the chopped vegetables into the pan and brown lightly. Add the herbs, wine and the bones (if using) and season with sea salt and pepper. Top up with water until the braise is just covered, then bring to a simmer and spoon away any foam rising. Cover the pot and let cook for 1½ hours, until the kid is tender. Remove from the heat and let cool.

Roll out two-thirds of the pastry and line a buttered pudding basin, approximately 18–20cm x 12–15cm. Roll out the remaining piece to just fit on top.

When completely cooled, decant the whole braise into the pastry-lined pudding bowl. Lay the disc of pastry atop and pinch the edges to seal. Lay a sheet of greaseproof paper over the pastry, then two sheets of foil. Tie this tightly with string. Sit the pudding on an inverted plate in a pan of simmering water coming two-thirds up the side of the pudding. Seal the pan tightly and let simmer for 2½ hours, checking from time to time if more water is required. Once done, remove the bowl from the pan. Lift away the foil and greaseproof paper. Tie a napkin around the bowl and take to table.

Game pie

Feeds 6

suet pastry (see page 253)
1 organic egg yolk and 1 teaspoon of double cream, to glaze

For the filling

300g shoulder of beef
300g haunch of venison
2 legs of hare
150g sliced smoked streaky bacon
4 small onions
3 carrots
4 sticks of celery
4 soup spoons sunflower or vegetable oil
500ml chicken stock
750ml red wine
50ml Madeira
6 bay leaves
a small sprig each of thyme, summer savory, and parsley
marrow bones for a chimney (optional)

Trim the beef, venison and hare and chop into roughly 2cm pieces. Cut the bacon into thick strips. Peel the vegetables and chop into small pieces. Heat half the oil in a pan over a brisk heat, and fry the meat and bacon in batches until browned thoroughly. Lift into a colander over a bowl and continue thus until all is done. Add the rest of the oil to the pan, tip in the vegetables and brown lightly. Add the stock, wine, Madeira and the herbs tied in a neat little bundle. Return the browned meat to the pan and bring all to a simmer, lifting away any detritus arising on the surface. Cover and let the braise cook gently for 2 hours, until the meat yields to the touch. Should there be an excessive amount of sauce, up the heat and let it bubble away until the sauce is reduced, just covering the meat. Once done, remove from the heat, and let the braise cool.

Preheat the oven to 180°C. Roll out the pastry slightly larger than the width of the pie dish, to ensure a neat overhang. Spoon the cooled braise into a pie dish. Place the marrow bone or preferred chimney piece in the meat (optional) and lay on the pastry, with incisions cut for the chimney as the mantle of pastry drapes over the pie. Tidy the edges. Brush the pastry with egg wash (the egg yolk beaten with the double cream) and bake for 50 minutes, until browned and piping hot.

Pastry recipes

BUSY LIVES LEAVE PRECIOUS LITTLE TIME for making pastry from scratch, so by all means buy pastry ready-made. But spare a thought for the quiet satisfaction of making your own. Rough puff pastry seems involved but in fact is mostly about the 20 minutes resting time between turns, which is whiled away preparing other ingredients such as vegetables and herbs. Suet crust is swiftly made and requires no rests or turns at all. Shortcrust pastry is made with relative ease. All pastry freezes well, so any unused pastry can be wrapped and frozen.

Rough puff pastry

500g plain flour, plus extra for dusting
500g cold unsalted butter, cut into small squares
a big pinch of salt
250ml cold water

Sift the flour onto a wide surface or into a large bowl. Add the cold butter and salt, then, using your fingertips, work the butter into the flour until it resembles coarse crumbs. Slowly add the water, about 50ml at a time, working deftly until all the water has been added. The dough will not be even but needs to be shaped into a rough ball and covered and refrigerated for 20 minutes.

Lightly flour the surface and roll the ball into a rectangle, 40cm x 20cm approximately. Fold this in three and turn 90°. Roll into the same sized rectangle again and fold in three. Cover and refrigerate for 20 minutes. Repeat this two more times, turning each folded rectangle 90°. Chill the pastry for an hour, or overnight, or freeze for future use.

Shortcrust pastry

250g plain flour, sifted, plus extra for dusting
a pinch of salt
125g cold unsalted butter, cut into small pieces
2 teaspoons caster sugar
1 organic egg
2 teaspoons cold water

Put the flour and salt into the bowl of a food processor. Add the butter and sugar, then combine to make a fine crumb. Crack the egg and yolk into a cup, add the water and beat with a fork. Add to the bowl and work until a dough forms. Tip the dough onto a lightly floured surface and knead lightly until smooth. Divide into two, wrapping one half tightly in greaseproof paper for use another day, storing in an airtight container in the freezer for up to 3–4 months. Form the other half into a round, cover and refrigerate for at least an hour or overnight before using.

Shortcrust pastry with lard

150g unsalted butter
70g lard
330g plain flour
1 organic egg yolk
120ml very cold water
a pinch of salt

Work the butter, lard and flour nimbly to make a fine crumb. Beat the egg yolk with the cold water and salt and add to the pastry. Deftly mix, then knead into a dough. Wrap tightly in greaseproof paper and refrigerate.

Flaky shortcrust pastry with lard

360g plain flour, sifted
170g cold unsalted butter
60g cold lard
3–4 soup spoons ice-cold water

Place the flour and a pinch of salt in a wide, deep bowl. Cut the butter and lard into even-sized pieces, add to the flour and cut with a knife into small pieces. Rub with your fingertips so the pieces fall like flakes back into the bowl. There is no need to make a fine crumb. Add the ice-cold water and mix lightly into a ball. Shape the ball into a disc and cover tightly with greaseproof paper. Refrigerate.

Ricotta pastry

70g unsalted butter
225g ricotta
225g plain flour, plus extra for dusting

Allow the butter to soften before using. Place the butter, ricotta, flour and a pinch of salt in a bowl and mix. Knead the dough gently until smooth. Cut one-third of the dough away, then form two flat rounds, wrap them in greaseproof paper and refrigerate.

Suet pastry

225g self-raising flour
115g shredded suet
1 organic egg yolk
7–8 soup spoons whole milk

Sift the flour into a wide bowl. Add the suet and a pinch of salt. Add the egg yolk to the milk and beat. Deftly mix all into a soft dough and cover. Roll out to the required size on a lightly floured surface.

POTATOES

EARTHY DELIGHTS

Potato pancakes, smoked eel, poached eggs and horseradish

Sarladaise potatoes

Potato, Jerusalem artichoke and celeriac gratin

Potato & wild mushroom cakes

Rumbledethumps

Potato & artichoke salad

Jansson's temptation

Pommes Anna

Potato & olive cakes

Potato salad

WILL THERE BE JERSEYS OR AYRSHIRES FIRST? Dad asked this question every year as spring approached, impatient for a bowl of new potatoes with butter and parsley, a ritual that defines spring as much as sunshine, pea shoots and all the other green things that appear so suddenly after the winter chill.

And sure enough, Bobby Milroy, our greengrocer at the Sinderins on the Perth Road in Dundee, would finally get one or two little baskets of Jersey Royals or Ayrshires, usually the former, since the latter, grown on the west coast of Scotland, a bit further north and that much colder than the Channel Islands, came later. Dad ate new potatoes almost daily throughout their brief season, finishing off with a very good early from Cornwall which arrives at the beginning of summer, shortly after Jersey Royals.

A 'new' potato, regardless of size, is easily identified, having only papery flakes covering the milky-hued potato within, requiring but a rub and a scrub to clean prior to cooking. Once the skin sets and becomes firm during August and September, the highly esteemed new potatoes become mids, which in this cook's opinion can be even more flavoursome than their costly siblings. To optimise a crop of new potatoes and keep them small, you simply need to plant them closer together.

Jersey potatoes have been granted a DOP, a geographical indication deeming this potato worthy of government protection and ensuring they can only be grown on the Channel Islands with seaweed harvested from the Jersey shoreline. Ayrshire earlies also have a DOP.

These potatoes are but three of the varieties grown in the British Isles and Ireland, a tiny number compared to myriad varieties grown around the world. As Alan Davidson wisely observed, such is the scale of the subject of the potato it is either a paragraph or fifty pages.

Some UK varieties, such as Maris Piper, Kerr's Pink and King Edward, are lauded as 'all-rounders', growing well wherever they are planted and good for boiling, baking, steaming, mashing, roasting, gratins and of course chips. These varieties are admired by independent growers and supermarkets alike, and may well be among the varieties sold in bags marked for a particular type of cooking. There is efficiency in this degree of sorting and grading, but often these potatoes have been in storage for a long time, which diminishes flavour and nutrients.

It's always worth looking out for different varieties of potato grown locally that may not make the supermarket shelves but turn up at a greengrocer or on a market table near you. Cooking in Soho and Hackney, I rely greatly on deliveries, often by post, from growers as far flung as Hereford, Cornwall, Northumberland and Kent. The miles travelled are compensated for by produce grown free of chemicals on carefully nurtured land.

Among our favourite suppliers are Lucy and Anthony Carroll, who grow potatoes on their farm in Northumberland. So successful were they that they began taking their potatoes to a farmers' market in Berwick, where they caught the attention of a great many folk and restaurants, laying the foundations for Carroll's Heritage Potatoes, a splendid business with an excellent website listing the varieties grown and how they like best to be cooked.

Carroll's grow familiar varieties such as Pink Fir Apple 1850, Alberta, King Edwards, Maris Piper, Yukon Gold and Mayan Gold, as well as those less well known, such as Aura 1951, Arran Victory 1918, Violetta and Sharpe's Express. Even more beguiling are their heritage varieties, with curious names such as Mr Little's Yetholm Gypsy 1899, a variety developed by Mr Little in the Scottish Border village of Yetholm, the Gypsy capital. They have a distinctive swirled blue, white and red skin and a white floury flesh. The Shetland Black 1923 is another historic variety. It has a dark purple skin and when cut open a blue antioxidant ring is exposed.

A prized variety is the Ratte. This was the potato chosen by the most famous French chef of his day, Joël Robuchon, to make his legendary mashed potato, of which stories abound concerning the amount of butter he added to cooked and sieved Ratte potatoes. His recipe states 250g of butter to 1kg of mash, but this might just be false modesty. A somewhat healthier alternative was made with olive oil and a splash of cream by an equally renowned chef, Frédy Girardet, author of *La Cuisine Spontanée*, who cooked in Crissier in Switzerland.

A waxy potato is not the first choice for mash in the British Isles, and certainly not the further north you go. It's fair to say that Scotland and Ireland excel at floury, soft-hearted potatoes that make the cloud-like mash I remember from my childhood. This memory is bolstered by Jane Scotter at Fern Verrow, a biodynamic farm in the foothills of the Black Mountains in Herefordshire, who grows potatoes that are chosen to fuel comfort and nostalgia as much as for quality and flavour. Among impeccable fields of flowers, leaves, herbs, fruits and vegetables, she grows varieties such as Cara, Charlotte and Arran Victory, superb for roasting (requiring a gentle steam for a few minutes before roasting. It is worth mentioning that most potatoes steam very well as an alternative to boiling).

Considering the history of the potato, its origins in the high altitudes of the Andes and its journey through time and place to become one of the world's most valued crops, it seems right that potatoes – and their growers – should be afforded a great deal of respect. As my father realised, and I have come to learn, it takes a surprising amount of effort to ensure a bowl of new potatoes graces the table every year.

When considering potatoes: a few notes on sizes and grading

Most potatoes are sown early in the year and harvested from late spring/summer onwards. They are harvested almost to order through the summer, with one huge effort required in the autumn to dig through September and October and harvest the last potatoes before the first frosts appear.

Grading by size

A new potato, regardless of size, has flaky skin easily removed by rubbing and a light scrub. Most new potatoes are sold when small and, if larger, are simply sold as large or baking potatoes.

Once the skin of a potato 'sets', it's no longer a new potato. Roughly speaking, when a potato can no longer be rubbed clean, when the skin has set and must now be peeled, it has become a 'mid'.

There is little difference between first early potatoes and second early potatoes, which also includes new potatoes. These potatoes continue through May, June, July and August.

'Tinies' is a term coined by Lucy and Anthony Carroll for a rogue, very small size of potato that does not fit when grading sizes. With each dig, some tinies will emerge – some varieties produce lots, or very few or none at all, so making enquiries is advised.

Large potatoes are fully grown, harvested in the autumn before the first frosts.

What are they good for?

A few varieties and their uses

All-rounders, good for pretty much anything: Cara, Kerr's Pink, Maris Piper, Maris Peer, Nicola, Alberta, King Edward, Désirée.

Steaming, boiling: varieties of new potatoes and earlies such as Jersey (Royals), Charlotte, Ayrshire and Cornish and all the other earlies.

Roasting: all-rounders and earlies; particularly good are Arran Pilot/Victory, Ayrshire (these should be gently scrubbed before simmering briefly so as not to break up and collapse in the pan. Drain thoroughly and roast in goose, duck or pork fat or olive oil for 45 minutes to 1 hour).

Frying: all-rounders, also Aura, Mayan Gold, Yukon Gold.

Galettes: all-rounders, also Mayan Gold, Yukon Gold, King Edward.

Gratins: all-rounders, also Mayan Gold.

Floury mash: all-rounders, Pentland Crown, Ayrshires, Arran Pilot/Victory.

New potatoes for simply boiling and serving with butter and parsley: Jersey Royals, Ayrshire earlies, Cornish earlies, Charlotte, Pink Fir, Mr Little's Yetholm Gypsy.

Potato pancakes, smoked eel, poached eggs and horseradish

GIVEN THE RECIPE FOR THESE PANCAKES BY HIS MOTHER, La Mère Blanc, Georges Blanc, having become famous at his restaurant in Vonnas near Lyon, published it in his book *Ma Cuisine des Saisons*. Originally cooked like blinis, as fame grew so did their stature, the individual blini pan becoming as famous in kitchen shops as the pancakes themselves in kitchens.

I loved best the version Alastair Little cooked at his restaurant in Soho, kindling an abiding love of smoked eel, although a discreet veil should be drawn over his opinion of Mr Blanc.

Feeds 2

450g floury potatoes, such as King Edward
95g self-raising flour
150ml double cream
150ml full-fat milk
3 whole organic eggs, plus 2 whites
350g smoked eel fillet
2 rashers of unsmoked streaky bacon
2 room-temperature organic eggs, for poaching
2 soup spoons light oil, such as sunflower
150g horseradish cream (see page 146)
a small bunch of chives, very finely chopped

The batter, smoked eel, horseradish cream and chives can all be prepared earlier in the day.

Peel the potatoes, rinse well and cut into even-sized pieces. Place these in a steamer over a gentle heat until fully cooked. Put the potatoes, hot from the steamer, into a food processor with the flour, cream, milk, a pinch of salt and black pepper, the 3 whole eggs and 2 egg whites and beat vigorously until smooth. Decant the batter into a container, cover and refrigerate for at least an hour.

Cut the fillet of eel into 1cm-thick slices and sit them on a plate to one side.

While the batter chills, heat the oven to 160°C. Lay the rashers of bacon on a wire rack over a baking tray (or in a grill tray) and bake in the oven until crisp, roughly 12 minutes. Lower the oven to 120°C to keep the bacon warm.

Bring a pan of water to the boil. Add a pinch of salt and gently poach the 2 eggs for 3–4 minutes, until the white is firm and the yolk runny. Place these in a dish and keep warm in the oven.

Heat a non-stick frying pan roughly 19cm in diameter over a moderate heat. Lightly oil the pan, then pour in a large ladle of batter and cook for around 2 minutes, until puffed at the edges. Carefully flip and cook on the other side until brown. Remove to a warm dish in the oven and repeat for the other pancake.

Place each pancake on a plate, lay on the pieces of smoked eel and add a spoonful of horseradish cream. On this sit a warm poached egg, the rashers of bacon and finally a scattering of chives.

Sarladaise potatoes

A BAKING SHEET OR STONE IS VERY USEFUL HERE. You will need an 18cm cast-iron skillet. At the restaurant we make individual Sarladaise, using small cast-iron pans about 10–12cm in diameter.

Feeds 6

a sprig of rosemary
4 cloves of garlic, peeled and thinly sliced
200g goose or duck fat
1kg large potatoes, such as King Edward or Mayan Gold

Preheat the oven to 200°C. Put a baking sheet or stone in to heat.

Pick the rosemary leaves and put them into a pot with the garlic and the goose or duck fat. Place over a gentle heat to infuse for 2–3 minutes. Peel the potatoes and slice thinly. A mandoline makes swift work of this.

Sit an 18cm cast-iron skillet over a moderate heat. Pour 80g of the goose or duck fat infusion over the bottom of the pan. Lay a concentric circle of potato slices around this and continue until you reach the sides of the pan. Lay on a few spears of rosemary and sliced garlic from the infused fat. Season lightly with sea salt and black pepper. Add a spoonful of the fat. Repeat the overlapping circles of potato, rosemary, garlic, sea salt, pepper and a teaspoonful of fat until no potato remains. Pour on any remaining fat. Excess can be drained from the dish after cooking, passed through a sieve, cooled and stored in sealed jar, to be used at a later date. The centre will be peaked slightly higher than the sides. Up the heat and when the sides of the pan are bubbling merrily, place in the oven on the heated baking sheet or stone.

Cook for 25 minutes, then open the oven. Use the bottom of a frying pan to press down gently on the potato cake. Remove the frying pan and continue to cook for a further 20–25 minutes, until the potatoes are a deep mahogany. Remove from the oven and let sit for 5 minutes. With a spatula, carefully loosen the cake round the edges, moving the spatula towards the centre, lifting gently as you go. Place a dish or a board over the pan and invert in one swift move, having a care for any spillage of hot fat.

Potato, Jerusalem artichoke and celeriac gratin

THIS CAN ALL BE PREPARED IN ADVANCE, for assembly and cooking later in the day.

Feeds 6

750g potatoes such as King Edward or Maris Piper, peeled
750g celeriac, peeled
750g Jerusalem artichokes, peeled
100ml whole milk
300ml double cream
a nutmeg

Heat the oven to 160°C.

Slice the peeled potatoes thinly. Place the slices in a bowl and run these under cold water until all trace of starch is washed away, then pat dry. Slice the celeriac thinly. Slice the Jerusalem artichokes thinly, roughly 3mm thick.

Lay the slices of celeriac evenly over the base of a wide, deep ovenproof dish. Season lightly with salt and black pepper. Add a layer of Jerusalem artichoke slices, then lay over the slices of potato.

Warm the milk and cream and season with sea salt, freshly ground black pepper and freshly grated nutmeg, then pour gently over the vegetables. Place in the oven and bake for 1 hour, until golden brown. Insert a knife to ensure the vegetables are quite cooked. Let the gratin sit for 10 minutes or so before serving, warming through if required.

Potato and wild mushroom cakes

Feeds 6

125g dried porcini
1 onion
25g unsalted butter
3 soup spoons olive oil
1 clove of garlic
a small handful of curly parsley
1kg potatoes such as King Edward or similar, or Mayan Gold, boiled in their skins and left to cool
1 organic egg
50g finely grated Parmesan
a handful of plain flour
light vegetable oil

Soak the dried mushrooms in water and leave until quite softened, at least 20 minutes.

Peel and finely chop the onion. In a pan over a moderate heat, melt the butter and add the olive oil, then add the onion and cook gently until softened and coloured only lightly, at least 20 minutes.

Lift the mushrooms from the water and squeeze lightly to remove any excess. (Check too for any grit adhering to the mushrooms. A careful rinse is a wise manoeuvre.) Chop the mushrooms coarsely. Add them to the onion and cook gently until slightly darker and no liquid remains in the pan, roughly 15 minutes.

Peel the garlic and chop finely, add to the pan, stir well, cook for a minute, then remove from the heat. Chop the parsley and add to the pan of onion and mushrooms.

Heat the oven to 150°C.

Tip the cooled boiled potatoes, the mushrooms and onion, egg and Parmesan into a bowl. Season with salt and black pepper. Mix with your hands until all is brought together in a rough mix. Form into coarse round cakes and refrigerate for 30 minutes or so.

Tip the flour onto a plate and season thoroughly. Warm a frying pan on the stove and, when hot, add a few spoonfuls of vegetable oil. Lightly dip the cakes in the flour, pressing only gently. Sit them in the oil to fry gently until crusted and golden, about 12–15 minutes, then turn and repeat. Lift the cakes from the pan, put them into an ovenproof dish and continue until all are done.

Keep these in the warm oven and serve piping hot, with fried eggs or another grating of Parmesan.

Rumbledethumps

SCOTLAND AND IRELAND HAVE A WEALTH OF DISHES using cooked potatoes, cabbages, swedes, spring onions and herbs, usually mashed. In truth, variations of this dish can be found throughout the British Isles. All these are excellent vehicles for leftovers, but made fresh from scratch they are lighter and much more delicious.

I look to F. Marian McNeill for impeccable detail in research and sage advice on matters of Scots regionality. Rumbledethumps is one of them, a name derived from rumble, which means to mash, and thumped, which of course means beaten down. It's not dissimilar to the Highland dishes kailkenny, made with cooked potatoes, cabbage and cream, and colcannon, with claims of origin in Ireland and the Highlands of Scotland, often cooked with carrots or turnips added. Clapshot, an Orkney dish, is made with equal quantities of swede and potato cooked each in its own pot, then drained, mashed and beaten together with butter, a splash of cream perhaps, and a flurry of thinly sliced chives and spring onions, splendid with haggis, served every year on January 25th to honour the Scots poet Robert Burns.

Feeds 6

750g mealy potatoes, such as Kerr's Pink, King Edward or Golden Wonder
75g unsalted butter, plus a little extra for mashing
2 small onions, peeled and finely chopped
750g Savoy cabbage, coarsely chopped
1 soup spoon chopped chives
1 bunch of spring onions, trimmed and very thinly sliced

Peel the potatoes, cut into large, equal-sized pieces, rinse well, then put into a pan of salted water and bring to the boil. Simmer until cooked through.

Melt the butter in a small pan and cook the onions over a low heat until softened, about 20 minutes. Lift the potatoes out of the water with a slotted spoon and set to one side. Add the chopped cabbage to the potato water, bring back to the boil and cook until tender, about 2–3 minutes. Drain the cabbage, return to the pan with the potato, cooked onion, chives and spring onions, and smash together until a slightly coarse, rough mash is achieved, seasoning as you go. Add more butter if necessary, or even a soup spoon of milk.

Potato and artichoke salad

A LOVELY SALAD THAT EATS WELL AS IS and accompanies pork, kid, lamb, guinea fowl and fish such as cod, brill and grilled mackerel too. Such a salad is also a pleasant excuse to explore salad leaves such as different cresses, chicories and mustards.

Feeds 6

12 small potatoes (about 750g), such as Ratte
9 small artichokes
juice of 1 lemon
3 soup spoons extra virgin olive oil
2 cloves of garlic, peeled and finely chopped
1 shallot, peeled and finely chopped
2 small sprigs of rosemary, leaves picked and chopped
3 sprigs of thyme, leaves picked and chopped
a small bunch of flat-leaf parsley, leaves picked and finely chopped

Scrub the potatoes and place in a pan of salted water. Bring to the boil, then turn down the heat to a simmer and leave to cook until tender, roughly 25 minutes. Drain, cool and peel if you feel an urgent need. Halve lengthways and set aside.

Trim the artichokes of outer leaves and slice off the tips. Slice off any attached stalk that might be soft. Slice the artichokes thinly and toss in the lemon juice.

Heat a wide frying pan and add 1 soup spoon of olive oil. Tip in the sliced artichokes and lemon juice. Add 50ml of cold water and bring to a simmer, seasoning lightly with sea salt and freshly ground black pepper. Cook until all the liquid evaporates and the artichokes are tender, adding a little more water if required. When the slices are cooked, up the heat and let the artichokes take on a little colour; a gold crisp to the edges will suffice. Remove to a dish.

Wipe the pan and add the other 2 spoonfuls of olive oil. With due care, place the cooked potatoes cut side down in the hot oil and cook gently without disturbing, until browned and crusted.

Add the garlic and shallot, frying for just a minute, then add the chopped rosemary and thyme. Add the artichokes and the chopped parsley and season with much black pepper and a pinch of sea salt.

Jansson's temptation

I LIKE TO THINK THIS DISH came over with the Vikings and liked it so much it stayed. Slipping in a few more anchovies can add a little extra vigour. It's traditionally made with fermented anchovies, to be found online and in Scandinavian shops, but made with a good-quality anchy results in a very good dish indeed.

Feeds 6

1kg large potatoes, such as King Edward, peeled
3 large onions, peeled
90g unsalted butter
12 salted anchovy fillets
300ml double cream, mixed with 100ml full-fat milk

Preheat the oven to 180°C.

Rinse the peeled potatoes very well, then cut them first into 5mm-thin slices, then again into thin batons. Wash the batons again under very cold water until it runs as clear as can be. Slice the onions thinly.

Use half the butter to liberally coat an ovenproof dish. Pat the potatoes dry. Cover the bottom of the dish with half the potato batons, then half the onions. Season lightly, and lay the anchovy fillets evenly over the onions. Add the remaining onions, then the remaining potatoes, and finally dot with the rest of the butter. Pour over three-quarters of the cream and milk.

Bake for 30 minutes, until golden brown, then pour in the remaining cream. Press the potato down with the back of a large spoon and bake for a further 15 minutes. This partners very well with lamb and pork and is excellent with a green salad.

Pommes Anna

I HAVE NOT HELD A POMMES ANNA MOULD in my hands since my early days in London at a gentlemen's club on St James's Street called Boodle's. I had arrived there one winter's morning, having left Scotland to continue an appenticeship as a chef. The food at Boodle's was a mix of British and French classic dishes cooked with excellent ingredients, always fresh and mostly prepared that day.

I remember each day's deliveries piled beside a huge butcher's block in the kitchen, us chefs in our tall hats with a kerchief tied round our necks despatching meat, fish and vegetables hither and thither, including, of course, sacks of potatoes, tumbled into the yawning mouth of that extraordinary machine, the potato rumbler, which performed the rapid peeling of potatoes en masse.

The choice of vegetables on the menu always included two potato dishes, one boiled of course and one other, which on occasion was pommes Anna, a cake formed of thinly sliced potatoes. The slices, never rinsed, were dipped in warm clarified butter to line an eponymous mould sat over a moderate heat. You quickly learned the knack of layering the potato so that it overlapped and held in place the slices lining the mould, which would crisp golden in the oven while the potato cooked to a softened interior. Golly, they were good.

The moulds for pommes Anna were made of copper and lined with tin. They always shone, bright as a pin. Straight-sided, shaped like a hat, the moulds had two elegant handles, making them easier to hold when decanting. With a shiver of nervous care, praying they had crisped, cooked and coloured enough so as not to stick, the cakes were judged done only by the tell-tale edges, coloured a deep gold. A small sharp knife was carefully worked around the sides to ensure the glistening cake appeared without a hitch in a state of glowing perfection, to much relief and, I will admit, some satisfaction.

The Anna makes a splendid cake with a deep crust and a yielding softness within, perfect when cut into wedges and served with cuts of beef such as bavette, onglet, rump and loin, or fillet of lamb, hogget, mutton, pork and venison, and, of course, goes very well with roast chicken.

I have often thought about a copper mould for making this lovely dish, as pleasing to look at as it is to eat and good with so many things. A wider, shallower cake, a galette so to speak, shaped and cooked in a cast-iron skillet or frying pan, is as delicious as those cooked in the hatted moulds at Boodle's. The sliced potatoes require clarified butter, which is easy enough to make. Melt some butter in a saucepan over a moderate heat and spoon away any foam or whey that rises. Carefully ladle the butter through muslin into a bowl, leaving behind the white solids.

Mayan Gold and Yukon Gold cook a treat in this recipe, King Edwards work very well, and good results were also enjoyed with baking and roasting potatoes from a local greengrocer.

Feeds 6

2kg potatoes, such as Yukon Gold, Mayan Gold, or King Edward
200g unsalted butter, clarified and kept warm

Put a baking sheet in the middle of the oven and preheat the oven to 220°C. Peel the potatoes and slice thinly (a mandoline makes short work of this).

Place a 25cm cast-iron skillet over a gentle heat. Pour in a small ladle of clarified butter. Place a potato slice in the centre of the skillet and lay the rest of the slices around, overlapping. Continue thus until reaching the edge. Pour over a little more clarified butter and season evenly. Repeat with another layer of potato, continuing thus, adding butter, salt and black pepper as you go. Cover with a sheet of foil and place a lid on top.

Place on the baking sheet in the oven and bake for 45 minutes. Lift the lid and remove the foil. Press the cake down lightly with the bottom of a frying pan. Remove the frying pan and cook for a further 30 minutes, until the edges of the cake have coloured deep gold.

Insert a small knife into the cake for doneness; there should be no resistance. Press down lightly with a frying pan one last time. Remove

the cake from the oven and let sit for 5 minutes. Carefully work a spatula round the edges, lifting slightly to loosen the cake. Work the spatula gently towards the centre to free any slices that are sticking. Shake the pan gently to see if the cake shifts free. Place a board or dish on top. With one swift move, invert. Tap the bottom of the skillet. Lift the skillet away and serve.

Potato and olive cakes

GOOD WITH A SALAD OF LEAVES, with a few fillets of anchovy, a spoonful of crumbled or thinly sliced cheese, such as a mild feta or Parmesan, and black olive crumbs (see page 74). I also like this with a fried egg on top and perhaps a few olives and a couple of capers.

Feeds 6

1kg King Edward potatoes, peeled and halved
120g black olives, pitted
a small bunch of spring onions
a small sprig of thyme
a small sprig of rosemary
2 soup spoons chopped flat-leaf parsley
2 cloves of garlic, peeled and finely chopped
1 small organic egg, beaten
2 teaspoons fennel seeds, ground in a pestle and mortar
3 soup spoons extra virgin olive oil, plus 2 more for frying
a tiny pinch of salt
a plate of lightly seasoned flour

Preheat the oven to 200°C.

Steam the potatoes until tender, 30 minutes or so. Chop the black olives into small pieces. Thinly slice the spring onions. Pick the leaves and spikes of thyme and rosemary and chop finely, then place, along with all the other ingredients, except the flour, in a bowl and mash together until deftly but coarsely mixed. Divide into 12 balls, shape into cakes, then lightly dip each cake into the flour.

Heat an ovenproof frying pan and just cover the bottom of the pan with a soup spoon of olive oil. Lay in some of the cakes, leaving room between them to avoid any steam rising. Cook undisturbed until the edges colour well, then turn carefully and place in the heated oven for 5 minutes. Lift the cakes onto a dish and repeat until all are done.

PS: A pleasing thought is to dip both sides of the cakes, once floured, in beaten egg then breadcrumbs and fry… very good with aïoli.

Potato salad

POTATO SALAD EATS WELL WITH ALMOST EVERYTHING, from bacon, to smoked fish, to cold roast meats and much more besides. This is a robust recipe for cooler days when vigour is required.

Feeds 6

1kg potatoes of a waxy persuasion such as Pink Fir, Charlotte
2 soup spoons extra virgin olive oil
1 soup spoon organic cider vinegar

For the dressing

1 soup spoon organic cider vinegar
2 soup spoons Dijon mustard
6–7 soup spoons extra virgin olive oil
2 small onions, peeled and finely chopped
a bunch of spring onions, thinly sliced
1 soup spoon salted capers, soaked in cold water for 30 minutes and chopped
a small bunch of flat-leaf parsley, finely chopped
a small bunch of dill, finely chopped

Wash the potatoes thoroughly and boil them in their skins in lightly salted water. Once cooked, drain and, when cool enough to handle, peel. Coarsely chop the potatoes, dress with the 2 soup spoons of olive oil and 1 soup spoon of vinegar, and leave to cool.

To make the dressing, stir a big pinch each of sea salt and freshly ground black pepper into the vinegar until the salt has dissolved. Stir in the mustard and beat in the olive oil. Tip in the chopped onions, sliced spring onions, capers, chopped parsley and dill, and taste for seasoning. Tip this dressing on to the potatoes, mix well and serve.

SALADS

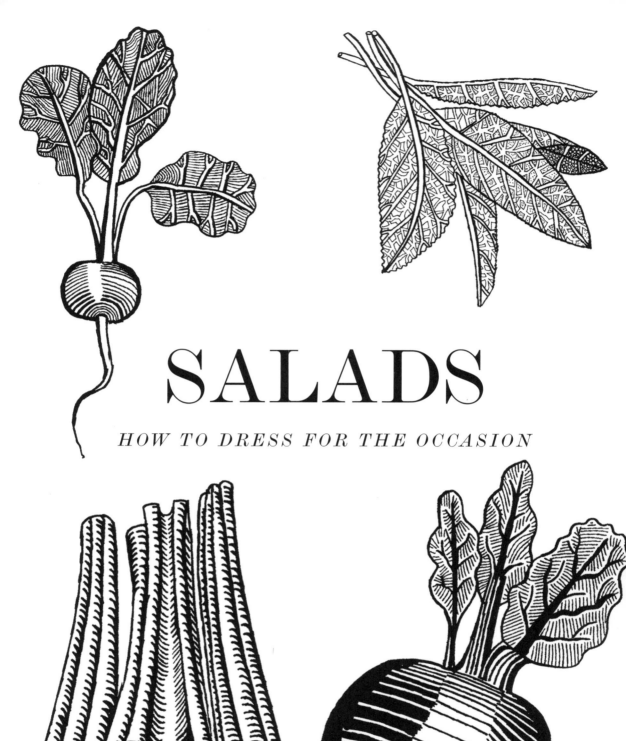

HOW TO DRESS FOR THE OCCASION

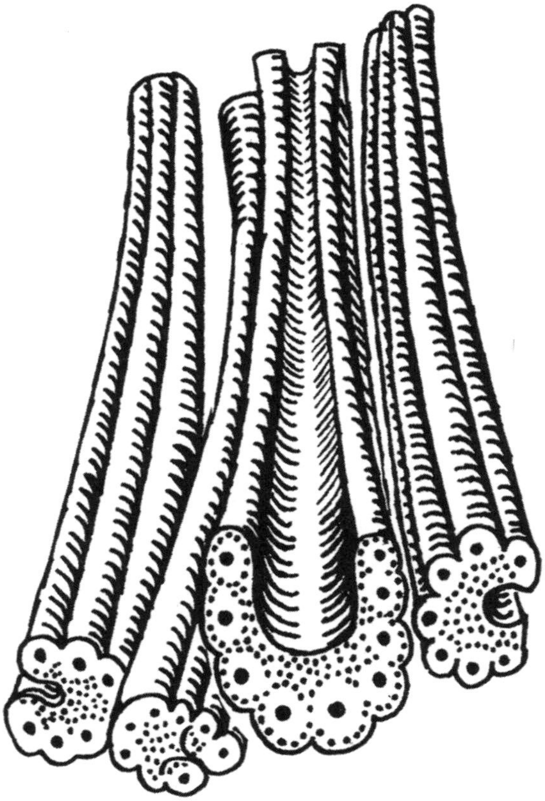

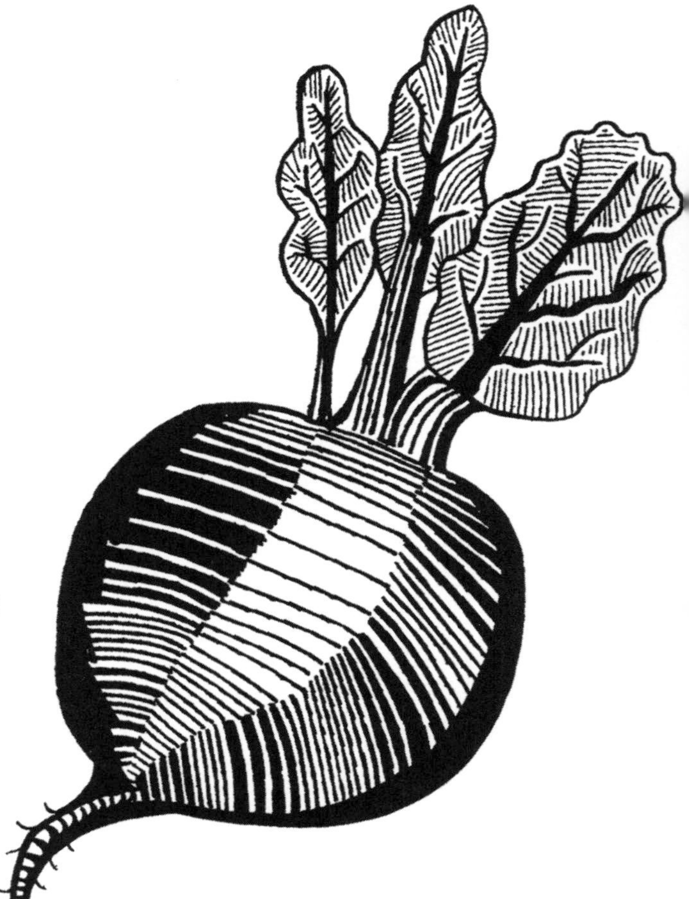

Dandelion, bacon, chicken livers & croutons

Puntarelle & anchovy salad

Green tomato salad

Tomatoes, lovage & goat's curd

Beetroot, soft-boiled eggs & horseradish

A dish of tomatoes, curds & herbs

A good vegetable salad

Kohlrabi, apple, celeriac and celery rémoulade

A list of leaves, vegetables & herbs

THERE IS SOMETHING SO PLEASING about the morning ritual of deliveries into the kitchen that ushers in the day with the boisterous business of delivery folk carting in boxes, trays and bags filled with produce. More often than not, the biggest and best of deliveries are those of fruit and vegetables, salad leaves and herbs from traders and importers, foragers and producers further afield.

The boxes are piled up in the kitchen, requiring a familiar choreography of unpacking and storing before the cooks gird their loins, gauging with practised eye where and how best to begin with enough good things to ensure a busy day's preparation ahead.

One of the first chores for the larder, the area in the kitchen responsible for the preparation and serving of salads, is taking the trays, boxes and bags of lettuces and leaves to pick through and sort, removing blemished leaves, washing and drying. It's quite a performance, bowls and colanders filled with leaves in varying shapes and hues: mustards, peppery rocket, chicories and soft-leaved heads of every red and green, variegated, some flecked, some resolutely uniform, some slender-stemmed, some large-leaved. Put them all together and you can create salads of extraordinary variety.

Good suppliers, growers and producers of these leaves are as important to a kitchen as the cooks themselves. Good cooks need to know as much about the provenance of their vegetables and leaves as they do about their meat and fish.

In all the kitchens I have worked, not to mention at home, produce has been at the fore. The memories remain vivid of weekly deliveries from the market at Rungis in Paris to the kitchen at Bibendum of trays of mesclun, a mixture of every sort of brightly coloured gathered leaves. At Alastair Little, some of our salad leaves were supplied by the redoubtable Frances Smith, who had worked with Christopher Lloyd at Great Dixter, and Joy Larkcom, who had revolutionised salad and vegetable production in the UK in the eighties. Frances grew all manner of leaves, herbs and vegetables at her quail farm near Appledore in Kent. The leaves, snipped early in the morning and delivered that day, were a revelation of delicate flavours, textures and appearance. Frances described them all in newsletters which I would keep and pore over, to remind myself of the addition of sorrel and mustard, of a particular red orach, or a memorable delivery of Good King Henry that had turned the most viridian hue of green when cooked, or a wonderful bag of wildly heated mustard leaves, perfect with a dish of grilled onglet.

After Frances retired, I began to work with Jane Scotter at Fern Verrow, a biodynamic farm in the foothills of the Black Mountains in Herefordshire. They used to sell their wares every Saturday in among the arches at Spa Terminus in London's Bermondsey. Jane grows lettuces of every variety and colour, each year blousier than the last; spinach of every shade of green; rockets both wild and domestic, small- and large-leaved; mustards from deepest reds, and huge to delicate pale-green japonicas; chicories of every shape and shade of red and green imaginable, their names alone, Tardivo, Treviso and Castelfranco, forming a road map through the Veneto…

And then there are the cresses, ranging from wild to land cress, kales of every type imaginable, beet leaves, chards and salsify shoots, dandelions, claytonia and purslane. There are herbs, too – mint, parsley, tarragon, chervil, tiny snippings of sweet cicely, fennel and basil but also lovage and angelica, alexanders, marjoram, summer savory, sorrels, domestic, wild and an oh-so-very-pretty wood sorrel that closes when it is cold, hiding within itself.

Jane Scotter was in the vanguard of growing seasonally for flavour and quality rather than conformity in size and shape, planting the first seeds at Fern Verrow in 1996. It is heartening that more and more growers and producers are experimenting with seeds of different varieties of vegetables and leaves.

For ingredients gathered in the wild, I speak with foragers who know well where, when and what to pick without damage to delicate, sometimes tiny ecosystems. Such provender requires as much respect and attention as produce grown in a pot, on a ledge, in a garden, on an allotment or a farm. Foragers play an increasingly important role, supplying in excellent condition such plants as wild cress, dandelion, chickweed, hairy bittercress, wood sorrel – and sea vegetables from the coasts: sea beet, sea aster, purslane and both rock and marsh samphire.

It is no surprise that one of the best sources for finding produce is on the internet, Instagram in particular, where an astonishing array of foragers, growers and farmers' markets announce what's best that day, sometimes with short films such as those, eagerly awaited, by the witty, knowledgeable and indefatigable Andy Harris, proprietor of the Ealing Grocer. Most days he takes viewers on a guided tour of the superb produce displayed for sale at the shop. It is worth noting that cooks are encouraged to buy where possible produce intact and should never be deterred by the odd blemish and yellowed leaf on plants grown and stored free of chemicals and plastic bags. Nipping leaves from sprigs of herbs is more pleasing by far than snipping open a sealed bag with a pair of scissors.

The simplest salad of soft green leaves, from a Bibb or Romaine, with a bunch of peppery-leaved watercress, blades of flat-leaf parsley and picked mint, is quick to prepare. To this can be added chicories, their bitterness tempered with dressings as simple as a squeeze of lemon juice and a measure or two of extra virgin olive oil. More complex dressings can be made with chopped olives, capers, anchovies and chilli, to be spooned over finished dishes or for dipping leaves and cut vegetables. Chopped pistachios and almonds, pine kernels and walnuts mixed with pieces of bread tossed in olive oil and baked crisp add bite and crunch.

Dandelion, bacon, chicken livers and croutons

A ROBUST SALAD THAT USED TO APPEAR often on menus but fell away over time. Today's readily available wispy, pale-yellow dandelion is a faint imitation, so it's worth seeking out puntarelle or Catalogna, chicories which are closely related to dandelions and are ideal for this salad.

Feeds 6

3 or 4 thick slices of crusty bread, cut into large croutons
2 big handfuls of sturdy dandelion, or puntarelle or Catalogna, or failing that escarole, possibly mixed with watercress
2 soup spoons sherry vinegar
1 teaspoon Dijon mustard
4 soup spoons extra virgin olive oil
1 soup spoon walnut oil
200g freshest chicken (or duck) livers
150g best streaky smoked bacon, cut into lardons

Preheat the oven to 180°C. Place the pieces of bread on a baking tray and bake for 12 to 15 minutes, until golden and crisp.

Trim the salad leaves of any blemishes, despatching any in distress. Tear the leaves and cut the stalks into small pieces. Wash well, drain and dry thoroughly.

In a bowl, whisk the sherry vinegar with a good pinch each of sea salt and freshly ground black pepper. Add the Dijon mustard, whisk, then add 3 soup spoons of olive oil and the walnut oil.

Trim the chicken (or duck) livers. Heat a wide frying pan. Add 1 soup spoon of olive oil to the pan, followed swiftly by the bacon. Cook the bacon gently with a wooden spoon, standing well back until all the pieces have separated. The bacon will colour quickly, so lift the pan from the heat and lift the bacon from the pan.

Lightly season the chicken livers and lay each carefully in the hot oil. Let cook until coloured, roughly 2 minutes. Turn the livers and cook for another minute. Remove the pan from the heat and lift the livers from the pan.

In a large bowl, place leaves, bacon, chicken livers, croutons and the dressing. Mix well, taste for seasoning, then take swiftly to table.

Puntarelle and anchovy salad

I ONCE ATE THIS SUPERB SALAD AT A TRATTORIA in Milan, made with the tips only and a few tiny tendrils of puntarelle still attached, dressed with anchovies and lemon. I find the long tendrils cut from the tips are excellent in other dishes such as warm salads made with squid or cuttlefish. It is important to split the tips of puntarelle and slice as finely as possible. A traditional Roman 'tapu', a piece of wood with a wide hole drilled through the middle, with a sturdy mesh tacked on, is traditional for pushing the shoots through before dropping them into cold water to crisp and curl.

It is worth noting that salted anchovies are wonderful but increasingly rare. If you chance upon them, they are easy to prepare, requiring a thorough soaking to dispel excess salt and rinsing in cold water. The two fillets are then pulled from the spine of the fish, bones and head despatched.

Feeds 6

1 head of puntarelle
12–15 anchovy fillets
1 clove of garlic
6 soup spoons extra virgin olive oil
a fair few grinds of the pepper mill
juice of 1 lemon

Tear away any stalk and leaf attached to the shoots of the puntarelle. If you have a tapu, partially push the shoots through just as far as the tips. Or separate the shoots, cut away the tips, halve what remains and slice as thin as can be. Soak in cold water to curl and crisp. Drain and dry thoroughly.

Coarsely chop the anchovy fillets. Finely chop the garlic, then crush to a paste. Place in a bowl along with the olive oil and the black pepper. When ready to serve, mix the anchovy dressing and the puntarelle with the lemon juice in a big bowl and take to table.

Green tomato salad

I LOVE FRIED GREEN TOMATOES but I also love them, as here, quartered and blistered in hot oil in a frying pan with a few other lightly charred vegetables dressed with lemon, capers and olive oil. This salad is good with so much, by itself, or you can use it to accompany grilled and roast meats, or cheese, curds and grilled bread.

Feeds 6

2 soup spoons small salted capers
6–8 green tomatoes
4 soup spoons extra virgin olive oil
1 heart of leafy celery and bright and fresh leaves
1 bulb of fennel
a bunch of Tropea onions or spring onions, or 3 small leeks
1 lemon, unwaxed, boiled for 20 minutes until fully softened
a bunch of mint, leaves picked
a bunch of flat-leaf parsley, leaves picked

Rinse the capers of any adhering salt and let them sit in water for 30 minutes.

Cut the tomatoes into quarters or sixths, depending on their size. Heat a frying pan and cook the pieces of tomato in 1 soup spoon of the olive oil over a moderate heat until blistered and coloured dark. Remove from the pan and set aside.

Trim the celery and fennel of any blemishes, including the leaves and fronds, and chop both into small pieces roughly the size of a fingernail. Trim the onions or leeks and chop similarly.

Add one more spoonful of olive oil to the pan, reheat, then add the celery, fennel and onions. Place a lid atop and cook over a fierce heat until the vegetables become bright and have caught around the edges, taking on dark flecks of colour, about 5–10 minutes.

Halve the boiled lemon and discard the pulp within. Chop the softened peel into small pieces. Add these to the cooked tomatoes, vegetables and herbs in a bowl, with the drained capers and remaining 2 soup spoons of olive oil. Mix deftly and taste for seasoning, then tumble upon a dish to serve.

Tomatoes, lovage and goat's curd

LOVAGE, WITH ITS HIGHLY ACCENTED, slightly bitter flavour of celery, makes excellent company for a tomato. Adding goat's curd tempers the ebullient herb, making this an estimable trinity. This is a salad perfect for using many different sizes and varieties of tomato.

Feeds 6

6 soup spoons extra virgin olive oil
250g goat's curd
75ml natural yoghurt
a small bunch of lovage, leaves picked and chopped
a small bunch of flat-leaf parsley, leaves picked and chopped
6 large ripe tomatoes
1 soup spoon very good red wine vinegar, e.g. Banyuls
(see page 198)

Beat 4 soup spoons of the olive oil into the goat's curd and yoghurt in a bowl. Into this stir the chopped lovage, half the parsley and some salt and black pepper. Blithely spoon the curd on to a dish in heaps and mounds, reserving one soup spoon.

Blanch the tomatoes in a pan of boiling water (unless using ripe summer tomatoes, in which case no need to blanch), then drain, cool and peel. Coarsely chop the tomatoes into large pieces. Put these into a bowl with the vinegar, the remaining olive oil, the reserved soup spoon of the curd mix and some salt and black pepper. Dress the tomatoes in this mixture, then tumble them over the heaps of goat's curd on the plate.

Throw the remaining parsley over in a flurry and finish with the remaining 2 soup spoons of olive oil. This is good served on a big dish.

Beetroot, soft-boiled eggs and horseradish

THIS BOLD, BRIGHT SALAD NEVER LOSES ITS APPEAL whenever it is made, which is often. Very good on its own, this salad also eats well with cured and smoked fish as well as with thinly sliced ham, or cold roast lamb, beef or pork. The dressing is simplicity itself to make, a salad cream if you will, and don't be shy with grating horseradish over the beetroot, both delighting in each other's exuberance.

A few rules, well, musings really, on the business of choosing, preparing and cooking beetroot. There are so many varieties of beetroot in gorgeous pinks, purples and a gold, a particular variety I love called Flaming Badger. The cook can indulge in all manner of variations with different varieties and colours. I like the small new season's tender beetroots both steamed and baked in foil, or, if there is time to soak, in a diable. Steaming beetroot results in a delicately cooked vegetable, while roasting beetroot in foil or a diable results in a rich intensity. Ensuring the beetroots are of a similar size and shape and regardless of which method of cooking chosen, beetroots take roughly the same time to cook. Larger beetroots, later in the season, are best boiled until tender.

A diable should be soaked for at least an hour in cold water. Tumble in the beets, cover and bake in a preheated oven set at 180°C until the beetroots are tender, taking from 30 minutes to 1 hour depending on size and age. (See page 370.)

Feeds 6

1kg small beetroots, gold, pink and purple
1 teaspoon caster sugar
2 soup spoons red wine vinegar
6 freshest organic eggs, at room temperature
2 big handfuls of assorted salad leaves, e.g. mustards, soft-leaved rocket, watercress and cress, escarole or Grumola
a small bunch of chives, finely chopped
1 soup spoon flat-leaf parsley, leaves picked and finely chopped
25–40g fresh horseradish, peeled
1 soup spoon extra virgin olive oil

For the mustard cream

2 teaspoons organic cider vinegar
2 teaspoons caster sugar
1 soup spoon Dijon mustard
150ml double cream

Trim the beetroots, retaining any leaves still fresh enough for the salad. Place the beetroots in a steamer, or simmer in a pan of water until tender.

Once tender, let cool. When cool enough to handle, peel away any skin still adhering. Cut the beetroots in half. In a bowl dissolve the teaspoon of caster sugar in the red wine vinegar, tip in the beetroots and mix together with a big pinch of black pepper. Set to one side.

Place the eggs in boiling water and cook for 5 minutes. Cool under running water and peel. Store in cool water.

In a bowl whisk the cider vinegar and 2 teaspoons of caster sugar until the sugar dissolves, then add the mustard and whisk until smooth. Add the cream, mixing well. Cover and refrigerate until needed.

Tumble the salad leaves onto a handsome dish, lay on the beetroot, then cut the eggs in half and place them among the beetroot. Spoon the mustard cream wildly over the salad. Strew with the chives and parsley and grate the horseradish vigorously over the whole salad. Scatter over a few drops of olive oil and serve.

A dish of tomatoes, curds and herbs

THIS SALAD RELIES WHOLEHEARTEDLY on superb ingredients for both the cooked and uncooked parts. Goat's or cow's curd, ricotta or mozzarella are served with baked tomatoes dressed with a sauce vierge, made from the ripest tomatoes chopped and dressed with shallots, garlic, parsley and basil in a sublime olive oil. Such a dish is best prepared at the height of summer when tomatoes are at their most delicious. All can be prepared earlier in the day. Whenever I slice garlic for roasting tomatoes, I always think of the opening scene in *Goodfellas* when Pauli is using an illicit razor blade to slice the garlic as thinly as possible so that it liquefies in the pan with the oil… perfect for pouring on grilled bread.

Feeds 6

For the baked tomatoes

6 plum tomatoes, such as San Marzano
1 clove of garlic, peeled and sliced as thin as can be
3 sprigs of thyme
2 sprigs of rosemary
2 soup spoons extra virgin olive oil
2 buffalo mozzarella or burrata or stracciatella

For the sauce vierge

4 ripest Bull's Heart tomatoes and 4 San Marzano
2 shallots
2 cloves of garlic
1 red chilli (mild if possible), or a pinch of dried chilli flakes
a small bunch of mint
a small bunch of basil
a small bunch of flat-leaf parsley
1 soup spoon best red wine vinegar, e.g. Banyuls (see page 198)
4 soup spoons extra virgin olive oil, a doozy such as Capezzana

Preheat the oven to 150°C.

To bake the tomatoes, remove the eye and halve the tomatoes lengthways. Lay them side by side in an earthenware dish. Lay the garlic over the halved tomatoes. Pick the thyme and rosemary, then scatter the leaves and spears evenly over the tomatoes and lay on the stripped branches. Evenly season with a little sea salt and a good few grinds of a pepper mill. Spoon over the olive oil. Place the dish in the oven and leave to cook for 45 minutes or so, longer if required, checking from time to time that they are not cooking too fast or discolouring. Remove from the oven and leave to cool.

To make the sauce vierge, bring a pan of water to the boil. Remove the eyes of the Bull's Heart and San Marzano tomatoes. Plunge the tomatoes into the boiling water for 10 seconds, then remove and leave to cool. Peel the tomatoes and coarsely chop.

Peel the shallots and garlic, removing any trace of green shoots, and slice as thinly as possible. Finely chop the chilli (if using). Pick the herbs, tearing the mint and basil, finely chopping the parsley. Put the vinegar in a bowl with a little salt and pepper and mix until the salt dissolves. Add the olive oil. Add the chopped tomatoes, sliced garlic and shallots, then the torn and chopped herbs. Mix deftly.

Place the baked tomatoes on a dish. Tear the mozzarella over the tomatoes and season evenly with sea salt and pepper. Spoon over the sauce vierge and serve.

On occasion, I have grilled slices of red onion until lightly charred, then cooled and coarsely chopped them to scatter over the salad when serving.

A good vegetable salad

WE NEED MARKETS. Apart from the bustle and sense of community, nothing inspires the cook more than wandering among tables and stalls piled high with abundant produce surrounded by stacks of crates and boxes full to brimming. I am a market junkie, to borrow a phrase from culinary historian Jessica Harris, and am grateful for travels abroad and time spent perusing many markets around the world, the vast outdoor market in Turin or the venerable farmers' market in San Francisco, markets in Morocco, Transylvania and the labyrinthine passageways of Hanoi in Vietnam, each time bowled over by what has been on offer.

I count myself fortunate to live near a few farmers' markets and a fair few good fruit and vegetable shops.

I brush aside the grumbles and comments of folk who mutter about stalls of cooking and craft that dominate the street markets of Britain, believing wholeheartedly that the more we support the traders, the better the markets become. En route to a favoured vegetable stall it is hardly a chore to walk past folk selling all manner of clothes, crafts and other things, and there is always the happy chance you might find much to please, and at the very least you will have the bag of produce you went for in the first place with a view to preparing something good, perhaps a salad.

Salads are mostly composed of gathered ingredients prepared, cut, cooked or raw, in a dressing of oil and vinegar or in a more involved recipe. One recipe that should be a triumph of seasonal produce is a vegetable salad, made from all manner of delights chopped small and usually dressed with a generous measure of mayonnaise. Done well it is delicious, but to eat a good one is rare, suffering as it does from commercialisation and some pretty eccentric variations, such as one eaten in a flash restaurant where the salad was enclosed in a sugar casing mounted in a wooden frame tasting like something spooned from a tub lifted from the shelf of a supermarket.

Put aside such thoughts and instead, acquire, trim, peel and cook the freshest vegetables, the best on offer, for this prosaic salad dressed with a bright pesto of almonds, spinach and wild garlic. As with all salads, it is good to consider different olive oils and vinegars as well as a choice of salad leaves such as wide-leaved rocket, a bunch of spinach, mustard leaves, watercress, wild cress, land cress, lamb's lettuce. Depending on the season and availability, the cook can pick and choose whichever vegetables, leaves and herbs are at hand, taking full advantage of what is abundant at the time.

Feeds 6

a bunch of carrots, roughly 4 or 5, trimmed and peeled
350g new potatoes, such as Ratte, Charlotte or Pink Fir, well scrubbed
150g small turnips, topped and tailed
100g green beans, topped and tailed
100g runner beans, topped, tailed and sliced
100g broad beans, blanched and peeled
100g shelled peas
12 spears of asparagus, if in evidence
a small bunch of mint, leaves picked
a small bunch of flat-leaf parsley, leaves picked
juice of 1 lemon
1 teaspoon red wine vinegar, e.g. Banyuls (see page 198)
2 soup spoons extra virgin olive oil

For the pesto

150g whole blanched almonds
25–30g wild garlic, leaves picked, washed and dried, then coarsely chopped (or 2–3 cloves of garlic, peeled and finely chopped)
100g baby spinach, washed
a handful of flat-leaf parsley, leaves picked
a small bunch of tarragon, leaves picked
150ml olive oil

Cut the carrots in half and cook in a pan of salted boiling water until tender. Simmer the potatoes until just done, roughly 12–15 minutes, then drain. Simmer the turnips until cooked, about 8–10 minutes. Boil another pan of salted water and cook the beans and peas until tender. Cut the spears of asparagus in three, then plunge them into boiling salted water and cook for 3–4 minutes. Drain and cool. Tear the mint and chop the parsley.

In a bowl large enough to hold all the vegetables, mix a generous pinch of sea salt with the lemon juice and vinegar and stir until the salt dissolves. Add the olive oil and a pinch of black pepper. Tumble all the vegetables and herbs into the bowl with the dressing and mix deftly.

Place the almonds, garlic, spinach, parsley and tarragon, olive oil and a pinch of sea salt and black pepper in a food processor and grind to a coarse paste. Decant into a bowl and cover.

Lay the leaves holus-bolus on a large dish. Tumble the vegetables onto the leaves. Serve the pesto in a bowl alongside and spoon liberally over the vegetables.

Kohlrabi, apple, celeriac and celery rémoulade

A FEISTY SALAD THAT PAIRS WELL with grilled mackerel, onglet and smoked or cured fish. I believe wholeheartedly in making plenty of mayonnaise, vital when urges for a ham sandwich mount. For this salad, use half the recipe for mayonnaise and keep the rest in a sealed jar in the fridge.

Feeds 6

1 heart of leafy celery
300g celeriac
1 kohlrabi
2–3 apples
juice of ½ a lemon
1 heaped teaspoon Dijon mustard
1 level teaspoon English mustard
50–75g freshly grated horseradish

One, some or all of the below

50g baby spinach
50g land cress
50g leafy rocket
a small bunch of flat-leaf parsley, leaves picked and chopped

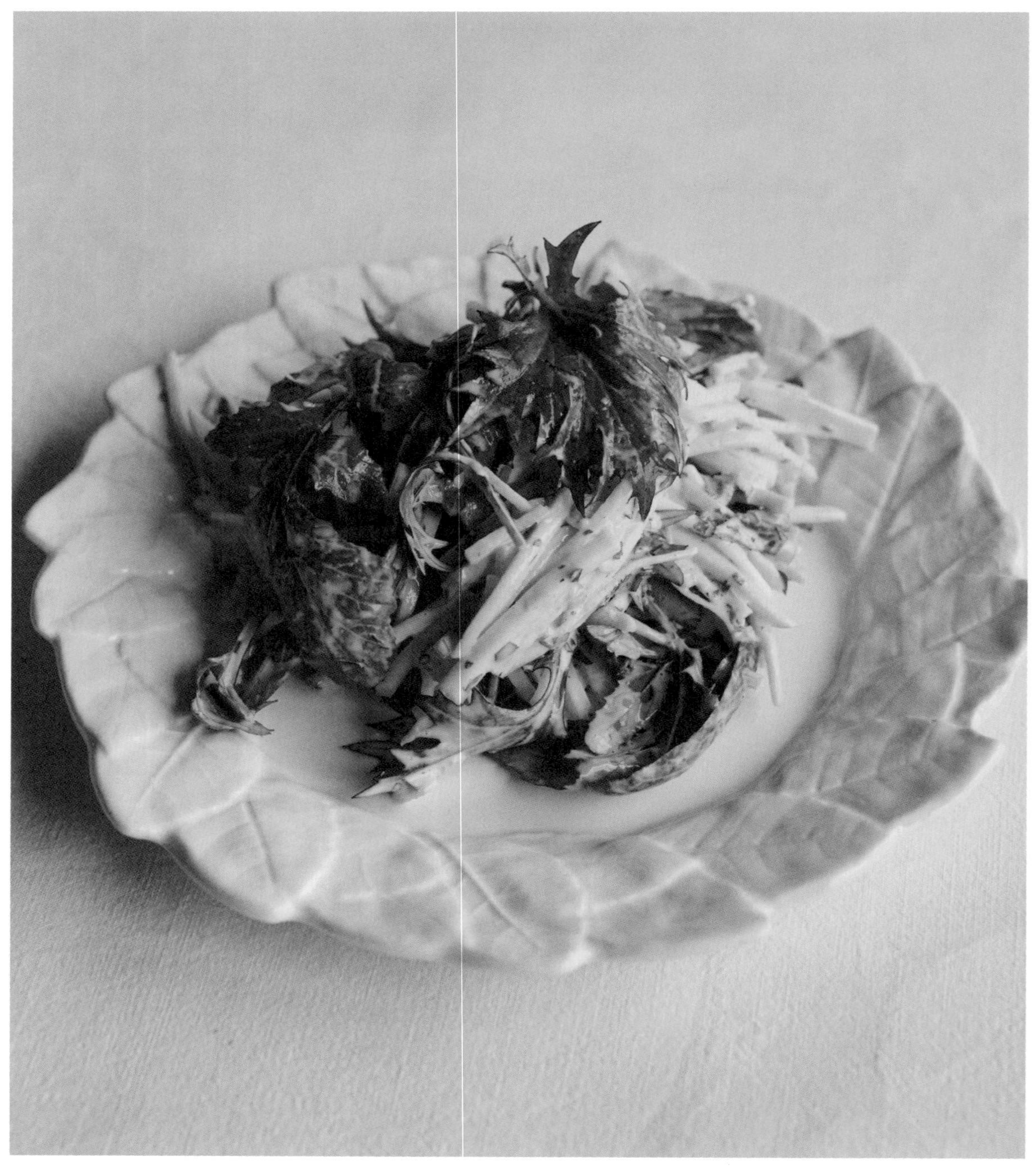

For the mayonnaise

2 organic egg yolks
1 teaspoon organic cider vinegar
1 teaspoon Dijon mustard
a few drops of Tabasco
200ml peanut or vegetable oil
50ml olive oil
juice of ½ a lemon

To make the mayonnaise, beat together the egg yolks, vinegar, a pinch of sea salt, the Dijon mustard and a drop or three of Tabasco in a bowl. Add the peanut or vegetable oil drop by drop, whisking thoroughly. Continue thus until the sauce thickens, then start adding the oil a spoonful at a time. Then slowly add the olive oil and drops of lemon juice and taste for seasoning. Cover and refrigerate.

Thinly slice the celery heart. Peel the celeriac and kohlrabi, slice thinly and cut into fine strips. Slice the apples thinly and cut into fine strips, tossing them in lemon juice as you go to stop the slices browning.

Place all the strips in a large bowl with the two mustards, the horseradish and a big pinch of freshly ground black pepper. Mix well. Add half the mayonnaise, then the leaves and chopped parsley. Mix deftly and serve.

A list of leaves, vegetables and herbs for the kitchen in general and salads in particular

Leaves

LETTUCE

There are so many varieties of lettuce in a riot of textures, colours, shapes and sizes:

Blousy, soft-leaved green lettuce, such as Webbs.

Little Gem (home-grown can be quite different in taste, colour and appearance to those more familiar in a plastic bag).

Oakleaf.

Corn salad or lamb's lettuce.

Romaine.

Bibb.

CRESSES

As vital as they are lovely, prized for their delicate leaves and hint of pepper:

Land cress, an ace leaf curiously rare and underrated.

Watercress, a peerless leaf, brilliant with everything. Watercress sandwiches were once sold on the streets of London. Now there is a thought for a fast-food snack.

Garden cress, even rarer than land cress. Worth seeking because it's beautiful to look at and has a good flavour.

Hairy bittercress, small-leaved, wonderful with a salad of leaves and cresses.

Wild cress is a foraged leaf of great character and flavour.

SPINACH

Bunches of small-leaved and stalked spinach are a treat in late winter and early spring, the tender young leaves as well as the small bunches of those cut from early crops.

RED ORACH

Prized for its colour, a small, three-cornered leaf, very attractive, adds texture and flavour. Also known as atriplex or garden spinach.

SALAD BURNET

A pretty, fern-like leaf that is welcome in a tumble of mixed leaves.

CLAYTONIA

A delicate stem and very beautiful. A bright, clean taste.

CHICKWEED

To be had from a forager, excellent with other leaves.

PURSLANE

Justly prized for salads.

MUSTARD AND PEPPER

Mustard, best picked when small. Large leaves are coarser in texture and more bitter and hotter to taste. Taste for potency. Excellent with thin slices of beef crusted with pepper.

Mizuna, a delicate, beautiful leaf with a surprising heat.

Mibuna, with similar properties to mizuna.

Rocket, prized for a peppered flavour – the soft-leaved varieties are often better than the wild varieties, which can prove tough-stalked.

CHICORIES AND ENDIVES

Members of the dandelion family. Both red- and yellow-leaved chicory are excellent dressed in salads.

Endives dressed in a vinaigrette made with much mustard are good with all manner of dishes. They are also good chopped and lightly fried in olive oil, or cut in quarters and baked with a spoonful of olive oil and a squeeze of lemon juice to serve, or mixed with chopped herbs to accompany roast lamb or pork.

FRISÉE

Only the tips of the commercially grown, wispy yellow plant widely available have worth. Frisée should be a coarse tangle of crisp and profuse blades coloured a dark green through to a fierce yellow.

ESCAROLE

Superior by far to a commercial frisée, this chicory, possessed of a mild bitter taste, is excellent just dressed in olive oil and vinegar and for all manner of salads.

DANDELION

Often wild but cultivated in Italy and France. To be had from a forager or from a grocer who imports vegetables, salads and herbs from Italy.

PUNTARELLE

A marvellous green comet of a vegetable with slender shoots that stream out in varying lengths from the tightly packed cluster of curiously shaped buds that resemble the heads of asparagus, but there the similarity ends. Puntarelle buds are not only hollow, but crisp, and are best eaten sliced as thin as can be or pushed through a *tapu* before being plunged into cold water to crisp and curl. Most famously a tradition in Rome, puntarelle are dressed with anchovy, olive oil and lemon.

CATALOGNA

A chicory very like the long tendrilled leaves of dandelion and the stalks of puntarelle, with a wider leaf and serrated edges.

GRUMOLA

A small, tightly packed chicory that comes red, green and variegated and is utterly delicious.

SORREL

Domestic and wild, the leaves are flavoured with a lemon-sharp tang. Wood sorrel has tiny, charming leaves belying an excellent though surprising tang.

CELERY LEAF AND CELERY HEARTS

Excellent chopped small for slaw, the leaves picked and added to a leaf salad.

KALE

Young leaves are best picked small, their stalks good sliced thin for slaw.

BEETROOT LEAVES

Best picked small and early in the season. The stalks can be sliced thin for slaw.

CHARD

Young, best picked small for salads, the stalks good for slaw.

PEA AND BEAN TENDRILS AND SHOOTS

Excellent in soups and salads and best when freshly snipped from their plants. Shoots, leaves and buds of peas and broad beans, salsify and celeriac, picked young and fresh, are worth gathering when the opportunity arises.

Roots and stalks from plants such as chervil, parsley, sweet cicely and chicories as well as leaves are worth tasting, as these can be chopped small and added to a slaw for dressing salads. Alexanders and more robust flavours are very good, in small quantities, though have a care they do not startle and overwhelm in slaws.

Herbs

BORAGE

Often dried and added with a pinch of thyme to stocks, soups and braises of pulses, meats and grains.

THYME

A plant of many varieties and flavours. I prefer plain thyme. A few sprigs of plain thyme, picked, the leaves stirred through or tied in a bundle, is a joy for simmering beans, lentils, soups, and braises of fish as well as meat.

ROSEMARY

Requires judicious use, as the flavour can overwhelm and become bitter. It is wonderful with roast lamb or pork and also for potatoes cooked crisp in duck, goose or pork fat.

SAGE

An excellent herb when used sparingly, as the flavour is pronounced and can overwhelm. The leaves are best picked and cooked fresh. Particularly good when cooking onions to accompany dishes with pork, lamb, kid and liver.

SAVORY

Summer savory is a tiny-leaved herb not unlike thyme but with a softer, less pronounced flavour. Good in all manner of cooking, summer savory is excellent in a pan of gently simmered broad beans. The estimable spring and early summer dish of vignarola, with young artichokes, peas, broad beans, asparagus and new potatoes, delights in a pinch or two of fresh or dried summer savory. Winter savory is more pronounced and requires care so as not to let it become overpowering. Use as with summer savory but in smaller quantities, as it lacks the delicacy of the summer version.

BAY LEAF

Good for making stock with vegetables, fish or meat; a pan of softening onions intended for a dish of liver or braises of beef or lamb; simmering beans and lentils; pot-roasting vegetables, be they potatoes, carrots or Brussels sprouts; laying on terrines; and infusing custards, creams and syrups for poaching fruit.

TARRAGON

One of the quartet often known as *fines herbes* (the other three are chervil, chives and flat-leaf parsley) that delight as much in an omelette as they do on all manner of salads, or strewn on cheese and curds spread on grilled or toasted bread. Tarragon is also very good in tomato soup, as well as in pale cream sauces for a roast rack of lamb, or poached fish and chicken. Add a few leaves to a syrup for poaching pears or peaches.

CHERVIL

A delicate leaf that can be added to eggs for omelettes or in small sprigs to leaf salads, and suits being added to chilled cream soups such as those made from celery, fennel, leek and potato.

CHIVES

These suit all manner of dishes, particularly salads, soups and sauces such as vinaigrette, mayonnaise and yoghurt. They can be scattered on innumerable dishes, from potato to tomato and onion salads. Best sliced as thin as can be and scattered fresh.

FLAT-LEAF PARSLEY

Use tender young whole leaves for chopping in salads and dressings. With age, the leaves become sturdier, requiring careful picking and chopping or slicing thinly for salads and dressing.

CURLY PARSLEY

Has a pronounced flavour ideal for finishing soups, such as those made with lentils, and braises. Chop finely and add to robust sauces for poached meats such as ham or smoked fish that delight in the mineral qualities of this herb. The stalks are excellent for stock.

BASIL

Estimable torn into salads and soups, basil has a particular affinity with tomatoes. It's also excellent with cheese, ricotta and other curds. Basil is famously ground with garlic, pine nuts and extra virgin olive oil to make pesto alla Genovese. Variations with young spinach, rocket and flat-leaf parsley with the use of almonds and, on occasion, walnuts are also to be considered.

SWEET CICELY

A delicate aniseed flavour that is delightful in salads, in small fronds, adding much to syrups for poaching fruit and infusing custard.

MINT

Famously partners lamb and potatoes, the leaves torn, the stalks tied in a bundle and simmered with new potatoes. Mint has almost as many uses as flat-leaf parsley for adding to salads and sauces, dressings and fresh chutneys, particularly with yoghurt. Popped on a pudding and dusted with icing sugar, mint seems as sad as a flag stuck in the ice by an explorer – it's a herb much better used as an ingredient than a pointless garnish.

CORIANDER

Makes a marvellous fresh chutney when rendered smooth with yoghurt, spiced with cumin and ground coriander. Chopped into salsas, sauces and salads of spiced, grilled, roast and chopped vegetables, meats, fish and shellfish, judicious use of coriander suits all manner of cooking, particularly dishes inspired by those of the Levant, the Americas and Asia.

FENNEL

Seeds of fennel, both fresh and dried, are excellent in all manner of dishes, from infusing for tea or vinegar, nibbling, adding to syrups for poaching fruit or pouring on to cakes, particularly those made with lemon and orange, to studding biscuits. Ground with rosemary, savory, thyme, oregano and lemon peel, and mixed with extra virgin olive oil and an aromatic pepper, fennel seeds are delightful on grilled fish and shellfish.

The fronds of fennel are good chopped with lemon peel, sea salt and pepper in a light cure to rub into hake or cod and then left for a few hours or overnight. The fronds also give a pale, delicate colour as well as flavour to a chilled soup that is particularly good in summer.

The bulb of fennel makes very good salads, sliced as thin as can be and eaten raw. Cut thick or quartered, fennel is excellent roasted or grilled with olive oil.

LOVAGE

Potent but superb on tomatoes. Chilled lovage soup is a miraculous 'potage santé'.

MARJORAM

A forceful presence, matching that of thyme or rosemary. Marjoram is often preferred dried, to be added in pinches. That said, a few picked leaves of marjoram on sliced tomatoes with a little chopped shallot, oil and vinegar are delicious.

OREGANO

A favourite use for oregano is in 'salmoriglio', a dressing made of chopped fresh oregano, garlic, lemon peel and olive oil, spooned over grilled fish in particular but also grilled meats. Also very good in small measures in tomato soup.

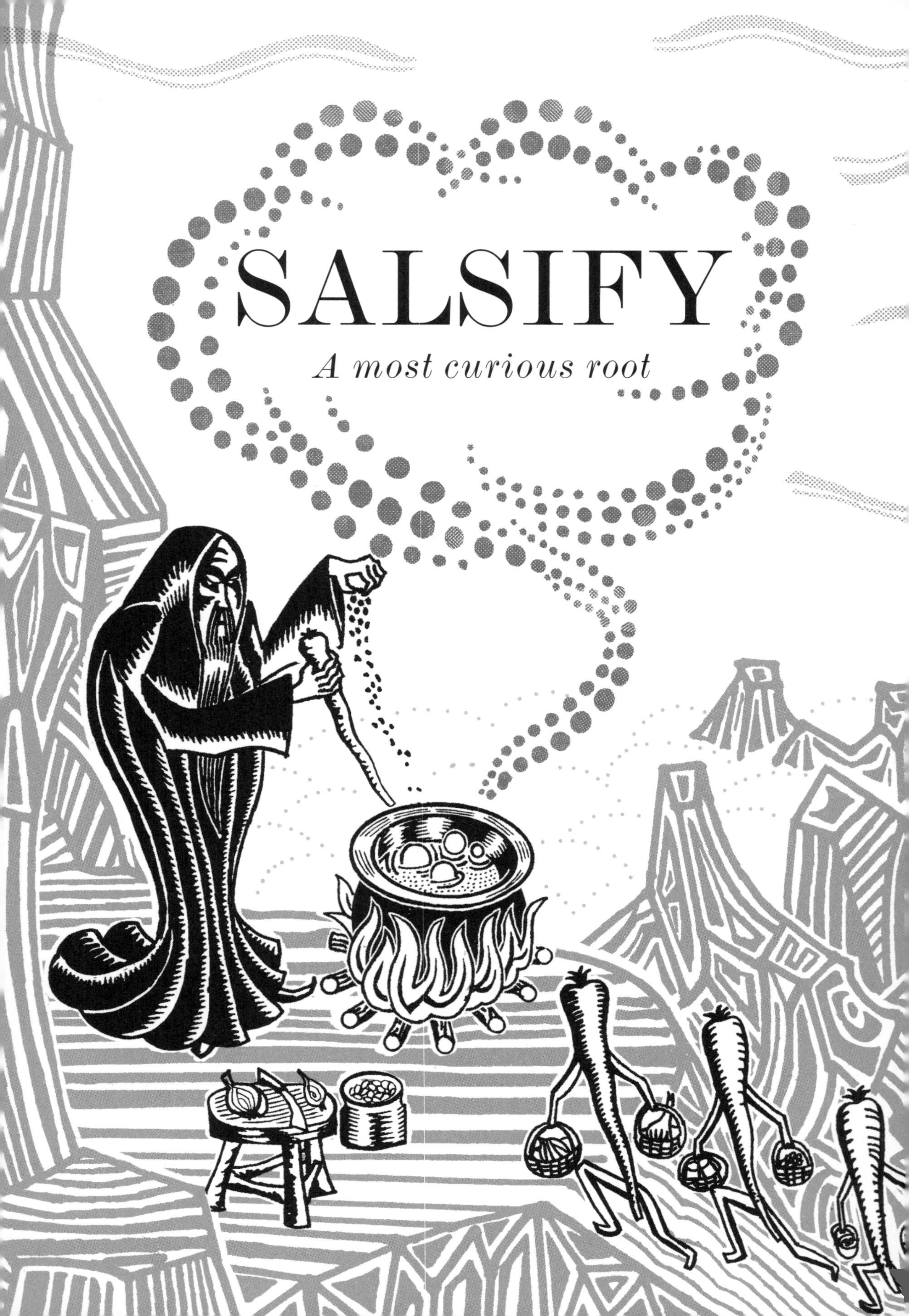
SALSIFY
A most curious root

Baked salsify
Salsify risotto
Suppli

SALSIFY APPEARS AS WINTER'S GRIP TIGHTENS. It's a vegetable that has an elegant and delicate flavour at odds with its appearance – a dark, earthy root, long and slender, enclosed in a covering of bark echoing the barren, bleak silhouettes of trees in the thrall of winter. It looks as though it'd be more at home in an apothecary's storeroom. But a scrape of the peeler reveals a surprising whiteness that will discolour swiftly after being pared. Plunge it into a bowl of water with a couple of slices of lemon to prevent that happening, but beware, too much lemon and the delicate, elusive flavour of salsify will disappear.

Once peeled, salsify cooks easily, boiled in lightly salted water until just done. Letting the salsify cool in the water, then rolling it in leaves of brick pastry, liberally buttered, seasoned and generously strewn with finely grated Parmesan, then baked crisp in a hot oven, makes an excellent little something hot with drinks or as a starter at table.

The very end of the season for salsify falls just as asparagus arrives. Both asparagus and salsify, cooked and served stacked like a small bonfire, are excellent as a bite with drinks.

Baked salsify

ONE PACKET OF FEUILLES DE BRICK has about 12 leaves within, so best to use them all, which means a dozen sticks of salsify are required. These keep well in the fridge for a day or so.

Feeds 6

12 sticks of salsify
1 small lemon, thinly sliced
75g unsalted butter
12 leaves of feuilles de brick
50g grated Parmesan

Preheat the oven to 200°C.

Wash the salsify thoroughly, then peel and place in a bowl of cold water with a couple of slices of lemon. Once all the salsify are peeled, rinse well and place in a pan of cold water. Lightly salt the water,

bring to the boil and simmer until the salsify is tender (anywhere between 15 and 25 minutes), having a care not to overcook, lifting more slender salsify from the pan to allow any larger ones to cook fully. When all are done, let cool on a tray.

In a small pan, melt the butter. Brush one leaf of feuilles de brick with melted butter, then season with a little salt and black pepper and grated Parmesan. Cut in half. Place one stick of salsify at the curved end, the pole so to speak of each half, and roll tightly towards the cut edge, the equator of the disc. Repeat until all are done.

Place the rolled salsify on a baking sheet. Bake for 6–7 minutes on one side, then flip and bake for a further 3–4 minutes, until golden brown and crisp. Remove from the oven, place on a board, cut in half, then put on a plate and strew with more grated Parmesan.

PS: If feeling flush, much sliced truffle atop is very good.

Baked asparagus in Parmesan

As above but with a stick of asparagus, peeled and just cooked through. Proceed as for salsify.

Salsify risotto

THE DELICATE SOFTNESS OF SALSIFY, and for that matter, scorzonera (black salsify, which can also be used here), cooked in rice until just done, is as simple and soothing as it is lovely.

Artichokes, sliced thinly and cooked in similar fashion, are also very good.

Feeds 6

450–500g salsify
juice of 1 lemon
1 small onion
100g unsalted butter
a small branch of thyme, leaves picked
1.5l light, clear chicken or vegetable stock

450g Carnaroli rice
150ml white wine
100g finely grated Parmesan

Wash the salsify well, peel swiftly and put into a bowl of cold water with the lemon juice. Salsify varies in width, so halve or quarter the larger pieces so they are all the same size before slicing all thinly.

Peel and finely chop the onion. Heat the butter in a wide saucepan over a moderate heat, add a pinch of salt and cook the onion until softened, about 15 minutes. Add the sliced salsify, a pinch of thyme leaves and a good pinch of sea salt and 100ml of the stock. Simmer the salsify until just cooked and the stock is absorbed.

Add the rice and cook for a minute, then add the wine. Cook for 1 minute, then add a ladle of stock, stirring until the rice soaks up the stock. Add another ladle of stock. Continue thus until the rice is cooked, roughly 25 minutes. Add half the grated Parmesan to the pan and stir well. Taste for seasoning. Serve with the remaining Parmesan in a bowl alongside.

Suppli

SIMILAR TO ARANCINI, 'SUPPLI AL TELEFONO' are made from leftover risotto shaped into rounds, with a piece of mozzarella in the centre that, when cooked, melts, and if pulled stretches into strings like telephone wires.

To make suppli, shape leftover risotto into small cakes, each stuffed with a thumbnail-sized piece of mozzarella. Roll each cake in breadcrumbs and fry in olive oil over a moderate heat before finishing in an oven preheated to 180°C for 10–12 minutes. This is a pleasing dish served with a purée made from either spinach, cavolo nero or pumpkin.

SOUP

THAT RESTORATIVE BREW

Chestnut, bacon, bean & pumpkin soup

Chilled lovage & spinach soup

Chilled courgette & lettuce soup

Roast tomato soup, chilled

Jerusalem artichoke, celeriac & salsify soup, aka velouté

Cock-a-leekie

Kale, cabbage & bean soup

Chickpea, spinach, mussel & clam soup

Sorrel soup

Lentil soup

Mushroom soup

HEAP WITH HONOURS WHOEVER INVENTED SOUP. Second only to a salad, soup is the backbone of the kitchen, often inexpensive to produce and making short work of any ingredients loitering in the kitchen. This applies to ingredients bought in a supermarket or at a greengrocer's, or a box of vegetables, leaves and herbs bought online from a farm or indeed brought from a garden or allotment bursting at the borders with abundance or, all too often, if you are like me, the enthusiast who got carried away at a particularly inviting stall in a market.

There are two rules for making soup: use the freshest vegetables you can find (but keep in the back of your mind anything that needs using up – no pot ever suffered from the addition of an extra onion or carrot); and remember that an appetite for soup is largely weather-dependent. A tureen of chilled soup with the tinkle of a few ice cubes on a summer's day pleases greatly. As too does a pot of chestnut and bean soup in the autumn.

Making soup is a relatively straightforward affair, but, as with most cooking, much depends on the ingredients used and the care and patience afforded them. As a potter can tell by holding a cup whether it has been made with diligence or with speed, so too with food, for is a soup thrown together as pleasing as a soup made with care, a little patience and good ingredients?

Pans of pulses, grains and root vegetables or kale and cabbages sweetened by a sharp frost make soups to warm and nourish the soul in winter months. To add vigour to these winter vegetables, you could add white vegetables such as celeriac, Jerusalem artichokes and salsify, as well as dried mushrooms.

As the calendar progresses, grains and root veg give way to elegant, though hearty, bowls of celery and fennel soups packed with winter greens simmered until tender and then blended, followed by springtime soups made from chard or turnip tops, the great, long delicate stems of cime di rapa, or early courgettes, the first peas and asparagus.

Come the warmer months, the impatience for tomatoes mounts. A soup made with uncooked tomatoes is best done in summer when there is likely to be an abundance. But should the tomatoes be under par, halve them and lay them side by side in a wide dish strewn with a few sprigs of herbs such as thyme, summer savory, oregano, marjoram or rosemary for a deep, rich flavour, and roast them slowly in a gentle heat in the oven. Pass through a sieve. To brighten and lighten this soup, handfuls of fresh soft-leaved herbs such as lovage or tarragon, mint or basil can be added before serving. If you've only a got a few beautifully ripened tomatoes, chop them coarsely with herbs and olive oil to serve upon or alongside a soup of roasted tomatoes.

Much anticipated in the summer too are other chilled soups: elegant green bowls of spinach, lovage or sorrel, or a mixture of herbs, lettuces, cucumbers and courgettes, blended, adorned with liberal amounts of yoghurt and olive oil. It is of course of utmost importance that the soup be thoroughly chilled when served.

As summer wanes, wild mushrooms and pumpkins appear, to make soups that can be bolstered with herbs and newly harvested hazelnuts, cobnuts and walnuts, almonds and pistachios mixed with olive oil. Keep an eye out for fresh borlotti beans – they are particularly good cooked with the last of the summer tomatoes and green beans.

The Scots are good at making soup – and naming them too: Cullen skink, crappit heid, partan bree or cock-a-leekie. Such cooking is hardly unique to Scotland, but what is most interesting about these northern soups, apart from their ability to provide a whole meal in themselves, is the sheer wealth of ingredients available to make recipes from a rich heritage of tradition and a considerable French influence as shown in recipes for cock-a-leekie and pot-au-feu.

Most recipes for soup in that temperate land consist of vegetables, shellfish, fishes and all their parts, such as cod or smoked haddock, split peas and lentils, barley and much else besides, and they are, on the whole, robust and unblended – all the ingredients cooked in one pot and simmered over time, a meal in themselves, but made with plain water that allows the clear, vibrant flavour of the ingredients to taste of themselves.

There is rarely any need to make a stock prior to making soup – just fill a pot with vegetables, beans, lentils or barley, perhaps bolstered with pinches of dried herbs and dried mushrooms. Any meat required in the soup would come in the form of a ham hock, sometimes smoked, or just a piece of bacon, perhaps a piece of mutton or a whole fowl.

For the cook pinched for time, a soup can be made with just a quartet of potato, onion, celery and leek simmered in water for 30–40 minutes until tender. This will make a perfectly delicious vegetable soup in itself, to which can then be added any other ingredients that catch the cook's eye – from the abundant produce of a farmers' market, kitchen garden or indeed to whatever can be found in the bottom drawer of the fridge (e.g. fennel, squash, courgettes, cauliflower, broccoli and so on). Once the vegetables are quite cooked through, greens such as kale, spinach, watercress, parsley and other soft-leaved herbs can be added.

The vegetables are best left in large pieces and poached gently, resulting in a light though robust soup, leaves and herbs added at the last minute to wilt before blending. On that subject, if the soup is to be blended then consider please a deep fine-meshed sieve for the smoothest result; it's so worth the effort. To these soups can be added cream and fresh herbs finely chopped, or perhaps a spoonful of good olive oil.

It has always struck me as curious that recipes for chilled soups, something of a must for this cook, are not more to the fore. Chilled soups have a restorative, soothing quality that delights in the summer months. Vichyssoise is a venerable recipe, but it is worth considering that leeks are at their best in winter, when a chilled soup is perhaps not the most obvious choice.

There are a wealth of green vegetables such as late-season fennel, courgettes, spinach, celery and other leaves and herbs such as lettuce, parsley, sorrel and lovage that also make estimable chilled soup. I confess happily to serving, when available, the miraculous foraged leaf wood sorrel, small, delicate, very pretty and surprisingly flavoursome on chilled soups, one of the very few diminutive leaves and herbs that I enjoy cooking with.

For recipes that are more involved, time is as vital as a large, sturdy pot that allows the ingredients to cook gently without having to disturb them, except with an occasional stir. Uncrowded ingredients simmer gently side by side, imparting their flavour to the brew. Crowding grains such as barley or lentils in a small pan results in an unfortunate gloop. Avert this by gently simmering barley in plenty of water, at least 3 litres of water for each cup of barley (150g). Any superfluous liquor can be made into that estimable brew, barley water.

Soaking pulses overnight is to be commended because with prior soaking, dried beans or chickpeas, say, plump up, the skins softening, resulting in the beans cooking evenly and becoming tender. There is too the recourse of tins or jars of beans and chickpeas already cooked, which even the great Marcella Hazan recommends, from which much comfort can be taken.

Chestnut, bacon, bean and pumpkin soup

THE HARVEST OF PUMPKINS EACH AUTUMN appears with a show-stopping bravura. Arriving at a friend's house once I was grabbed by the hand and pulled outside to see the pumpkin patch – a huge compost heap that had been strewn with seeds. The coils and curls and spirals in and around, over and through huge leaves, revealing every colour and shape of pumpkin imaginable, was a sight to behold. The dark green and the grey ones seemed to be the best for eating; the orange gourds were given over for gargoyle portraiture. Pumpkins came in every form over the weekend, but I rather liked this recipe for a great pan of soup, which now appears on the menu at Quo Vadis as the nights draw in.

PS: You can of course spike, roast and peel your own chestnuts. Or you can use the cunning little packets of already peeled roast chestnuts on sale in delis and supermarkets.

PPS: Never stir the pot while cooking, for beans are fragile and must cook undisturbed, regardless of the cook's curiosity.

Feeds 6

2 small onions
3 sticks of celery
3 large carrots
1 smoked ham hock or 100g piece of salted/smoked bacon or pork
4 soup spoons olive oil
a small branch of rosemary
a small bundle of thyme
4 bay leaves
4 cloves of garlic, peeled
a big pinch of dried chilli flakes
250g dried borlotti beans, soaked overnight in plenty of cold water (or 2 x 400g tins)
1 small pumpkin, or a wedge of a pumpkin, roughly 1kg
250g chestnuts, vac-packed or cooked and peeled
Parmesan and a good extra virgin olive oil, to serve

Peel and coarsely chop the onions, celery and carrots. Chop the pork into small pieces, the size of the tip of a pinkie. Heat the olive oil in a wide heavy-bottomed pot and add all the pork, herbs, garlic, chilli flakes and vegetables. Stir well, cover with a lid and cook over a gentle heat, stirring from time to time, for roughly 1½–2 hours.

Rinse the soaked and drained beans until the water runs clear. Place in a pan with plenty of water over a high heat until boiling. Drain well and rinse lightly. Tip the beans on to the vegetables and cover with 4–5cm of water. Lower the heat and simmer for at least an hour or until the beans are tender.

Heat the oven to 180°C and roast the pumpkin whole for roughly 40 minutes, until it yields utterly, cooked through without any resistance when speared to check for doneness.

Lift the pumpkin from the oven and, when cool enough, peel the skin and pull the flesh from the seeds. Liquidise the cooked pumpkin and pour into the cooked beans. Chop the chestnuts coarsely and add to the pot. Heat the soup gently, stirring with care, seasoning with salt and black pepper. Place a piece of Parmesan on a board with a grater, to take to table, and serve the soup with grated cheese and a soup spoon of olive oil.

The cook might consider infusing a few soup spoons of extra virgin olive oil, say 100ml, by warming it gently for 5–10 minutes with a few spears of rosemary, a cracked unpeeled clove of garlic and a red chilli. Strain and decant into a pretty jug to set on the table.

Chilled lovage and spinach soup

LOVAGE HAS A COMMANDING FLAVOUR of celery, which is tempered when paired with other greens such as spinach and parsley. The green leaves and herbs are wilted in a simple brew of simmered vegetables, then blended, cooled swiftly and chilled. Equally potent are alexanders, so beloved of foragers and more and more beloved of cooks – and worth seeking out. These can be chopped small, seasoned with salt and pepper, dressed in a little olive oil and spooned atop the soup when serving.

Feeds 6

1 small onion
2 cloves of garlic
2 sticks of celery
1 small bulb of fennel
6 soup spoons olive oil
1 small potato
500g fresh, large-leaf spinach, washed very well (maybe even three or four times in a sink full of cold water)
100g flat-leaf parsley
100g lovage
white pepper, freshly milled

Peel the onion and garlic. Chop these, the celery and fennel into small pieces and cook, covered, over a gentle heat in the olive oil for 20–25 minutes, until tender, stirring from time to time. Peel the potato and cut into pieces; rinse well and add to the pot. Pour enough water into the pot to cover the vegetables and simmer until the potato is quite cooked, for about 20–25 minutes. Pile in the washed and drained spinach, parsley and lovage and stir well until wilted, 3–5 minutes, then blend in small batches.

To achieve a beautifully smooth finish, pushing the soup through a fine-mesh sieve while still hot is well worth the effort. Continue thus until all is done. Leave to cool. Season, mix well, cover and refrigerate for a minimum of an hour before serving. This soup keeps remarkably well refrigerated in a sealed container for 2–3 days.

The best consistency for this soup is that of pouring cream – add a little water if it's too thick. And on that subject, a spoonful of cream or a good natural yoghurt and a splash of olive oil is to be encouraged when serving. The soup can be heated if you wish: warm in a pan until it reaches a simmer (4–5 minutes). Don't boil.

Chilled courgette and lettuce soup

A LIMPID GREEN CHILLED SOUP, softly aromatic with tarragon and chervil. You can replace the courgettes with asparagus for an equally sublime soup.

Feeds 6

1 small onion
2 sticks of celery
1 small bulb of fennel
6 soup spoons olive oil
white pepper, freshly milled
1 small potato
5 medium-sized courgettes, or 12–15 plump spears of asparagus if considering this option
4 or 5 heads of soft green lettuce
1 soup spoon chopped chervil
1 soup spoon chopped tarragon leaves

Peel and coarsely chop the onion, then the celery and fennel. Warm a pot over a gentle heat, add the olive oil, tip in the vegetables, add a little salt and a pinch of white pepper, cover and cook gently, lifting the lid and stirring from time to time. Allow a good 20 minutes to half an hour to cook fully.

Peel the potato and chop into pieces. Rinse well and add to the pot. Add enough water to cover the vegetables. Top and tail the courgettes and wash well, or wash and trim the asparagus if using. Chop the courgettes and add to the pot, adding water enough again to just cover and return to a simmer. Cover and cook gently until the potato and the courgettes are quite soft.

Discard any blemished leaves from the heads of lettuce. Coarsely chop and wash the lettuce and drain. Add the lettuce, chervil and tarragon to the pot. Stir, then remove from the heat. Ladle the soup into a blender, in batches. It is worth considering pushing the soup through a fine mesh sieve to make it smooth. Adjust the seasoning. Cool swiftly, then cover tightly and refrigerate. Stored thus, the soup will keep for 2 days. Serve very cold.

Roast tomato soup, chilled

THIS TAKES A LEAF FROM THE NINETEENTH-CENTURY Italian writer Pellegrino Artusi, who, likening the ubiquity of tomatoes to the zeal of a priest busybodying his way into families, a benign presence doing good with so much vigour, was dubbed by popular wit as Don Pomodoro. Artusi was prompted by this to give a helpful recipe for a good tomato sauce.

Herein with little prompting except for a smile and an abundance of ripe tomatoes when at their peak in the summer, a recipe for a good tomato soup. I like to serve this sometimes with grilled bread spread with a light goat's cheese and a drop or two of extra virgin olive oil, with perhaps a leaf or two of torn basil. I bless the day I bought a 'mouli-légumes', which makes short work of giving this soup a consistency not too smooth for a lighter result.

Feeds 6

1.2kg ripest tomatoes
2 sprigs of rosemary
2 sprigs of thyme
2 sprigs of summer savory
4 soup spoons olive oil
2 onions
4 cloves of garlic
2 sticks of celery
1 small bulb of fennel
2 strips of orange peel
2 fresh red chillies

6 bay leaves
125ml white wine
a few leaves of basil, mint, tarragon or basil

Heat the oven to 180°C.

Cut the tomatoes in half and lay them cut side up in a roasting tray. Add the herbs, a little sea salt and freshly milled black pepper and 2 soup spoons of the olive oil. Bake in the oven for 1 hour, until flecked with colour and well roasted.

Peel the onions and garlic and chop along with the celery and fennel. Warm a pot, pour in the remaining olive oil and add all the other ingredients except the wine and fresh herb leaves. Cover the pot and, stirring from time to time, simmer thus for 30 minutes or so until quite softened. Pour in the white wine and 250ml of water and bring to a boil. Simmer for 5 minutes, then tip in the roast tomatoes and any tomato goodness resulting. Simmer all together for 30 minutes.

Push the soup through a sieve or a mouli and leave to one side until cooled, then cover and refrigerate.

Just prior to serving, shred the fresh herb leaves and stir into the soup. Have a bottle of extra virgin olive oil on the table, for people to add if they wish.

Jerusalem artichoke, celeriac and salsify soup, aka velouté

THE ROOTS OF GOOD COOKING ARE GROUNDED in the use of good ingredients, a principle I embrace wholeheartedly. This seemingly simple recipe is just that, making excellent use of three autumn vegetables: two roots, celeriac and salsify, and one rhizome, Jerusalem artichokes.

A basket filled with these marvellous-looking vegetables: a few handfuls of Jerusalem artichokes, all twists, turns and curves, an orb of celeriac, hopefully with bright-green stalks and leaves still attached, a bundle or two of salsify, wonderfully curious long stalks often tied like a faggot of wood, with very much hoped for shoots and sprouts still attached, a sure sign of being newly dug and as fresh as can be. My heart leaps when I see vegetables intact with their plumage attached and unfurled.

Justly prized for their singular delicate flavour, they seem to have miraculously eschewed the fate of many vegetables grown on a vast scale to feed the insatiable appetite of the supermarket. This is perhaps a price paid for a lingering suspicion, a hangover of witchcraft and alchemy perhaps, and a certain obscurity, but for whatever reason, as Jane Grigson wisely observed, their lack of success is odd. Personally, I like to think of this as a modest integrity.

A more obvious reason of course is they are not grown to a perfect shape and size, generally appear caked in soil and require a good wash and some awkward peeling, which, with a little practice, is swiftly done. Regardless, these vegetables are worth seeking out; I long unwaveringly for their return every year to grace an autumn menu.

This trinity of vegetables results in a soup wonderfully pale, rich and delicate. The recipe is simplicity itself, for the real work, after a swift peeling of course, is done in the pot when these remarkable vegetables soften through simmering, releasing their delicate flavour, and when blended smooth require only a spoonful of cream.

PS: Salsify was once known as the oyster plant, reportedly having a mild flavour of oyster, which after many years cooking and eating I have never found, though on occasion I have unwittingly bought a cousin, scorzonera, which is thought superior and has a light bitter taste. It is delicious.

PPS: Rarer still, if not almost vanished, is a long root vegetable called a skirret, which I think only avid gardeners grow. I wish I could find it to help fuel the cause of beleaguered root vegetables, so often taken for granted and all too often rather wanting in flavour and texture.

PPPS: It is worth noting that this soup is excellent with white truffles… Just a thought.

Feeds 6

300g Jerusalem artichokes
300g celeriac
300g salsify
50g potatoes
100ml double cream
white pepper, freshly milled

Wash and peel the vegetables and cut into similar-sized pieces. Place in a pot with a big pinch of sea salt. Cover with 1 litre of water, then place the pot over a medium heat and bring to the boil. Lower the heat and simmer until the vegetables are tender, roughly 25–30 minutes. Liquidise the soup and pass through a sieve. Pour in the cream and mix well, tasting to check if any more salt and a little freshly ground white pepper are needed. Warm gently without boiling before serving.

Cock-a-leekie

IN MANY WAYS THIS FAMOUS SCOTTISH SOUP is more akin to pot-au-feu, a dish in itself. Most recipes for cock-a-leekie, and there are many, include prunes and on occasion rice, which in times gone by was incorporated into soups to thicken. This seemed odd to me when I was a little boy growing up in Scotland and remains so. As for the prunes, I can only assume the Presbyterian leanings of the farmer quoted in *The Scots Kitchen* who noted that the man was an atheist who first polluted cock-a-leekie with prunes. From a culinary perspective, I agree wholeheartedly, for there are many other delightful uses for prunes elsewhere in a kitchen.

No, if I were to risk a shocked sensibility when serving cock-a-leekie, it would be for an accompaniment more suited to invigorating a brew of poached chicken and leeks, such as a fiery aïoli, that fine unguent of olive oil, eggs and much garlic, or indeed a salsa verde, a peerless sauce made from parsley, anchovies, capers, garlic and herbs. These are of course just suggestions, but rather good ones.

Feeds 6

4–6 medium-sized leeks
1 whole small organic chicken or 4 organic chicken legs, even better a capon
4 large waxy potatoes, peeled and coarsely chopped
3 sticks of celery (peeled if stringy)
3 bay leaves
4 whole allspice (a perfumed spice that lends much to this dish)
a generous bunch of curly parsley, chopped

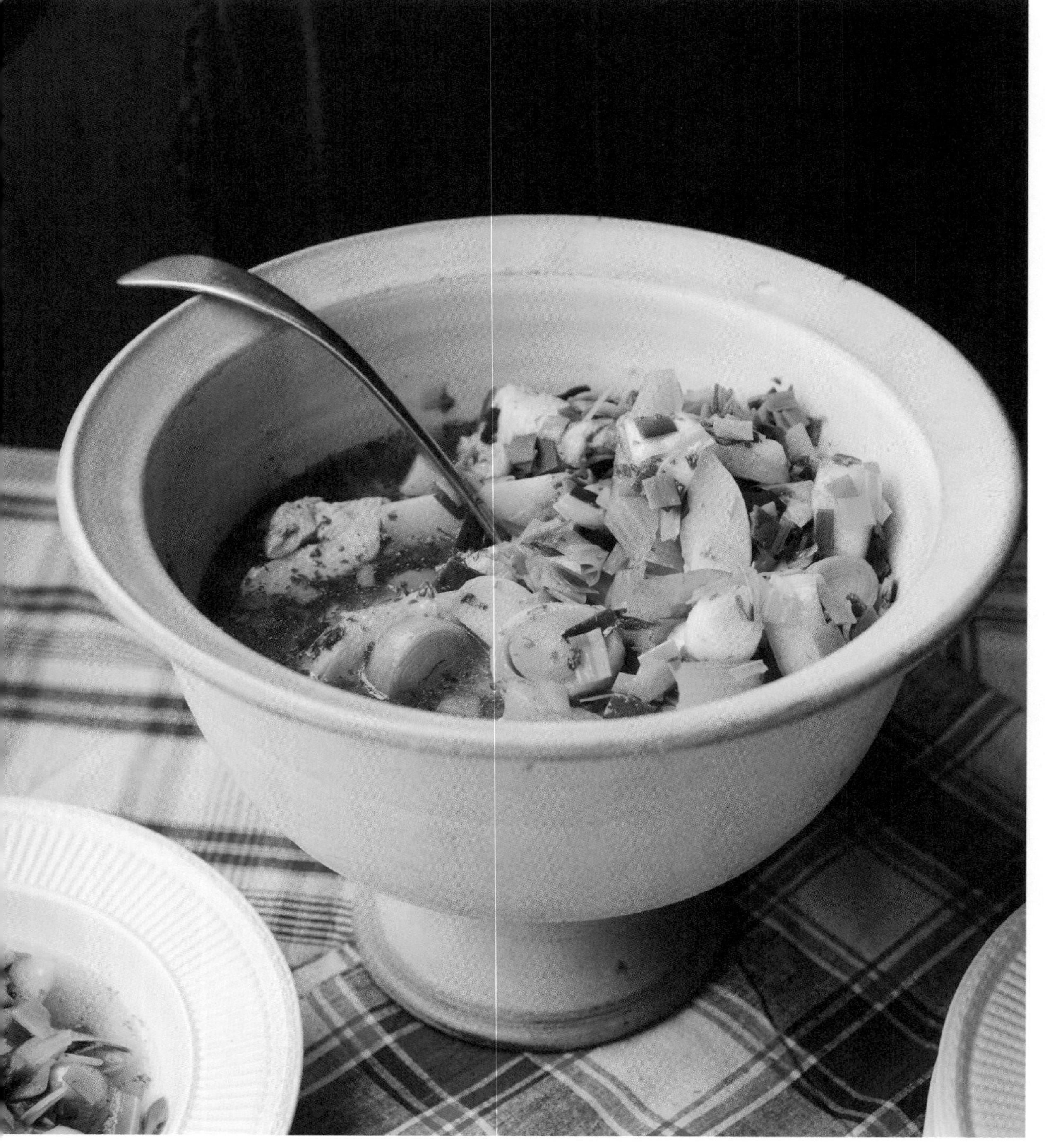

Trim the leeks and slice into short lengths, say 2cm or so. Wash these thoroughly in a fair few changes of cold water.

Place the fowl or legs in a large pot. Cover with water. Add the potatoes and the celery. Add the bay leaves and allspice. Place the pot on a stove. Bring to the boil, lower the heat and simmer for 5 minutes, then turn off the heat and leave all to steep for 20 minutes.

Lift the chicken from the broth. Return the broth to the boil and tip in the leeks. Boil for 5 minutes, then remove from the heat. Joint the bird and arrange the pieces in a large, deep serving dish. Heap the leeks and potatoes in the middle of the dish. Strew with parsley. Decant the remaining stock in the pan into a jug to serve alongside.

Kale, cabbage and bean soup

KALE IS INVIGORATED BY FROST, which makes the leaves of this sturdy green plant sweeter, more tender and a great deal more delicious, particularly when used in a warming broth of beans. Although rare and costly, a new season's just-pressed olive oil such as Capezzana (see page 197) from Tuscany lends an otherworldly quality to this soup. Such an oil is a rare treat, particularly in the winter when even a spoonful can elevate the simplest of dishes mightily.

Feeds 6

300g dried cannellini or borlotti beans, soaked for 24 hours in plenty of cold water
4 bay leaves
a small sprig each of rosemary, thyme, sage and summer savory, tied with string into a bundle of joy
tip of a teaspoon of dried chilli flakes
4 soup spoons extra virgin olive oil
4 carrots
1 onion
2 sticks of celery
500g leeks, both white and green parts
500g kale, still on the stalk
a very good extra virgin olive oil for serving (see pages 197)

Rinse the beans and put them into a pan with plenty of cold water. Pop in the bay leaves and the bundled herbs along with a pinch of dried chilli flakes.

Bring the beans to a simmer, spooning away any foam rising to the surface. Add the 4 soup spoons of olive oil. Let the beans cook gently for at least an hour, preferably 2, or longer if possible, under a lid, letting the thin outer skin become tender. At home as well as in the restaurant I often cook the beans very gently for 3–4 hours.

Peel the carrots and onion. Chop the carrots, onion and celery and add to the pan of beans. Cook gently for an hour or so. Check the beans to see if they are tender. Wash the leeks, then slice, green and all. Strip the kale from the stalks and chop the leaves coarsely. The stalk of the kale near the tips can be tender, so it's worth tasting. If so, slice thinly and add to the pan with the leeks and leaves. Return the lid and cook all together until just done. Taste for seasoning, and serve with a very good olive oil spooned on top.

Chickpea, spinach, mussel and clam soup

CHICKPEAS ARE A BRILLIANT LEGUME, delicious and nourishing, and when cooked at home, the resulting broth makes a brilliant instant vegetarian stock. There is a remarkable amount of theory regarding the soaking of chickpeas, from the stalwart Roman stallholders who leave their golden sunshiny pails of soaking chickpeas for 72 hours, water unchanged and used in cooking, to some restaurateurs who stipulate at least 48 hours' soaking, to those recipes that state they should be soaked overnight and cooked with a spoonful of bicarbonate of soda to eliminate any remaining hardness from stubborn chickpeas. A friend in Tuscany does not soak his chickpeas at all.

A rule of thumb is to soak dried chickpeas for as long as possible, preferably overnight, then they can be cooked in plenty of simmering water in a tightly lidded pot until tender in under an hour. Needless to say, they can take longer. Once cooked, the chickpeas are then drained and placed in a pot with plenty of water, and you can have them simmering while preparing all the other ingredients. I have to confess to having used tinned chickpeas with pleasing results for sure. I do feel it is worth noting that chickpeas that are already cooked, like so many jarred and tinned pulses, have all too often been cooked until too soft so cannot take much more cooking.

Feeds 6

2 small onions
4 cloves of garlic
1 bulb of fennel
6 sticks of celery
4 soup spoons olive oil
500g fresh large-leaf spinach
200g plump tomatoes
6 bay leaves
tip of a teaspoon of dried summer savory, or winter savory, or both
tip of a teaspoon of dried oregano
a pinch of dried chilli flakes
150g dried chickpeas (cooked as above), or 400–500g tinned or jarred chickpeas
1kg mussels
1kg clams

Peel the onions and garlic. Trim the fennel and celery. Chop the onions, fennel and celery coarsely. Warm a pan and add the olive oil, chopped vegetables and whole peeled cloves of garlic (the garlic becomes sweet and delicate through being cooked intact).

Pick the stalks from the spinach and wash the leaves thoroughly, as often as required to ensure no grit remains, it being a shame to spoil a soup for the sake of a rinsing. Drain and chop coarsely.

Boil a pan of water. Remove the eye from the tomatoes and plunge them into the boiling water for 10 seconds. Remove from the water, leave to cool, then peel and chop coarsely. Add them to the pan of cooked vegetables with the herbs and chilli flakes. Add the spinach a handful at a time, allowing it to wilt before adding the next, until all have yielded to cooking. Add the cooked chickpeas and the water in which they cooked, then bring the soup to the boil and leave to cook over a gentle heat for 30 minutes.

Debeard the mussels. Rinse the mussels and clams in several changes of cold water, until the water is quite clear of any trace of sandy grit.

After 30 minutes, check the soup for doneness. Should there be much liquid above the chickpeas, up the heat and boil it away, not stirring the pan too vigorously. Add the mussels. Stir well and cover with a lid. After a few minutes, add the clams, stirring lightly. After a few minutes, when all the shells have opened, discarding any that haven't, give one final stir, season accordingly, and decant into a great big bowl or tureen or simply take the pan to table.

Sorrel soup

THIS IS POTATO SOUP INVIGORATED WITH SORREL – 'potage santé', the very essence of simplicity. It's a delightful soup that soothes and comforts in a most homely and healing manner.

If sorrel proves scarce, you can substitute springtime nettles, though please do exercise caution and use gloves when picking to avoid being stung (the sting will be happily despatched upon cooking). Should wood sorrel be at hand, a few leaves scattered over the soup add a pleasantly surprising zip.

PS: The colour of this soup at best will be a pale olive green, as sorrel dulls upon cooking. For a more vibrant soup add a good few leaves of spinach or a handful of flat-leaf parsley.

Feeds 6

500g floury potatoes
2 small onions
4 sticks of celery
4 bay leaves
250g sorrel or 500g spinach and 100g flat-leaf parsley

Peel, chop and rinse the potatoes. Peel and chop the onions and celery. Place all in a pot with the bay leaves, a little salt and black pepper and 1.5 litres of water. Bring to the boil, then simmer for half an hour or until all the vegetables are thoroughly cooked. Stir in the sorrel (or other leaves if using) and cook for a few stirs until quite wilted into the soup. Blend and pass through a sieve. Taste the soup to check if the seasoning needs correcting.

Lentil soup

AS WITH LIGHTING A FIRE IN A HEARTH, making lentil soup warms and comforts. It is a recipe for a nourishing buck-u-uppo that banishes the cold, soothes and emanates well-being. The accompaniments are good bread and butter and perhaps a pot of English mustard with which to make sandwiches from the meat pulled from the ham hock once cooked. Mum always used to liquidise one third of the resulting soup, to pour back in. I love this and still finish the lentil soup thusly. Remove the bay leaves first. I also like the soup as a great pan of vegetables and lentils. Both thoughts have merit.

Feeds 6

6 carrots
1 potato
1 onion
1 stick of celery
1 leek, green part attached
1 smoked ham hock or 100g piece of smoked bacon
2 bay leaves
100g red lentils
80g yellow split peas
a small handful of chopped curly parsley

Peel the carrots, potato and onion. Chop these into small pieces, then chop the celery too. Trim the leek, both white and green parts, then slice into 1cm-thick rounds and wash thoroughly to ensure no grit should mar the soup.

Place the ham hock or bacon in a large pot. Tip in all the vegetables. Add the bay leaves, the red lentils and the split peas. Add enough water to cover the ham hock by about 5cm, as the lentils will expand through cooking. Place a lid atop. Put the pot over a high heat and bring to a simmer, stirring well from time to time. Once the soup is simmering, lower the heat and let cook for at least 2, preferably 3 hours. An occasional stir is all that is required. Should any frothing matter arise, spoon this away.

Lift the ham hock from the soup. (When cooled, pull the meat from the bone, sit it on a plate and serve with bread, butter and a blot of mustard alongside.) Season the soup with much freshly ground black pepper and a pinch of sea salt. Add sippets too, should you fancy (see page 75), and serve with the parsley on top and bread and butter.

Mushroom soup

THIS SOUP WAS A GREAT FAVOURITE OF DAD'S, and he was fond of serving it for dinner when folk came to the house. Dad's cavalier measuring of spirits was a joy to watch as he held a bottle of sherry over the pan and poured it into the soup.

Feeds 6

3 small onions
2 cloves of garlic
125g unsalted butter
1.3kg large flat-cap mushrooms (if possible, Portobello mushrooms)
1 teaspoon tip each of chopped thyme and summer savory
100ml white wine
200ml sherry
200ml double cream

Peel and finely chop the onions and garlic. Melt the butter in a wide-bottomed pan, add the onions and garlic and place a lid atop, cooking gently for 10–15 minutes, until softened and golden.

Check the mushrooms for any blemish or adhering matter. Coarsely chop the mushrooms and add to the pan along with the thyme, savory and a big pinch each of salt and black pepper. Stir well, replace the lid, and let the mushrooms cook gently, stirring from time to time. After 10 minutes or so, once the mushrooms are bubbling merrily, add

1.2 litres of water along with the wine and sherry. Bring to the boil, then lower the heat and simmer for 20 minutes until the mushrooms are fully softened. Add the cream and return to the boil, then remove from the heat and blend in small batches until smooth. Pass through a sieve into a clean pan and return to the heat prior to serving, tasting to check if any seasoning is required.

SWEET SOMETHINGS

Caramelised apple

Bramble brûlée

Baked rhubarb with blood orange & vanilla

Gooseberry fool

Apricot compote, cow's curd & pistachios

Strawberries, pepper, lemon & cream

Plum compote

Plum compote, ricotta and hazelnuts

Peaches in wine and bay leaves

Apple tarts

Coupe Danemark

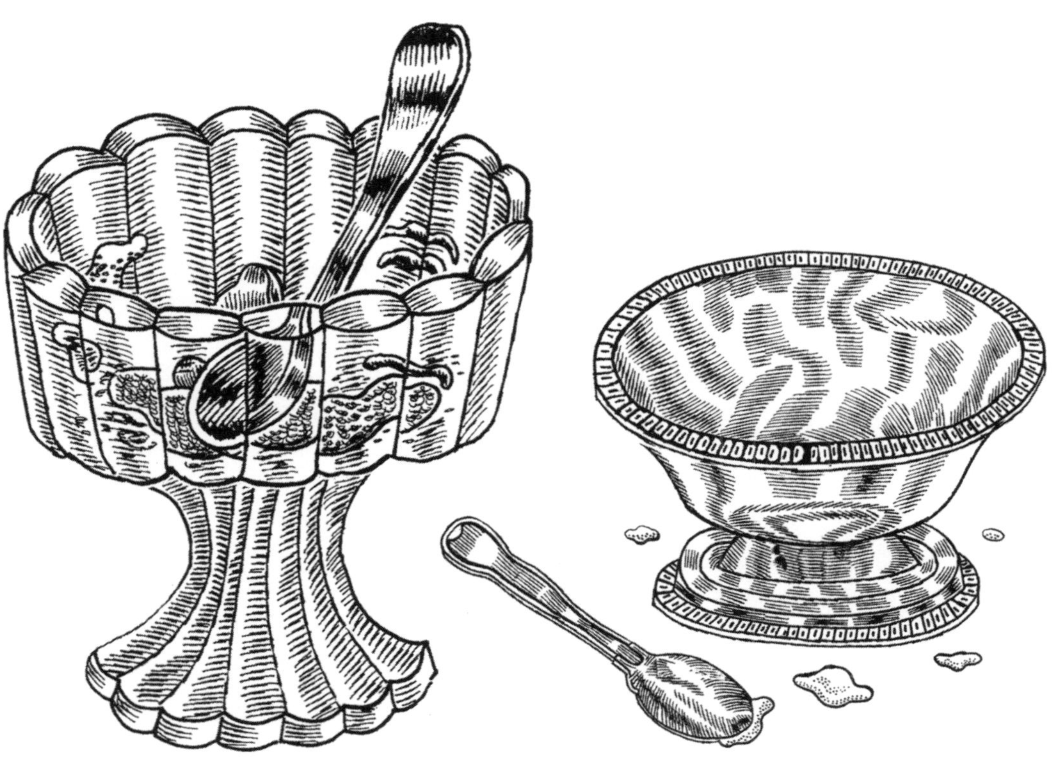

THERE IS ALWAYS ROOM FOR PUDDING – even if dining alone. Sometimes, only a spoonful or two of something sweet suffices, or a board of farmhouse cheese. The simplest and swiftest of puddings is a beautifully ripened fruit – an impeccable pear, peach or fig, by itself or with a piece of cheese.

Having a few good cheeses is always a wise move, whether you're feeding one or a host of guests. And if fresh fruit is not at hand, then perhaps it is a thought to have slices of those miraculous preserves, fruit cheese made from medlar, quince, damson or crab apple, often to be found at a cheese shop or good grocer. To add to a handsome plate of farmhouse cheese, I often buy from Brindisa pieces of some of the extraordinary confectionery made from pressing fruits and nuts together, such as one with dates and walnuts and another with prunes, walnuts and almonds. A stash of very good biscuits and oatcakes goes without saying.

When at their peak, at the height of summer, strawberries, fully ripened, heaped on a dish, are at their best eaten fresh, superb with just cream. But strawberries are also good sliced, dressed with lemon juice, a dusting of sugar and a few grinds of fragrant pepper to heap on shortcake and cream. Raspberries, at their best in late summer, are reason alone for homemade ice cream. When spooned upon scoops of freshly churned vanilla ice cream they are peerless and fair brimming with the warm embrace of nostalgia, particularly for this cook who grew up surrounded by fields of raspberries.

Fruits such as gooseberries, apricots, cherries, plums and peaches, every kind of berry and currant, grapes, elderberries, sloes, wild plums such as bullace and damsons, apples and pears can be made into glorious compotes that can be stored in sealed pots in the fridge, simmered with a little sugar, perhaps with vanilla, strips of lemon or orange peel, a bay leaf, a few leaves of scented geranium or an umbel or two of elderflower, perhaps already made into a cordial.

In the winter, lemons and oranges at the peak of their season can be made into curds for spooning on cakes, meringues, tarts, creams, custards – puddings as simple as they are lovely. Forced pink Yorkshire rhubarb, baked with the zest and juice of oranges and with vanilla, brightens the long cold days, creating an effect as startling as it is moreish. These winter preserves can be spooned over soft fresh cheese, ricotta, goat's and cow's curds, yoghurt with a whisper of honey or lots, and strewn with slivers of baked almonds or pistachios. The cook with time to spare could consider poaching peaches, quinces or pears in syrup to serve with a chilled custard infused with cinnamon or vanilla.

The recipes that follow are simple, reasonably swift to prepare, and, made with care and impeccable ingredients, are as delightful for solitary diners as they are for great gatherings.

Caramelised apple

For each person

1 apple, such as Cox's Orange Pippin, Egremont Russet or Braeburn
juice of ½ lemon
20g caster sugar
tip of a teaspoon of vanilla extract (optional)
6 whole almonds, sliced and cooked gently in a small pan with 25g unsalted butter and a pinch of caster sugar until golden

Peel and core the apple, cut it in half, then slice each half into 3 or 4 pieces and toss in the lemon juice.

In a wide, heavy-bottomed frying pan, dissolve the sugar over a moderate heat until it becomes a golden liquid, roughly 5–7 minutes, tilting the pan when necessary. Up the heat and when the caramel is frothing, carefully add the sliced apple with the lemon juice. Stand well back, as this will fizzle and splatter. Add the vanilla and when the furies have abated in the pan, stir gently. Leave undisturbed for 2–3 minutes while the apple slices absorb the caramel, taking on a bronzed hue, agitating and tilting the pan gently while continuing to cook until the apple pieces are tender.

Remove from the heat and tip the apple pieces on to a plate or dish. Best when served just warm. Strew over the almonds and serve with fromage frais, cream, custard, ice cream or a good Greek yoghurt.

Bramble brûlée

THIS IS A PUDDING MUM WOULD MAKE FOR US through the autumn on our return from gathering brambles picked from the hedgerows in and around the village. The pudding was a prize earned for the scratches and general dishevelment resulting from battle with the bushes. If brambles, as wild blackberries were always known in Scotland, were plentiful, and survived scoffing by us hungry pickers, jars of bramble jelly were made and stored with all the other preserves, each label painted by Dad and watched over with careful eyes against an always ravenous brood.

Mum would hold back a few handfuls of brambles and gently fold them through lightly sweetened, gently whipped cream that was then spooned into a shallow dish, strewn with demerara sugar and placed under a hot grill until the sugar caramelised and ran through the gently melting cream, richly marbled by a few bubbling brambles peeping through on top. The dish was then cooled and popped into the fridge.

Should brambles prove scarce, raspberries are very good here.

Turn on the grill.

For each person, add a large pinch of caster sugar to 100ml of double cream and whip lightly until soft peaks form. Gently fold through the brambles. Spoon into a shallow dish. Strew with a teaspoon of demerara sugar. Do not smooth.

Sit the dish on a tray and place under the hot grill. Rotate the tray after a minute or so to ensure the sugar caramelises evenly. Once coloured a deep mahogany, the caramel, cream and brambles on the surface running and bubbling somewhat, remove from the heat and let sit for a few minutes until cool enough to be refrigerated.

Baked rhubarb with blood orange and vanilla

SO SWIFTLY DONE. This is particularly good when blood oranges are in season and the winter forced rhubarb is still a bright pink. There is wonderful red-stemmed rhubarb worth seeking out as the season continues. Making lots of stewed rhubarb is a good idea, as it can be used for breakfasts, lunches and dinners throughout the week, served with bowls of curds, ricotta, natural yoghurt, with shortcake, biscuits and almond tart. Cooking times depend on the size, age and freshness of the rhubarb stalks. If the stalks are slender, cook for 8 minutes. Be aware that green rhubarb takes longer to cook than the pink.

This quantity feeds 6, but will keep very well, covered, in the fridge.

800g rhubarb stalks
3 blood oranges
a small thumb of ginger
½ a vanilla pod, split and seeds scraped
3 soup spoons caster sugar

Preheat the oven to 180°C.

Trim the rhubarb and slice into 6cm lengths, or thereabouts. Lay these side by side, but not touching, in a layer in a wide baking dish. Carefully grate the zest of the oranges, removing any excess pith. Peel and grate, or thinly slice, the ginger. Lay the zest and grated ginger on and around the rhubarb, with the vanilla pod.

Juice the oranges and mix the juice with the sugar and the seeds scraped from the vanilla pod. Pour this over the rhubarb. Cover the dish tightly with foil and cook in the oven for 12–15 minutes, until tender. Let cool undisturbed. Lift off the vanilla pod, rinse, dry and add to a jar of caster sugar or vanilla essence.

Serve with yoghurt or with a spoonful of lemon curd and a shortcake biscuit (see page 61).

Gooseberry fool

THE BEST WAY TO COOK GOOSEBERRIES destined for this quintessential fool, a delight of compote, cream and custard, is to bake them in the oven. Lay them in a single layer in a wide dish, sugar them liberally, cover with foil and bake, allowing the resulting flood of juice to disperse in a cloud of steam, producing the consistency of a compote.

As gooseberries occasionally coincide with elderflowers, a spoonful of homemade cordial or indeed an umbel or two of the elderflowers themselves laid among the fruits imbues them with an appealing muscat flavour.

1kg gooseberries, topped and tailed
150g caster sugar
2–3 umbels of elderflower or 1 soup spoon of homemade cordial (optional)

Preheat the oven to 180°C. In the widest dish possible, or several if needs must, arrange the gooseberries in one layer. Spoon the sugar evenly over the fruit (if pursuing the thought, add the elderflower or a spoonful of elderflower cordial; substituting the elderflower cordial for water will also work).

Cover the dish(es) tightly and bake for 35–40 minutes, checking from time to time they are not catching at the edges. Cool, pass through a sieve and refrigerate. This keeps well for a fair few days.

To make a gooseberry fool for one person:

Fold 1 soup spoon of baked gooseberries into 50ml of lightly whipped double cream or a soup spoon of the best Jersey cream, with a spoonful of homemade custard (see page 341) stirred into the mix. Heap the fool into a bowl and serve. Maple walnut biscuits are especially good with this (see page 56).

Custard

Makes 600ml

1 vanilla pod, split and seeds scraped, or 1 teaspoon vanilla extract
500ml whole milk
6 organic egg yolks
40g caster sugar
140ml double cream

Place the vanilla pod and seeds in a heavy-bottomed saucepan with the milk (if using vanilla extract, add this to the milk instead). Place over a gentle heat while the milk infuses, stirring from time to time.

In a bowl mix the egg yolks and sugar together. Just as the milk comes to the boil, pour half on to the egg mix, stirring all the while. Pour this back into the remaining milk in the saucepan, and return to a gentle heat, stirring until the custard thickens.

Remove from the heat and pour in the cold cream. Pour the custard through a sieve into a waiting bowl and stir for a few minutes until the steam disperses. Cool and refrigerate until needed, not just for gooseberry fool but other puddings too.

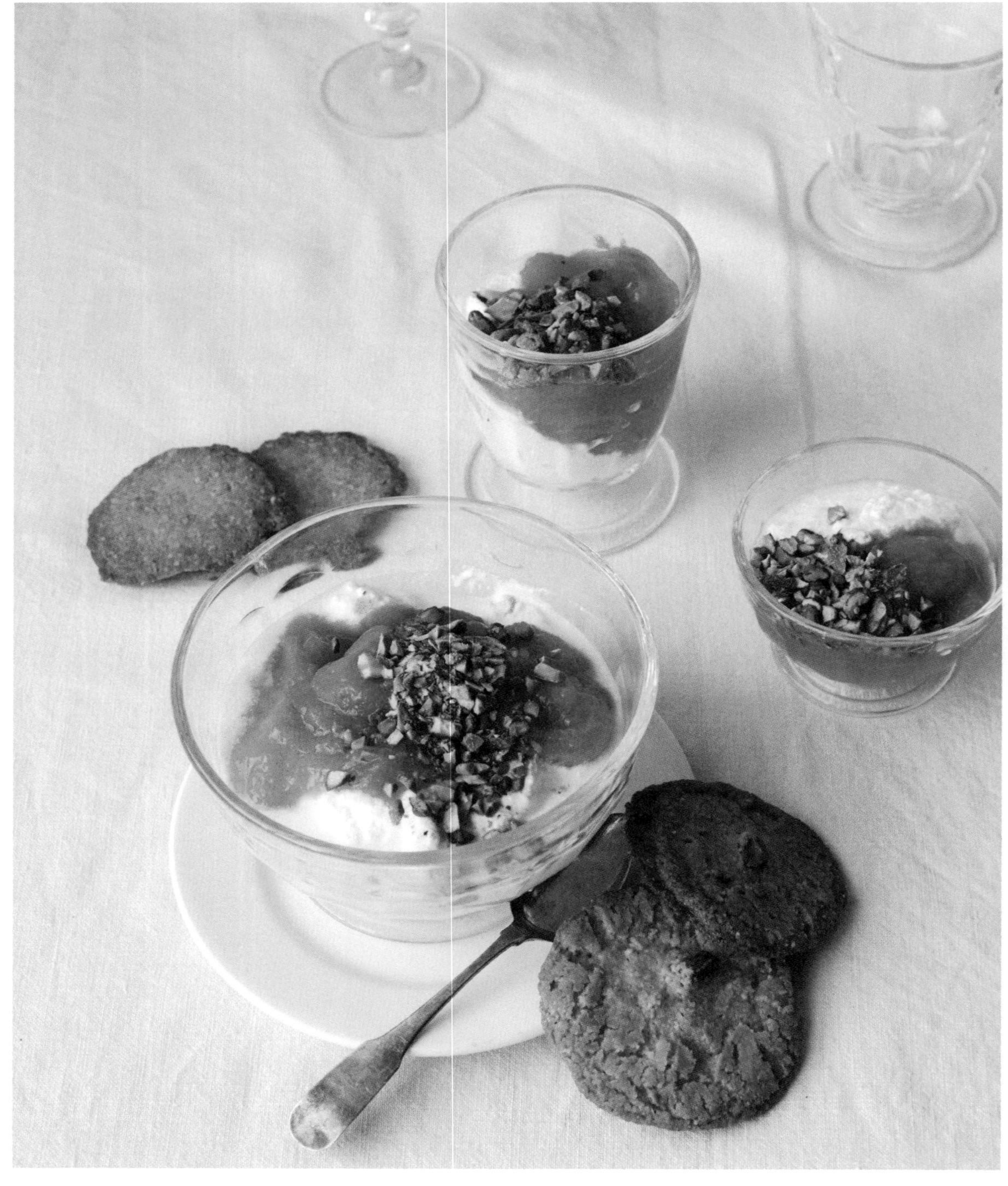

Apricot compote, cow's curd and pistachios

COW'S CURD IS THAT BIT LIGHTER and creamier than goat's curd, though both are equally delicious. Needless to say, ricotta or yoghurt make good company too. A pistachio biscuit would accompany this well. A thought for the cook with a little extra time is to crack the apricot kernels and take the pips from within. Gather them in a square of muslin and tie tightly.

For each person
25g cow's or goat's curd
1 spoonful apricot compote
1 teaspoon pistachios, roasted and chopped

For the apricot compote
12 ripe apricots, halved and stones removed
½ a vanilla pod, split and seeds scraped
4 soup spoons caster sugar
1 lemon

Coarsely chop the apricots. Place the vanilla pod and seeds in a pot with the apricots, sugar, 2 strips of lemon peel and the lemon juice. If using, add the tightly tied bag of apricot kernels (see introduction). Sit the pan over a moderate heat and, stirring gently – the merest agitation so the apricots retain some form – cook until the apricots soften and bubble gently. Cook for a few minutes longer, then remove from the heat and cool.

Spoon the compote over a generous spoonful of curd with the chopped pistachios. Store any remaining compote in a sealed container in the fridge. Keeps well for a fair few days.

Strawberries, pepper, lemon and cream

For each person

STRAWBERRIES ARE BEST eaten just picked from the patch, unadorned. Strawberries bought in punnets and never having seen the inside of a fridge are prized, and when served with cream, sugar and freshly churned ice cream prove irresistible. Worth considering, too, if the strawberries prove to be under par, is jollying the berries up no end by slicing and heaping them in a dish, each layer lightly sugared with a squeeze of lemon juice and a few grinds of black pepper. Left to sit for at least 10 minutes, a beautiful light syrup then forms. Serve with cream, or spooned over ricotta, crème fraîche or curds. Needless to say, these are also very good heaped on meringues, cakes, tarts or – best of all – shortbread.

Cheese

Bra is a tiny city in Piedmont in the north of Italy, near to all the great grapes of Barolo and Barbaresco, not to mention Alba down the road for truffles and countless other superb produce in this beautiful region. Notably, every two years, there is held in Bra, the birthplace of Slow Food, the Slow Food Cheese Festival. Here, for a few extraordinary days in the autumn, you will find cheese from around the world laid out on stalls through the streets of the town, with all the makers, producers and merchants offering samples and selling to an endlessly fluid crowd constantly on the move from stall to merchant to tent, eating cheese morning, noon and night. I have wonderful memories of time spent at the cheese festival, sometimes as a cook, sometimes as one of the crew marvelling at its uniqueness that makes so much sense of the singular business of making cheese.

Farmhouse cheese is such a vital part of eating well. The simplest choice of a hard cheese such as Cheddar, a semi-hard cheese such as Berkswell, a blue cheese such as Stichelton and a soft-rinded cheese such as Wigmore or a washed-rind cheese such as Riseley are the current favourites, all British classic cheeses, modern and traditional;

be they made from cow's, sheep's or goat's milk, cheese plays an integral part of being at table and sharing.

Standing at the counter of Neal's Yard Dairy while all around are arms outstretched offering and taking slivers of the miraculous choice of farmhouse cheeses in impeccable condition is one of life's great pleasures. Add to this mix exceptional Comté, Parmesan and mozzarella, chosen from among the finest cheesemakers abroad. And don't forget the remarkable array of curds, ricotta, crème fraîche and yoghurt. There is, too, always good bread, butter, biscuits and oatcakes, fruit cheeses and, when in season, a riot of apples, pears and plums. Needless to say, the milk and cream is superb. A kitchen stocked with such provender makes for very good cooking and eating.

A similar care and consideration for quality and flavour abounds at Brindisa, who champion some of the finest cheesemakers in Spain – in much the same way as Neal's Yard Dairy champion British farmhouse cheese. And indeed the same can be said for La Fromagerie and Mons, for their tireless work scouring Europe for the best cheese to be had, beautifully cared for until perfectly ripened for sale in their cheese rooms.

These named, and there are so many more, I have known almost my entire cooking life in London and they have taught me so much about seasonality, quality, locality, pasture, farming, dairy and the tireless work done by the cheesemakers and farmers to ensure we can always offer superb farmhouse cheese and dairy at our tables.

The great autumn harvest of cobnuts or filberts with new season's walnuts, plump figs, the best grapes, such as perfumed black muscat and fregola, and the ripest new season's pears, heaped around a favourite farmhouse cheese or three with, perhaps, a jar of honey alongside, slices of pressed dried fruits and preserves and a plate of biscuits and bread, makes for one of life's great pleasures. And for the cook at home, there is no greater gift surely, merely requiring the tasting of many cheeses, buying, unwrapping and arranging.

PS: We have not even touched on dishes made with cheese, but that is another story.

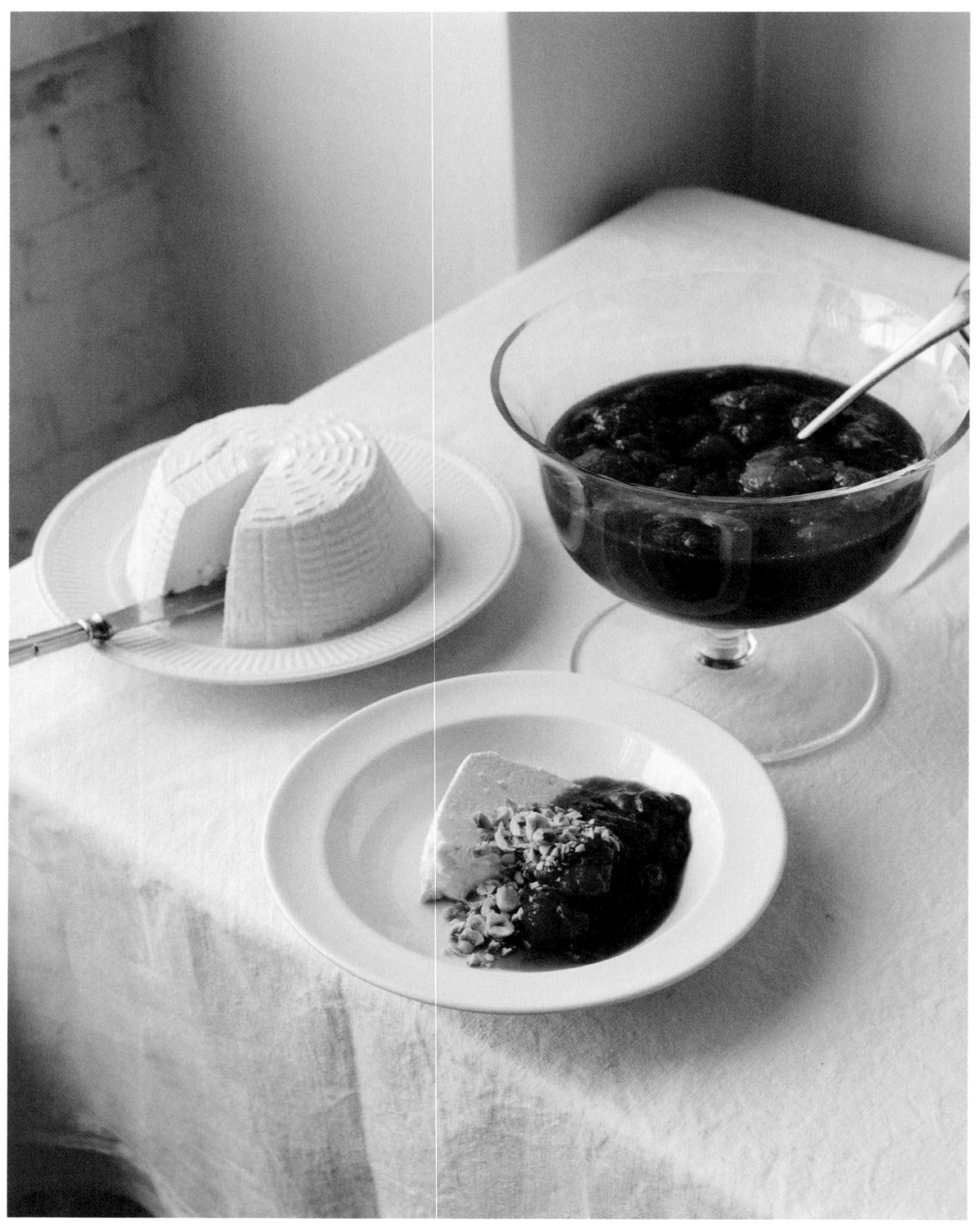

Plum compote

Makes 500g

500g plums
125g caster sugar
juice of 1 lemon
grated zest of ½ an unwaxed orange
1 vanilla pod, split and seeds scraped

Halve the plums, remove the stones (you can crack the stone, remove the kernel and tie the kernels in a piece of muslin and cook with the plums, which adds a good flavour of bitter almonds to the compote), and place in a heavy-bottomed pan with the sugar, lemon juice, grated orange zest and the vanilla seeds and pod. Place the pan over a moderate heat and stir gently until the sugar dissolves and the plums begin to bubble. Stir gently so as not to break the plums up too much, and cook for 10–12 minutes until the juice reduces by half. Cool and refrigerate until needed. It will keep in the fridge for at least a week.

In a film by Jim Jarmusch, *Paterson*, a name shared by a town and a bus driver who is also a poet, there is a scene with the poet standing in the kitchen, his wife baking for a stall at a farmers' market, and he quotes the poem 'This Is Just To Say' by William Carlos Williams.

I have eaten
the plums
that were in
the icebox

and which
you were probably
saving
for breakfast

Forgive me
They were delicious
So sweet
And so cold

Plum compote, ricotta and hazelnuts

For each person

1 heaped teaspoon ricotta
a pinch of sugar, if desired
½ teaspoon grappa or eau de vie de pruneaux, Quetsche, Mirabelle, Reine Claude, etc.
1 soup spoon plum compote (see 347)
a few shelled, rubbed roast hazelnuts (roasted in an oven at 180°C until golden, 5–6 minutes)

Beat the ricotta with the sugar, if using, and grappa or eau de vie to taste. Place in a bowl and serve with the plum compote, with the hazelnuts scattered over and a pistachio biscuit (see page 58).

Peaches in wine and bay leaves

GIVEN THAT A RIPE PEACH IS A RARE PRIZE, those requiring some encouragement might benefit from a glass of wine. Peaches sliced into a chilled Beaujolais or white wine lightly sweetened and scented with lemon and bay, or indeed a sweet wine, make a happy thought. Good with a biscuit too.

For each person

peaches (1 peach each, or half if they're really big)
a light dusting of sugar
2 bay leaves
a strip of lemon peel
125ml red, white or sweet wine

Slice the peaches thickly and toss lightly in a shallow bowl with the sugar, bay leaves and lemon peel. Pour over the wine, enough to just cover. Lay a plate atop to ensure the peaches are immersed. Cover well and refrigerate for at least 45 minutes before serving. Serve in a handsome bowl.

PS: Strawberries fare well prepared in this manner, especially if a few grinds of a pepper mill are added to the wine.

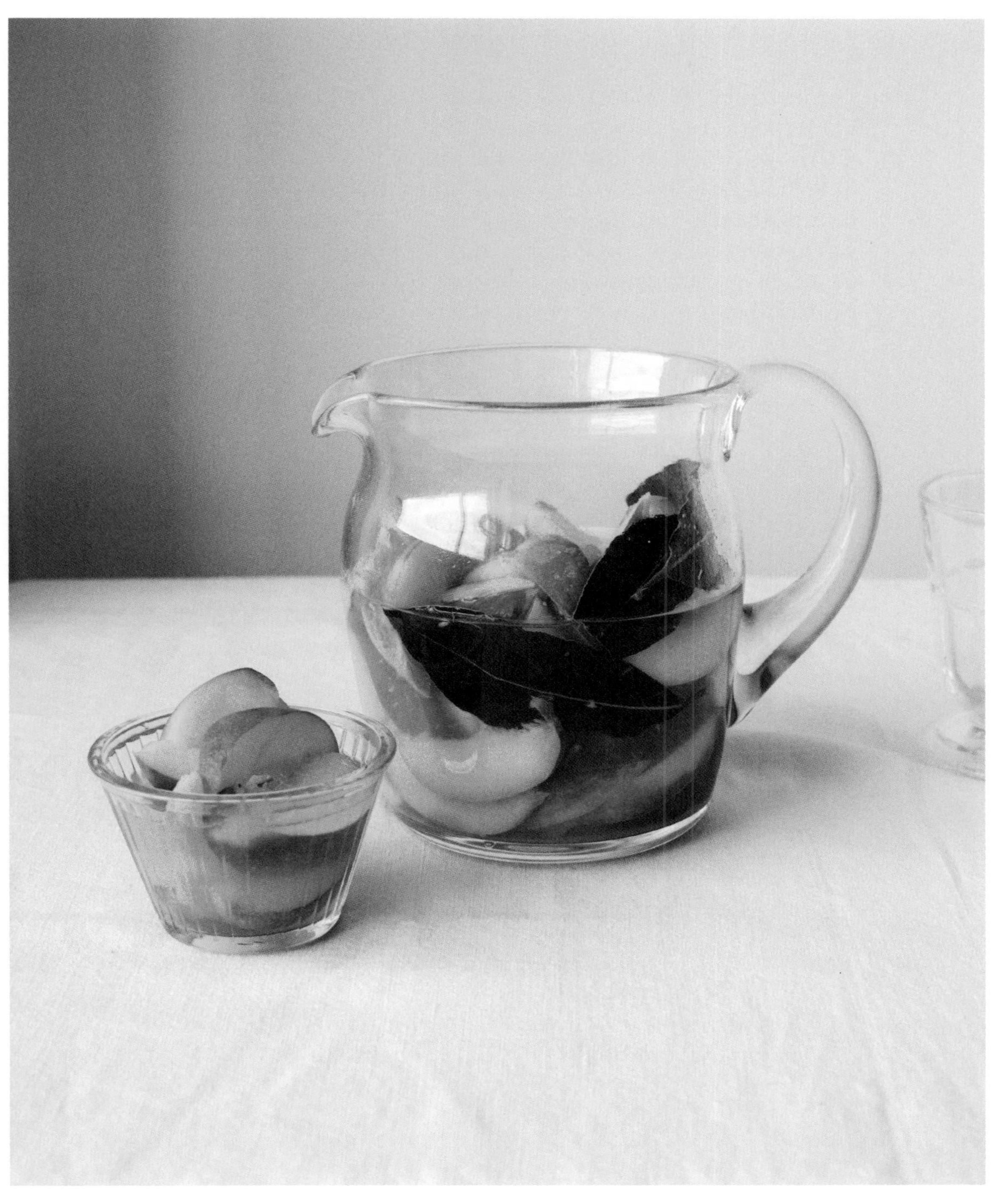

Apple tarts

I FIRST ATE A 'TARTE FINES AUX POMMES' at the Peat Inn in Fife on the east coast of Scotland when still a young apprentice in the late seventies. David Wilson, chef patron of this lovely restaurant in the middle of Fife, cooked much that had inspired him as he ate his way through the Michelin guide on travels through France. He was always very kind to a novice learning his craft and would tell me of the restaurants he ate at. Michel Guérard was named often, particularly when David set down a plate with a perfectly cooked disc of golden pastry with the thinnest slices of apple prettily arranged, just coloured at the edges, a caramel sauce around. I recognised the tart from Michel Guérard's book *Cuisine Gourmande*, which I had recently acquired, having devoured Mum's copy at home. 'I thought you might like this,' he smiled. I did. And still do. And when I cooked at Bibendum, only a few years later, Simon Hopkinson had a 'tarte fine aux pommes' on the menu, always individually prepared and baked to order, '15 minutes' as stated on the menu, although they always took longer, served with a gorgeous cream. Eddie and Sam Hart too had a 'tarte fine aux pommes' on their menu at Quo Vadis when they first opened on Dean Street. It is a lovely pudding, timeless, elegant and delicious, simplicity itself, the very best recipe to withstand the vicissitudes of time.

I have made this tart with pears, peaches, apricots and plums and enjoyed them immensely, but there is just that something about apple to which this cook happily returns again and again.

For each person

50g puff or rough puff or flaky pastry (see page 251)
1 apple, such as Egremont Russet, Cox's Orange Pippin or Jonagold
a squeeze of lemon juice
15g unsalted butter, melted
½ teaspoon caster sugar

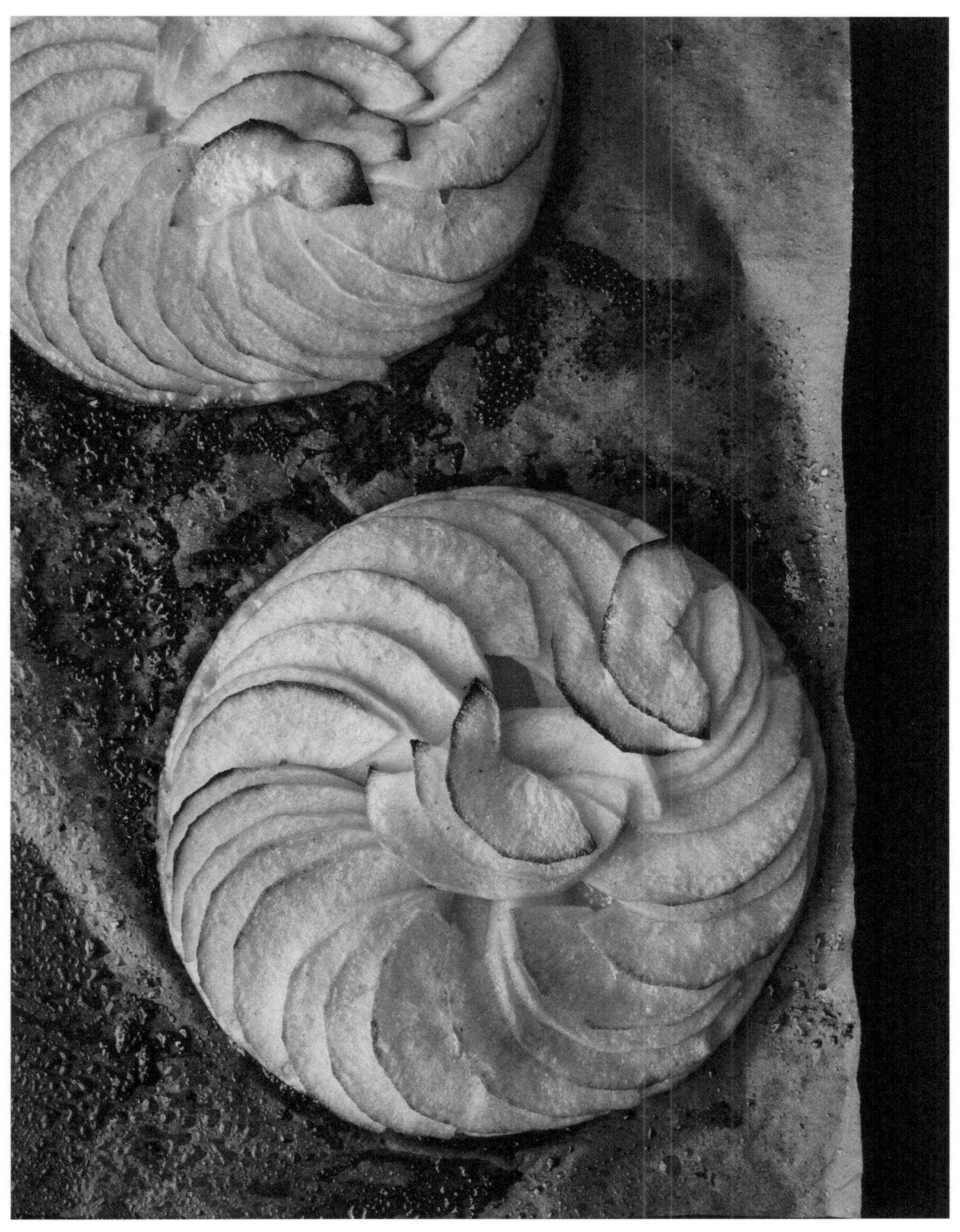

Preheat the oven to 200°C.

Roll the pastry out thinly on a lightly floured surface, roughly into a 12–13cm disc. (Remaining scraps can be rolled out to make kickshaws, see page 235.) Place on a baking sheet and prick with a fork. Refrigerate.

Peel and core the apple, halve it, slice the halves thinly and toss in lemon juice. Lay these concentrically and fairly evenly over the pastry. Brush the apple with melted butter. Evenly sugar the apple slices. (These keep remarkably well in the fridge if necessary.)

Bake in the preheated oven for 25 minutes until slightly risen and golden. Serve with very good cream. (If you make the tart in advance, warm it through just before serving.)

Coupe Danemark

WHILE WE WERE GROWING UP IN DUNDEE, our parents drove their brood everywhere to buy the best produce and always had a mild debate about which ice cream shop to visit out of the fair few ice cream parlours Dundee and its environs boasted. There was Robertson's on Castle Street in the centre of Dundee, who scooped vanilla ice cream straight from the churn, and whose demise inspired Dad one Christmas to give Mum an ice cream machine. There was Davie's in Lochee, alas long gone, but the great Italian ice cream makers remain, chiefly Visocchi's in Broughty Ferry and also Jannetta's and Luvian's in St Andrews.

These ice creams, scooped from their tubs, accompanied puddings galore, when apple pie always came 'à la mode', with a scoop of ice cream, but coupe Danemark was my favourite and also one of the very first puddings I ever served in a restaurant when I started my apprenticeship. And from time to time, it features on the menu still.

The dish is simplicity itself – a very, very good chocolate melted in cream, poured over vanilla ice cream and finished with a flourish of roast chopped almonds. In peak raspberry season, you could substitute raspberries for the chocolate.

For each person

50ml double cream
50g dark chocolate, at least 70% cocoa solids, e.g. from Pump Street or Valrhona
1 large or 2 small scoops of vanilla ice cream (see page 94)
whole peeled almonds, or pistachios or hazelnuts, roasted in the oven at 180°C for 5–6 minutes, and chopped

Bring the cream to a simmer in a pan, then add the chocolate and stir until melted and smooth. Pour over scoops of vanilla ice cream with whichever nut is chosen spooned over.

VEGETABLES

Picking, peeling, podding

Tomato salad

Broad beans with summer savory

Green beans, runner beans & bobby beans

Courgettes, yoghurt & dill

Potato, leek & egg salad

Jerusalem artichokes & chicory

A slaw of kohlrabi, turnip & sweet cabbage

Asparagus & wild garlic omelette

Turnip tops, chillies, anchovies, garlic & olive oil

Beetroots in a devil, carrots in a pot

TO MY MIND, you can never have enough vegetables. They are the mainstay of the kitchen, at the very heart of cookery, and the better the quality, the fresher they are, the better the dishes.

Seasonality is pure common sense and a good greengrocer is worth their weight in gold. The sheer variety of vegetables – billowing plumes of chard, fresh young onions with their long green shoots, so delicious when sliced thinly and steamed, beetroot with stalks and leaves attached, carrots with bright fronds, leeks with their fanned-out greens, uncut, bright and fresh, fresh peas, cauliflowers with bright-green leaves, cabbages that squeak, sprouting broccoli so fresh the leaves are good to eat as well, celery, green beans, tomatoes, courgettes – all offer the cook the makings of a vast spectrum of soups and rice dishes, countless salads, often warm and cold, to eat as is or as accompaniments to all manner of cooking.

Some vegetables require almost no preparation whatsoever and very little cooking. Think of asparagus, picked fresh, needing only a wash to dispel any grit (if older, peel or test for freshness by snapping the stalk at its most resistant point and discard the soft trimmings; use them and the peel in soup or in stock for risotto). Or the joy of a bowl of new peas or young green beans just picked and briefly cooked until tender with only a nut of butter and a pinch of sea salt. Or green leaves that cook in a very few minutes. Root vegetables such as freshly dug carrots that flash so bright when washed of soil and chopped, or the pale, mysterious salsify which takes a little longer, 20 minutes or so. A whole artichoke needs 45 minutes, but that gives you plenty of time to make a vinaigrette to create a dish as striking as it is simple.

There is a meditative quality to the ritual of preparing vegetables, picking, peeling, podding, washing and trimming as required. The following recipes are as simple as they are delightful to cook at restaurant and home alike.

The recipes can be adjusted by the cook depending on availability, with quantities scaled up or down accordingly.

Tomato salad

THE ONLY EFFORT REQUIRED FOR THIS ELEGANT, simple tomato salad is to find the ripest, best tomatoes. There are more interesting varieties of tomato grown in Britain these days, so it is worth seeking out growers and merchants who sell them. The best tomatoes are those imported from Italy at the height of summer, such as Marmande, bull's heart and, best of all, Cuor di Vesuvio. Use a good olive oil and equally good red wine vinegar, sea salt and a fully charged pepper mill. This salad, when in season, accompanies most things well, especially some bread, perhaps grilled and rubbed with garlic.

For each person
1 large tomato
1 small shallot
1 soup spoon red wine vinegar
2 soup spoons extra virgin olive oil

Cut the stalk from the tomato and plunge into a pan of boiling water. Count to 10, then take out the tomato and leave until cool enough to peel off the skin.

Slice the tomato thinly, all the way through, and put on a plate. Season well with crystals of sea salt and a fair few, say 6, grinds of a pepper mill. Peel the shallot, cut in half and chop each half finely. Lay these tiny pieces on the tomato, spoon over the red wine vinegar and the oil. Serve swiftly.

Broad beans with summer savory

A FELICITOUS PAIRING, the earliest broad beans are a delight eaten fresh from the pod, nibbled with pieces of cheese such as Berkswell or Pecorino or Parmesan. As the season gets underway the broad beans grow and thoughts of recipes to cook the blessed beans come to the fore. This simple dish is a joy on its own, paired with other vegetable dishes, or with a roast rack of lamb. It is best prepared when the beans are still tender and do not require a swift blanching and peeling.

PS: This dish sings when made with the freshest new season's broad beans. That said, frozen broad beans are a boon and very much worth considering.

For each serving
1 small white onion
1 soup spoon olive oil
200g broad beans in the pod, or 150g frozen
2 spring onions
a small sprig of summer savory, leaves picked
1 soup spoon chopped flat-leaf parsley

Peel and finely chop the onion. Cook it in olive oil over a gentle heat with a lid atop for 10–12 minutes, stirring from time to time until completely softened. Add the broad beans and a spoonful of cold water, a good pinch each of salt and black pepper, then simmer for 10–15 minutes, until tender, depending on size. Thinly slice the spring onions and add to the pot with the picked savory. Return the lid and simmer for 3 minutes. Add the parsley and taste for seasoning.

Green beans, runner beans and bobby beans

IN AMONG THE WEALTH OF SUMMER'S PRODUCE, newly picked green beans are eagerly awaited for salads, soups and braises. The extra fine and very fine and plain old fine are for those lucky enough to be close to the glorious vegetable gardens of France, Italy and other sunnier climes where such bounty is to be had with relative ease, with only the briefest time between picking and cooking. So tender are such vegetables that they wither quickly, so store and travel poorly.

Elizabeth David wrote of finding little French or string beans, which need only topping and tailing, making one of the most beautiful raw vegetable dishes imaginable, which should be served as with asparagus as a course of their own, when their exquisite flavour can be appreciated.

For those who fashioned a tall cone of poles for the plant to thrive upon, allowing for easy picking of beans hanging in clusters, a cap must be doffed. For the cook without a window ledge or a terrace, let alone a garden or allotment, it's off out to the shops in the hope that an intrepid merchant or a grower nearby or with a delivery service will have a plentiful supply. In Britain there will always be a great reliance on imports from faraway sunnier lands to bolster our short seasons that start later in the year.

There are also all the varieties of flat beans and runner beans, with differing colours of yellow, green and those fascinating beans coloured or just flecked with a deep purple that turns dark green when cooked.

A simple dish of beans is good for fuelling the cook's curiosity to find and try not only different varieties of beans but also the array of different onions in hues of white, yellow, pink and red, so wonderful raw, grilled or briefly cooked in a spoonful of olive oil with their long, spiked green stalks still attached, hopefully not tightly bunched with a rubber band, a practice as puzzling as it is unnecessary.

Excellent for one or more, this charming dish is very moreish, so make lots. Lovely as is, this also accompanies all manner of other vegetables, meats and fish. Any leftovers mixed with eggs make an excellent omelette the next day, or they can be heaped on grilled bread spread with ricotta or goat's curd, as well as being eaten in a salade Niçoise, or with chopped tomatoes in pasta.

While thinking of vegetables which when young and tender require only a nut of butter, those later in the season can be invigorated with different olive oils and vinegars such as a single varietal wine, cider vinegar or verjus, the sour pressed juice of green grapes.

The slicer designed for topping, tailing and despatching any string running the length of the runner bean, the most cunning of devices, is a wise investment for preparing this beguiling homage to the bean. The weights given are merely a thought; eat and cook as many as you wish.

For each person

1 pink Roscoff onion or a few shallots
1 soup spoon olive oil
1 soup spoon white wine vinegar, cider vinegar or verjus
150g green beans, bobby beans and/or runner beans
1 teaspoon extra virgin olive oil

Heat the oven to 180°C. Slice the unpeeled onion or shallots thinly. Warm a wide ovenproof pan, add the olive oil and lay in the slices. Season with sea salt and black pepper. Place in the oven and roast undisturbed for 12–15 minutes, until softened and coloured at the edges. Remove from the oven and leave to cool. Lift away the roasted skin, leaving only the softened onion within, and dress with the vinegar or verjus. Cover and leave to one side.

Top and tail the beans and slice the runner beans lengthways. Plunge the beans into a pan of vigorously boiling, lightly salted water and boil for 3–4 minutes. Drain and cool under cold water as briefly as possible.

Dress the beans with the shallots steeped in verjus and add the teaspoon of extra virgin olive oil. Toss well together and serve.

Courgettes, yoghurt and dill

THIS MODEST DISH PACKED WITH HERBS is possessed of surprising zip. Sliced thinly, the courgettes cook swiftly, undisturbed, with only a thin film of olive oil in the frying pan. Or, if cut into larger faceted shards, they can be cooked that bit longer until coloured well, tipped onto a plate, sea salt applied and a fair few twists of the pepper mill, then a spoonful of yoghurt stirred with chopped dill. So simple and excellent with so much.

PS: The cook might consider other herbs such as mint, parsley, sorrel or lovage.

For each person

2 small or 1 medium courgette
1 soup spoon extra virgin olive oil
2 spring onions, thinly sliced
finely grated zest of ¼ unwaxed lemon
1 teaspoon lemon juice (unnecessary if incorporating sorrel, which has a lemony taste)
1 teaspoon each chopped dill and flat-leaf parsley
1 soup spoon natural organic yoghurt

Trim the courgettes and wipe thoroughly, then cut into 5mm-thick slices. Warm the olive oil in a wide frying pan over a moderate heat and add the courgettes. Leave undisturbed for a few minutes, then stir briefly. Let cook and colour until just soft. Add the thinly sliced spring onions, lemon zest and a teaspoon of lemon juice. Taste for seasoning and mix well.

Tip the courgettes onto a large dish. Stir the dill and parsley into the yoghurt and spoon over the courgettes.

This is lovely as is, on grilled bread rubbed with garlic, olive oil and sea salt, with fish, on braised chickpeas and many good things.

Potato, leek and egg salad

A SALAD WITH SOOTHING QUALITIES well matched to steamed or poached fish such as lemon sole, plaice or smoked haddock. Two leaves I love are land cress and wild watercress, if I can find them. If you can't, use watercress instead.

For each person

2–3 small potatoes, such as Pink Fir, Ayrshire or Jersey
1 medium leek, green parts attached preferably
a pinch each of sea salt and freshly ground black pepper
1 teaspoon organic cider vinegar
1 teaspoon Dijon mustard
2 soup spoons olive oil
a small bunch each of land cress and wild watercress, or watercress, picked and washed and dried
1 hard-boiled organic egg, peeled
1 soup spoon chopped flat-leaf parsley

Scrub the potatoes and boil in lightly salted water until tender. Boil another pan of lightly salted water. Cut the leek into 2cm lengths, rinse well and cook in the boiling water for 3–4 minutes until tender. Lift the leek from the pan and lay on a plate to cool. Drain and slice the potatoes and set aside to cool slightly.

Make the vinaigrette in a large bowl: dissolve the salt and pepper in the cider vinegar, then add the mustard and olive oil and incorporate thoroughly. Add the potatoes, leeks and salad leaves to the vinaigrette and mix well. Spoon the salad on to a plate, grate over the egg and strew with the chopped parsley.

Jerusalem artichokes and chicory

A pleasingly simple warm salad.

For each person
1 spear of Belgian chicory
1 teaspoon lemon juice
an espresso cup of water
2 soup spoons extra virgin olive oil
2–3 Jerusalem artichokes
1 shallot, peeled and finely chopped
1 soup spoon chopped flat-leaf parsley
1 small branch of sweet marjoram, leaves picked

Thinly slice the chicory. Pull the slices apart and scatter over the bottom of a wide pan. Add the lemon juice, water, a spoonful of olive oil and a pinch each of sea salt and black pepper. Cover with a lid and cook very gently for 10–15 minutes, stirring from time to time, adding another splash of water if required.

Peel the artichokes and slice thinly. In another pan, fry these gently in a spoonful of oil over a moderate heat until softened. Be careful not to overcrowd the pan. Add the shallot, season with sea salt and black pepper and cook for a couple of minutes. Combine these with the wilted chicory, adding the chopped parsley and marjoram leaves. Mix with care. Eat as is or with a salad of green leaves and green beans.

A slaw of kohlrabi, turnip and sweet cabbage

I OFTEN SEE KOHLRABI AND TURNIPS piled in local shops and feel strangely cheated when their stalks and leaves have been clipped, for they are such an excellent measure of their freshness. The stalks can be chopped finely to add another little facet to this unassuming but pleasant dish that so well accompanies fish and shellfish, slices of cold meats, or grilled or roast duck or lamb or pork chops. This keeps well in a sealed container in the fridge for a few days.

Aigre doux is most often made with cider vinegar and honey, resulting in a sweet and sour condiment that is as good for dressing and finishing as it is for cooking. It is always pleasing to taste the subtle changes in dishes when using different oils, vinegars and other condiments.

Feeds 6

1 head of kohlrabi
1 small purple turnip
¼ of a sweetheart cabbage
1 teaspoon cider vinegar, aigre doux or verjus
1 teaspoon Dijon mustard
2 soup spoons extra virgin olive oil
1 teaspoon salted capers, soaked in cold water for 30 minutes
1 soup spoon finely chopped flat-leaf parsley

Peel the kohlrabi and turnip, cut into thin slices, then into thin strips. Shred or thinly slice the sweetheart cabbage and, if snappy and crisp, finely chop any remaining heart and stalk as well. Mix all three together in a large bowl.

In another bowl dissolve a pinch of sea salt and 4 grinds of a pepper mill in the vinegar, then add the mustard and olive oil. Mix well, then add the drained capers and parsley and mix again. Taste for seasoning, then toss the cabbage and the dressing together.

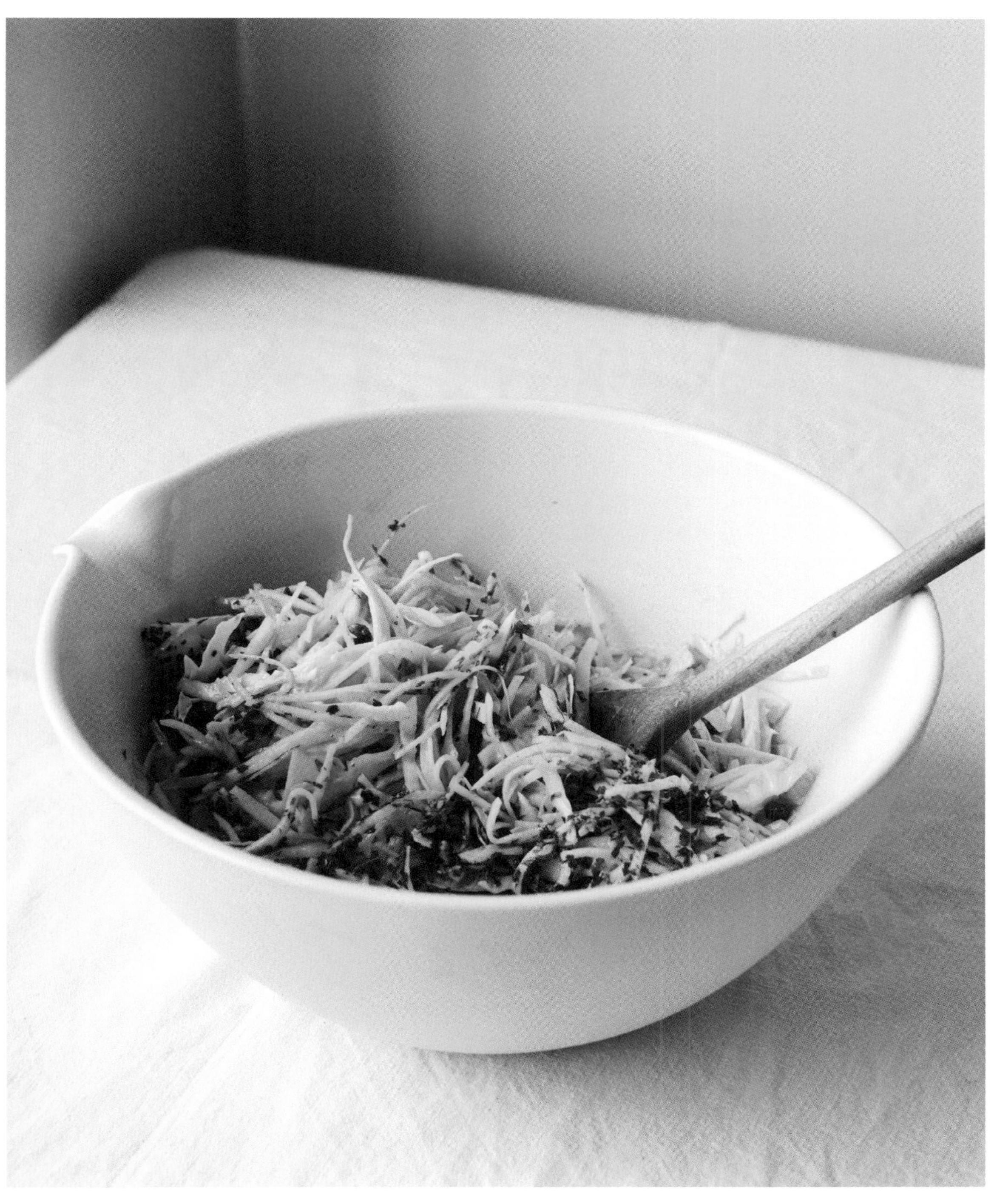

Asparagus and wild garlic omelette

PAIRING ASPARAGUS WITH POACHED EGGS is delicious, but equally good is an omelette. To add vigour, prepare the omelette with wild garlic, noted for its coltish exuberance which works very well here.

For each person

4–6 spears of asparagus
3 leaves of wild garlic
3 organic eggs
a small nut of unsalted butter
1 large soup spoon finely grated cheese, such as Parmesan or Berkswell

Heat the oven to 180°C.

Trim and, if required, peel the asparagus spears, then cut into short lengths. Boil in salted water for a few minutes until tender, then lift from the pan. Wash and chop the wild garlic. Beat the eggs well in a bowl and stir in the wild garlic.

Melt the butter in an ovenproof frying pan and add the cooked asparagus, mix lightly, then stir in the beaten eggs and season with sea salt and black pepper. Strew over the grated cheese. Pop the pan into the oven and bake until lightly coloured and just set in the middle, about 6–7 minutes, longer if required.

Bread and perhaps a green salad are good company.

Turnip tops, chillies, anchovies, garlic and olive oil

TURNIP TOPS WERE ONCE JUST THE STUFF OF LEGEND, but seem to appear more and more often as cime di rapa or rapini or broccoletti, as they are known in Italy. It's worth asking a greengrocer if there are any to be had from farms in the British Isles. From time to time the inquisitive cook can be pleasantly surprised. Buy lots, for the tops are so young and tender they reduce mightily when cooked. These are good as is, excellent on grilled bread and very good too with tagliatelle.

For each person
1 clove of garlic
4 plump anchovy fillets
a pinch of dried chilli flakes (or a little more if you fancy)
a pinch of summer savory or thyme leaves
a pinch of rosemary needles
2 soup spoons extra virgin olive oil
a big handful of turnip tops

Set a small pan of water to simmer. Peel and thinly slice the garlic and place in a heatproof bowl with the anchovy fillets, chilli flakes, herbs and olive oil. Place the bowl over the simmering water and leave until the anchovies dissolve, say 10 minutes or so, stirring from time to time.

Trim any stalk and leaf requiring dismissal from the turnip tops. Wash and drain. Set a wide pan over a high heat and add a small cup of water. Once boiling, throw in the leaves and cover with a lid. Boil vigorously for 5 minutes, until the stalks have little resistance when a sharp knife is inserted. Drain any excess water (hopefully very little, if any, left), then stir the anchovy sauce into the pan. Stir well and cook for a few minutes more without a lid, bubbling away any excess liquid prior to serving.

Beetroots in a devil, carrots in a pot

A DEVIL (OR DIABLE) IS A POT THAT REQUIRES SOAKING overnight, but the resulting vegetables are well worth the little thought and effort required. Beetroot cooked in a devil, earlier in the week, to then be stored in a sealed container for later in the week, is a boon for the cook alone or shy of time. If you don't have a suitable pot, cook them in a foil parcel instead.

Feeds 6

600g small beetroots
3 soup spoons extra virgin olive oil
1 teaspoon red wine vinegar
600g freshest carrots
100g fresh horseradish

Preheat the oven to 180°C. Remove any stalks and leaves from the beetroots. Place the beets in a baking brick or diable that has been soaked overnight (or on a piece of foil large enough to wrap them in). Lightly season with salt and black pepper, seal the brick or close the foil parcel and bake for 45 minutes to 1 hour until tender. When the beetroots are cooked, put to one side until cool enough to peel, then cut in half and dress with 1 soup spoon of olive oil, the vinegar, and some salt and black pepper.

Trim and peel the carrots. Cut into large pieces, roughly 5cm long, then place in a wide pan and add just enough water to cover. Add 1 spoonful of olive oil and a pinch of sea salt. Cook over a high heat until the water evaporates and the carrots are cooked through. Remove the pan to a trivet.

When ready to serve, return the carrots to the heat and warm through with a soup spoon each of water and olive oil. At the last minute, add the beetroots to the pan but don't stir, ensuring the carrots take on only a blush of beetroot. Cover and warm through, then tumble into a bowl.

Grate the horseradish and heap atop the vegetables. Toss all together at table. This accompanies grilled offal, grains such as emmer and barley, poached meats such as chicken breast or roast guinea fowl, or other vegetables such as rainbow chard and kale.

WALNUTS

THE REDOUBTABLE NUT

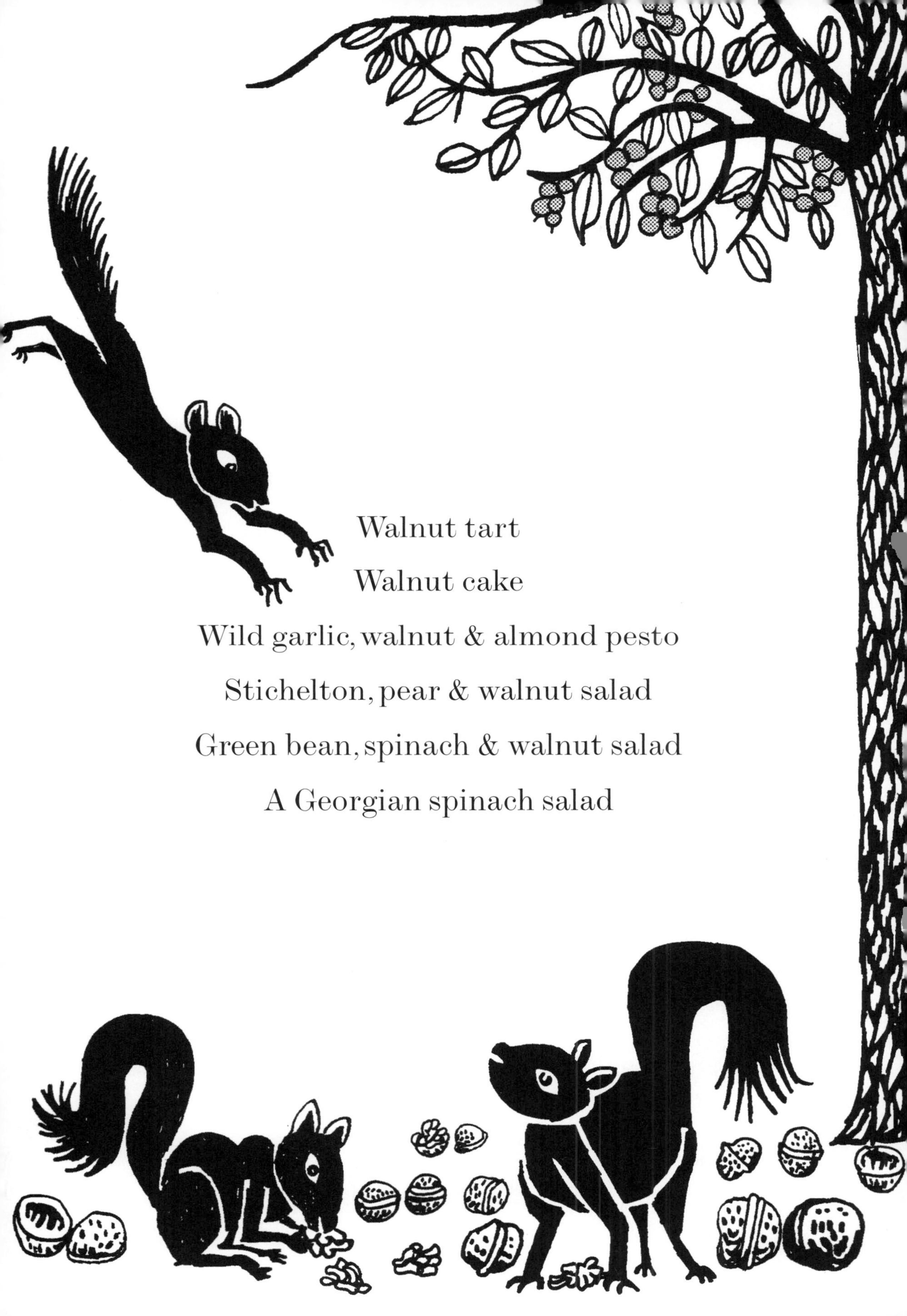

Walnut tart

Walnut cake

Wild garlic, walnut & almond pesto

Stichelton, pear & walnut salad

Green bean, spinach & walnut salad

A Georgian spinach salad

In times past, a fine friend carried the annual responsibility of bringing back walnut oil from the south-west of France. Each year he bemoaned the ever-reducing walnut harvest and the concomitant reduction in available oil. But, being a very good friend, he always managed to find two or three bottles, delivering them with all the stealth and hilarity of a hooch smuggler during Prohibition.

Walnut oil is so welcome, in small measures. It has a mighty presence in a dressing – a drop or two is all that's needed to grace a salad. (I revelled in the vinaigrette recipe from my days at Bibendum; we mixed 1 spoonful of French walnut oil with 5 or 6 spoonfuls of a superb Provençal olive oil, a spoonful of Dijon mustard and a spoonful too of a fine red wine vinegar. Seasoned carefully, this was a vinaigrette memorable enough to convince even Richard Olney that chefs in restaurants could dress a salad well.)

A salad in which walnuts feature is best made in January. Bitter leaves, a chicory such as escarole and a magnificent, late-harvest pear with a coarse texture and its stalk dipped in wax, tossed in a vinegar that might be quince or pear, prune or even a rare and exquisite pink Pineau des Charentes vinegar (see page 198), mixed with Stilton or Stichelton, and a fine-quality walnut.

As a rule, the paler the walnuts the better. If they're darker in colour, blanch and peel them to reduce a too intense flavour or any bitterness. If only I had access to the walnuts in Kazakhstan and Kyrgyzstan described by Roger Deakin in his book *Wildwood*, but as I don't, I seek out Turkish, Greek, French and Italian walnuts instead. Walnuts are at their best in late autumn, early winter.

There are sauces to be made with walnuts too: a French sauce called 'aillade', walnuts pounded with garlic and olive oil, excellent with fish; Turkish, 'tarator' by name, made using walnuts pounded with tahini, yoghurt and olive oil.

And then there's the baking: walnut tarts, walnut cakes and biscuits, too, that are as splendid for elevenses as they are at teatime or even as a pudding.

Walnut tart

WHEN I WAS FIRST IN LONDON, a great friend from Dundee used to make this tart regularly as a pudding following a great pan of moules marinière. We both loved this recipe (from Jane Grigson's *Good Things*) so much we even baked it together.

Feeds 6

250g sweet shortcrust pastry (see page 156)
75g maple syrup
75g golden syrup
125g unsalted butter, softened
100g soft dark brown muscovado sugar
3 organic eggs
250g shelled walnuts, coarsely ground
finely grated zest and juice of 1½ unwaxed lemons

Preheat the oven to 180°C.

Roll out the pastry on a floured surface and use it to line a tart tin measuring approximately 21–22cm x 4cm. Chill for 20 minutes, then remove the tart tin from the fridge, line with baking parchment and fill with baking beans or uncooked rice. Bake in the preheated oven for 25 minutes, checking from time to time to make sure the edge of the pastry is not discolouring. Remove from the oven and carefully lift the paper and baking beans from the pastry. Leave to cool.

Measure the maple and golden syrups into a small saucepan and warm very gently.

Place the butter and muscovado sugar in a bowl and beat until smooth. Crack the eggs into a jug and beat well. Add the beaten eggs a little at a time to the butter and sugar, beating continuously until all are incorporated. Gently add the lightly warmed syrups. Then add the walnuts, lemon zest and juice and a pinch of salt. Mix well, pour into the baked pastry case and bake for about 45 minutes, until golden brown and risen.

As with most tarts, served just warm with a splendid thick Jersey cream is best.

Walnut cake

Feeds 6, with a little spare for elevenses the following day

350g walnuts, shelled and peeled weight
4 organic eggs, separated
225g caster sugar
finely grated zest of 1 unwaxed lemon
50g unsalted butter, melted and still just warm

Preheat the oven to 180°C. Line a 21–22cm x 4cm cake tin with baking parchment. Grind the walnuts coarsely.

In a bowl, mix the egg yolks and sugar, beating vigorously until voluminous. Beat the egg whites separately in a clean bowl until stiff peaks form. Partially fold the coarsely ground walnuts into the beaten egg yolks and sugar. Add one-third of the beaten egg white and fold in well. When mixed, fold in the remaining egg white, lemon zest and melted butter.

Decant the batter into the lined tin. Bake for 45 minutes until quite cooked through. Let the cake cool. Eat as is or serve with ice cream and chocolate sauce.

Wild garlic, walnut and almond pesto

AS A RULE OF THUMB, use 1 part wild garlic leaves to 2 parts of spinach and parsley. This is very good with 100g of fresh horseradish grated on top, to serve with grilled mackerel.

Feeds 6

150g wild garlic
a large bunch of flat-leaf parsley
150g young-leaved spinach
125g whole blanched almonds
125g walnuts
2 soup spoons walnut oil
250ml extra virgin olive oil

Snip the stalks from the leaves of wild garlic. The stalks are good for the stock pot, making soup or steeping in vinegar. Pick the parsley leaves and the spinach. Wash the leaves, drain and dry well.

Place the almonds and walnuts in a mortar or a food processor and grind coarsely. Add the leaves in handfuls and grind to a thick paste, adding the walnut oil as you go to loosen the pesto. Season with salt and pepper. Place in a jar or a sealed container. Smooth the surface and cover with a thin layer of olive oil. The pesto keeps well, chilled, for 3–4 days.

Stichelton, pear and walnut salad

THIS PLEASING SALAD IS BEST in the winter months when walnuts, pears and Stilton are at their peak. It is worth keeping an eye out for interesting varieties of pears such as Passe-Crassane, so distinctive with their stalks topped with a drip of red wax.

Colston Bassett is a pasteurised Stilton, the only Stilton permitted, and Stichelton is unpasteurised, and made from the last culture taken from the last unpasteurised Colston Bassett Stilton that was stored and preserved by Randolph Hodgson at Neal's Yard Dairy.

Feeds 6

2–3 ripe pears
1 soup spoon very good vinegar (you can get quince vinegar from the Vinegar Shed, see page 390)
250g Stichelton or Colston Bassett Stilton, or any good blue cheese
75g membrillo or quince cheese
100g walnuts, coarsely chopped
3 big handfuls of mixed leaves such as escarole, soft green lettuce, rocket, spinach, chicory or even watercress
3 soup spoons walnut oil
2 soup spoons extra virgin olive oil

Halve and core the pears, then slice thinly. In a big bowl, toss the pears in the vinegar to prevent discoloration. Crumble the Stichelton

over the pears. Cut the membrillo into small pieces and scatter over the Stichelton, then strew with the chopped walnuts. Add the leaves, a little salt and black pepper and the walnut and olive oils. Mix together, taste for seasoning and serve.

Green bean, spinach and walnut salad

THIS IS VERY GOOD WITH PORK – either a solitary chop or a roast. The pesto keeps well under a film of oil, covered and in the fridge, for up to a week.

Feeds 6

125g walnuts
3 cloves of garlic, peeled and sliced
juice of ½ a lemon
2 soup spoons tahini
80g rocket
120g baby spinach
150ml extra virgin olive oil
500g green beans (search out different varieties such as runner, bobby and green)

Put the walnuts and sliced garlic into a food processor and grind to a fine paste. Add the lemon juice, tahini, rocket, spinach and olive oil with a good pinch of sea salt and plenty of black pepper. Pulse again until a coarse, soft paste forms. Tip the paste into a bowl, cover with a light film of olive oil and put to one side.

Put a big pan of lightly salted water on to boil. Into this plunge the green beans and boil until tender, about 3–4 minutes. Drain and cool under running water and, when ready to serve, put the beans in a handsome bowl, spoon the paste on top and mix well, adjusting the seasoning.

This paste is also great with fish, meat, pasta or even spooned over bread.

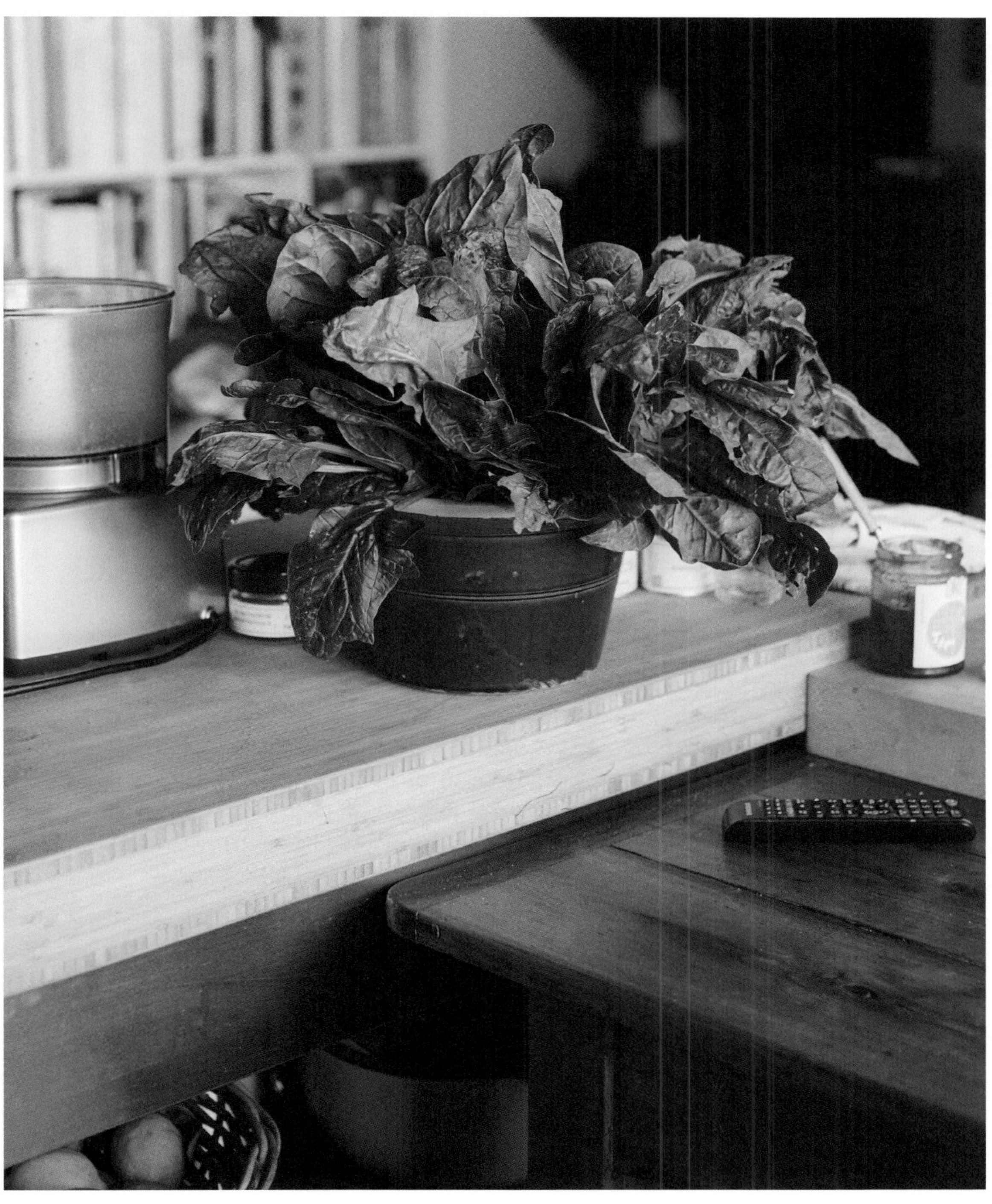

A Georgian spinach salad

THIS RECIPE IS INSPIRED BY A GEORGIAN PESTO called 'pkhali', used to dress 'ekala', mildly soured leaves that look like young vine shoots. It's similar to a recipe cooked by Olia Hercules for us at Quo Vadis which filled the kitchen with the extraordinary smell of walnuts cooking in blue fenugreek. If you can't get blue fenugreek you can substitute 1 teaspoon of coriander seeds, ground with half a teaspoon of fenugreek seeds. Wild asparagus, or hops, would also be excellent in this recipe.

Feeds 6

4 small cloves of garlic, peeled
a big pinch of dried chilli flakes
1 level teaspoon dried blue fenugreek
250g walnuts
3 soup spoons white wine vinegar, cider vinegar or lemon juice
600g spinach, beetroot tops or Swiss chard
1 small bunch of wild sorrel, if available
1 soup spoon extra virgin olive oil

Grind the garlic, spices and walnuts in a pestle and mortar or food processor until they become a soft paste, adding the vinegar or lemon juice as you go. Add a pinch of salt and black pepper.

Pick all the leaves through, removing any excess stalks, and wash thoroughly. Put the leaves and stalks into a wide pan with the soup spoon of olive oil over a medium heat until tender, 2–3 minutes, boiling away any excess water, then add the walnut paste and mix well.

WILD GARLIC

A MOST EXUBERANT
NOT TO MENTION ABUNDANT LEAF

Wild garlic purée

Wild garlic, rocket & anchovy sauce

Wild garlic & olive oil mash

As winter wanes and impatience for green shoots and leaves mounts, I speak often with my greengrocer, asking when the first wild garlic will be in. Wild garlic is a leaf that grows in abundance, equally at home on the towpath of a canal as in a sea of bluebells in a wood.

Prized for its sweet garlic flavour and brilliant kick – an exuberance that belies its charming flowers and soft, green-leaved appearance – wild garlic usually arrives in April, but has been getting earlier and earlier these last few years, before departing again towards the end of June.

In its wild state, it's vital to respect the leaf and the land on which it grows, so find a good greengrocer who delights in stocking such things and will have contact with growers and foragers who pick responsibly and wisely, and deliver leaves of wild garlic in a good condition.

I always buy too much and so have become adept at making dishes that use generous amounts of the leaves – and the flowers too, if still bright and fresh – which can be put into the fridge for use over the coming days (a purée that can be added to a fiery aïoli, excellent with fish such as sea bass, or added to mashed potatoes or salsa verde).

A pesto makes excellent work of an abundance of wild garlic leaves, ground with young spinach leaves, parsley, almonds and walnuts. The very first pickings of wild garlic are surprisingly mild and can be used in handfuls. The resulting pesto is particularly good on vegetables such as potatoes, greens and beans or to accompany roast or grilled vegetables, pasta, meats and fish. As the season progresses, the flavour of wild garlic becomes more pronounced, possibly requiring some caution.

A few suggested dishes for wild garlic, not so much recipes as a gathering of good things on a plate:

- Poached chicken, asparagus and new potatoes with wild garlic aïoli
- Roast guinea fowl with a salad of spinach, potatoes, peas and green beans dressed with wild garlic pesto
- Roast cod, wild garlic and mashed potatoes

Wild garlic purée

Feeds 6

250g wild garlic leaves
200ml extra virgin olive oil

Trim the wild garlic leaves, wash and drain. Blanch the leaves for 30 seconds in a pan of boiling water, then drain and leave until cool enough to handle. Squeeze the leaves to remove as much water as possible, then place in a blender with half the olive oil and blend until smooth. Continue blending and add the remaining olive oil in small measures, adjusting the seasoning as you go.

Wild garlic, rocket and anchovy sauce

THIS ROBUST SAUCE IS AN EXCELLENT COMPANION to all manner of grilled or roast vegetables and grilled or poached meats.

Feeds 12

2 cloves of garlic
75g anchovy fillets
125g wild garlic leaves
125g wild rocket
100g flat-leaf parsley
125ml extra virgin olive oil
¼ teaspoon freshly ground black pepper

Peel and coarsely chop the garlic. Place the anchovy fillets and garlic in a food processor, then add the leaves, olive oil and pepper and grind to a coarse paste. Decant into a bowl and refrigerate until needed.

Any leftovers can be stored in a jar under a film of oil, sealed and kept in the fridge for up to 5 days.

Wild garlic and olive oil mash

EXCELLENT WITH grilled meats, fish and vegetables.

Feeds 6

750g potatoes, such as King Edward or any 'all-rounder'
2–3 large spoonfuls of wild garlic purée (see page 387)
a small handful each of leaves such as wild cress, watercress, rocket and spinach

Peel the potatoes, put into a pan of boiling water, simmer until tender, then drain and mash. Stir in the wild garlic purée. Heat through and taste for seasoning. Add any leaves if so wished.

C'est tout.

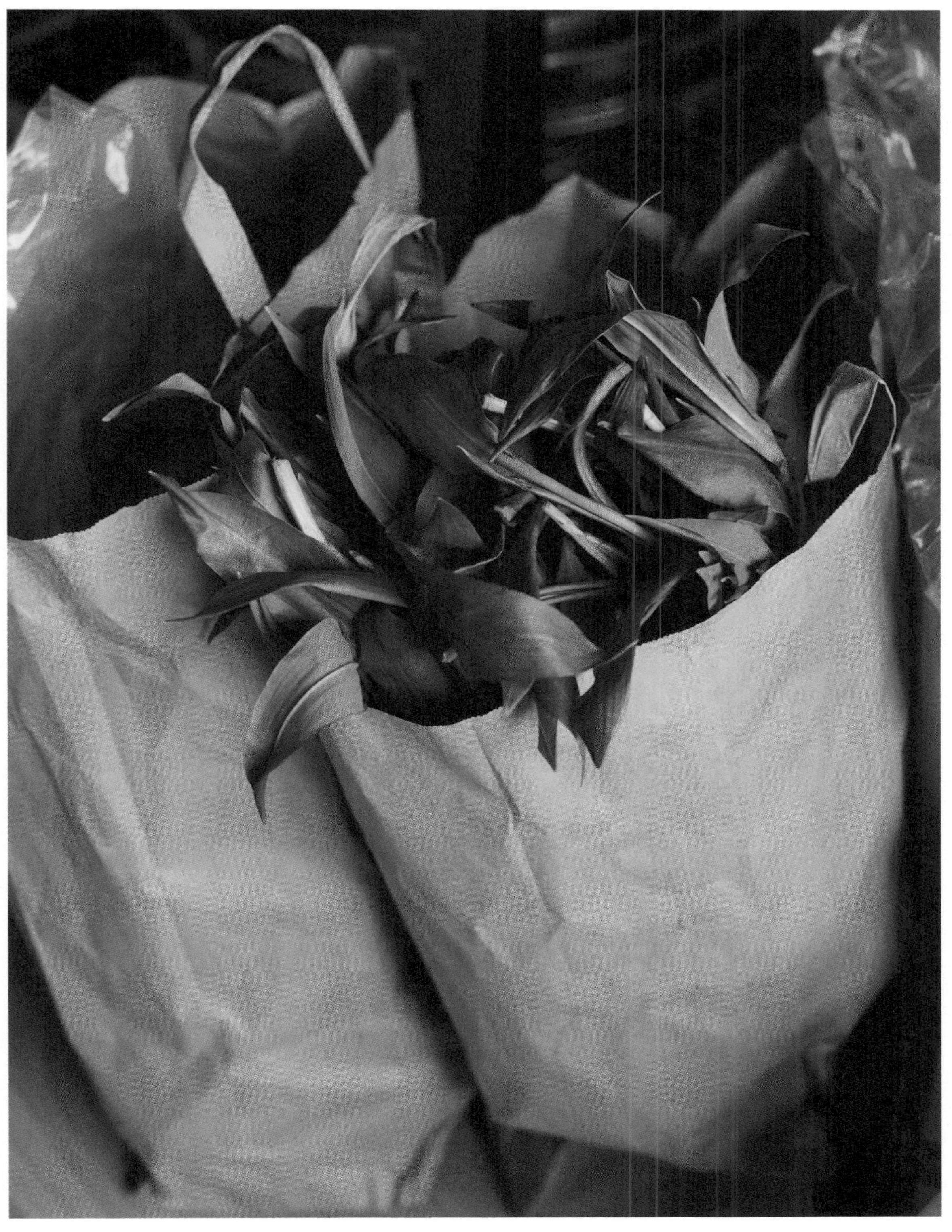

A list of great stockists

GROWING UP IN A FAMILY that thought nothing of jumping in the car to journey for something delicious remains still a joy. It's also my job to keep abreast of what's good, what's great, what's just in and destined for the pot as soon as possible. There is much to please when wandering a market, enjoying the familiarity of trusted and favourite traders and producers as well as the plentiful new farmers' markets that spring up with the enthusiasm of shoots in the spring. Finding what is best locally is now not only common sense, it's a pleasure that should be embraced wholeheartedly. I enjoy the game of plotting a course between markets, shops and the supermarket and of course the internet, though nothing beats that spontaneity of a stall heaped with good things that make you tear up the shopping list…

Stoke Newington Farmers' Market

Marylebone Farmers' Market

Broadway Market
broadwaymarket.co.uk

Spa Terminus
spa-terminus.co.uk

Maltby Street
maltby.st

Green Lanes

Brindisa
brindisa.com

Natoora
natoora.com

Jane Scotter
thelandgardeners.com

Shrub Provisions
shrub.london

La Fromagerie
lafromagerie.co.uk

H G Walter
hgwalter.com

Vinegar Shed and The Ealing Grocer
theealinggrocer.com

The Olive Oil Merchant
oilmerchant.co.uk

Philip Warren Butchers
philipwarrenbutchers.co.uk

Swaledale Meats
swaledale.co.uk

Huntsham Court Farm
huntsham.com

Neal's Yard Dairy
nealsyarddairy.co.uk

Coombeshead Farm
coombesheadfarm.co.uk

Postcard Teas
postcardteas.com

Sarah Green
sarahgreensorganics.co.uk

Turkish Food Centre
tfcsupermarket.com

Ethical Shellfish
ethicalshellfishcompany.co.uk

Fin & Flounder
finandflounder.co.uk

Secret Smokehouse
secretsmokehouse.co.uk

London Smoke and Cure
londonsmokeandcure.co.uk

Ben's Fish
bensfishmersea.co.uk

Devon Eel Company
devoneel.co.uk

Fresh Olive Company/Belazu
belazu.com

La Sovrana
instagram.com/la_sovrana_italian_az.agricola

Poilane
poilane.com

Puntarelle
puntarelle.co.uk

Valvona & Crolla
valvonacrolla.co.uk

Leila's Shop
leilasshop.co.uk

Pump Street Chocolate
pumpstreetchocolate.com

I Camisa & Son
icamisa.co.uk

Lina Stores
linastores.co.uk

Algerian Coffee Stores
algeriancoffeestores.com

Maison Bertaux
maisonbertaux.com

E5 Bakehouse
e5bakehouse.com

London Fermentary
londonfermentary.com

Barony Mill
baronymill.com

4 Cose
4cose.square.site

Fisher & Donaldson, Dundee
fisheranddonaldson.com

Zazou Emporium Vanilla
zazouemporium.com

Souschef
souschef.co.uk

Index

D

E

P

Q

R

S